tasteofhome
Casseroles

tasty hamburger casserole / **44**

special seafood casserole / **127**

creamy corned beef casserole / **27**

hawaiian ham bake / **99**

taste of home
Casseroles

A TASTE OF HOME/READER'S DIGEST BOOK

Editor-in-Chief: Catherine Cassidy
Vice President, Executive Editor/Books: Heidi Reuter Lloyd
Creative Director: Howard Greenberg
North American Chief Marketing Officer: Lisa Karpinski

Food Director: Diane Werner, RD
Senior Editor/Retail Books: Faithann Stoner
Editor: Janet Briggs
Associate Creative Director: Edwin Robles Jr.
Art Director: Rudy Krochalk
Content Production Manager: Julie Wagner
Layout Designer: Nancy Novak
Copy Chief: Deb Warlaumont Mulvey
Copy Editor: Susan Uphill
Recipe Asset System Manager: Coleen Martin
Recipe Testing & Editing: Taste of Home Test Kitchen
Food Photography: Taste of Home Photo Studio
Administrative Assistant: Barb Czysz

THE READER'S DIGEST ASSOCIATION, INC.
President and Chief Executive Officer: Robert E. Guth
Executive Vice President, RDA, &
President, North America: Dan Lagani
President/Publisher, Trade Publishing: Harold Clarke
Associate Publisher: Rosanne McManus
Vice President, Sales & Marketing: Stacey Ashton

For other Taste of Home books and products, visit us at tasteofhome.com.

For more Reader's Digest products and information, visit
rd.com (in the United States)
or see rd.ca (in Canada).

International Standard Book Number (10): 1-89821-876-4
International Standard Book Number (13): 978-0-89821-876-3
Library of Congress Control Number: 2011930379

Pictured on front cover: Italian Pasta Casserole, p. 67.
Pictured on back cover: Almond Cranberry Squash Bake, p. 159;
Meatball Rigatoni Alfredo, p. 25; Southwest Creamy Pasta Bake, p. 63.
Pictured on front flap: Dijon Scalloped Potatoes, p. 157.
Photo Credits: Stacked Pans, HelenaRakhuba /Shutterstock.com, p. 4.
Tip Box Kitchen Tools, Booka/Shutterstock.com.

Printed in USA.
3 5 7 9 10 8 6 4 2

table *of* contents

<< two-tater
shepherd's pie
37

hearty, comforting

Casserole, hot dish, potpie, strata, bake...no matter what you call it, it means convenient, comforting, home-cooked food.
Taste of Home Casseroles **is brimming with 377 delicious hot-dish recipes that are guaranteed to be delicious and satisfying.**

smoked pork chops
with sweet potatoes / **114**

WHY CASSEROLES ARE SO POPULAR:

- Many are either a convenient meal-in-one. Or, just add a salad or vegetable, and dinner is ready!

- Cleanup is easy—there's just the baking dish to wash.

- You're free to do other things while it bakes.

- Many can be assembled one day, then refrigerate and baked the next day.

- Casseroles are great for large family gatherings and potlucks.

- Leftovers make a delicious lunch or quick dinner.

- Most reheat easily in the microwave.

- Full of flavor, casseroles make you feel warm and cozy.

one-dish bakes

Casseroles offer an endless variety of food combinations. As you page through this book, you'll be amazed by all of the tempting dishes, from old-style classics to fresh combinations. Here's just a sample from the 10 chapters that follow.

The recipes in this collection were shared by home cooks just like you...they've been family tested and approved. And each dish was tested by a cooking professional at *Taste of Home*, the world's No. 1 food and entertaining magazine. So, when you make these recipes, you can cook with confidence knowing that they will turn out great, and other families have been delighted with them.

The casseroles in this indispensible cookbook are sure to become some of your family's favorite dishes. They'll be asking you to make them time and again!

breakfast

Egg bakes are great for lazy days or busy weekdays. Many featured here are prepped the night before, so while the family is getting ready in the morning, breakfast will be baking and they can start the day with a hearty meal.

<< pictured left

sausage-potato bake

prep: 20 min. • bake: 55 min. + standing

I not only make this casserole for breakfast, but sometimes for supper. To change it up a bit, you can substitute finely diced lean ham or crumbled turkey bacon for the sausage.
—Ruth Rigoni, Hurley, Wisconsin

- 1/2 pound bulk pork sausage
- 3 large potatoes, peeled and thinly sliced
- 1/2 teaspoon salt
- 1/4 teaspoon pepper
- 1 jar (2 ounces) diced pimientos, drained
- 3 eggs, lightly beaten
- 1 cup 2% milk
- 2 tablespoons minced chives
- 3/4 teaspoon dried thyme *or* oregano

Additional minced chives, optional

In a large skillet, cook sausage over medium heat until no longer pink; drain.

Arrange half of the potatoes in a greased 8-in. square baking dish; sprinkle with salt, pepper and half of the sausage. Layer with remaining potatoes and sausage; sprinkle with pimientos.

In a small bowl, whisk the eggs, milk, chives and thyme; pour over pimientos.

Cover and bake at 375° for 45-50 minutes or until a knife inserted near the center comes out clean. Uncover; bake 10 minutes longer or until lightly browned. Let stand for 10 minutes before cutting. Sprinkle with additional chives if desired. **yield: 6 servings.**

KITCHEN TIP

Red potatoes are great to use in casseroles. To thinly slice them for casseroles, you can use a sharp knife, but it is usually faster to use the slicing slot on a grater or mandoline. If you're really in a hurry, scrub the potatoes and slice them unpeeled.

broccoli-turkey brunch casserole

prep: 20 min. • bake: 45 min.

I have a lot of company at Thanksgiving, and I enjoy making new foods for them. I came up with this recipe as a great way to use up the leftover turkey. It's also great with cooked chicken, too.
—Kellie Mulleavy
   Lambertville, Michigan

- 1-1/2 cups fat-free milk
- 1 can (10-3/4 ounces) reduced-fat reduced-sodium condensed cream of chicken soup, undiluted
- 1 carton (8 ounces) egg substitute
- 1/4 cup reduced-fat sour cream
- 1/2 teaspoon pepper
- 1/4 teaspoon poultry seasoning
- 1/8 teaspoon salt
- 2-1/2 cups cubed cooked turkey breast
- 1 package (16 ounces) frozen chopped broccoli, thawed and drained
- 2 cups seasoned stuffing cubes
- 1 cup (4 ounces) shredded reduced-fat cheddar cheese, *divided*

In a large bowl, combine the milk, soup, egg substitute, sour cream, pepper, poultry seasoning and salt. Stir in the turkey, broccoli, stuffing cubes and 3/4 cup cheese. Transfer to a 13-in. x 9-in. baking dish coated with cooking spray.

Bake, uncovered, at 350° for 40 minutes. Sprinkle with remaining cheese. Bake 5-10 minutes longer or until a knife inserted near the center of the casserole comes out clean. Let stand for 5 minutes before serving. **yield: 6 servings.**

potatoes olé

prep: 25 min. • bake: 35 min.

I came up with this potato and egg recipe one summer when relatives came to visit. Everyone dug right in and commented on how delicious it was. To save time, you can use frozen hash browns.

—Lori Pierce
Cottage Grove, Minnesota

- 3/4 cup chopped onion
- 3/4 cup *each* chopped green, sweet red and yellow pepper
- 2 tablespoons butter
- 2 pounds red potatoes, cooked, peeled and cubed (1/4-inch cubes)
- 1 can (4 ounces) chopped green chilies, drained
- 5 eggs, lightly beaten
- 1 cup evaporated milk
- 1 cup (4 ounces) shredded Monterey Jack cheese
- 3/4 teaspoon salt
- 1/4 teaspoon pepper

Salsa and sour cream, optional

In a large skillet, saute onion and peppers in butter until tender. Add potatoes and chilies; toss to combine.

Transfer to a greased 2-qt. baking dish. In a large bowl, whisk the eggs, milk, cheese, salt and pepper; pour over the potato mixture.

Bake, uncovered, at 400° for 35-40 minutes or until a thermometer reads 160°. Serve with salsa and sour cream if desired. **yield: 8 servings.**

weekend breakfast bake

prep: 15 min. • bake: 30 min.

My family really enjoys this breakfast casserole on weekends or holidays. It's so quick to prepare and very filling. It's great for those on a low-carb diet, too!

—Melissa Ball, Pearisburg, Virginia

- 1 pound bulk pork sausage
- 1/3 cup chopped onion
- 4 cups (16 ounces) shredded Monterey Jack *or* cheddar cheese
- 8 eggs, lightly beaten
- 1 can (10-3/4 ounces) condensed cream of mushroom soup, undiluted

In a large skillet, cook sausage and onion over medium heat until meat is no longer pink; drain. Transfer to a greased 13-in. x 9-in. baking dish. Sprinkle with cheese. Combine eggs and soup; pour over cheese.

Bake, uncovered, at 400° for 30-35 minutes or until a knife inserted near the center comes out clean. Let stand for 5 minutes before cutting. **yield: 8 servings.**

italian sausage biscuit bake

prep: 20 min. • bake: 35 min.

This recipe is a keeper because all the components of a great breakfast go into one dish. It makes the morning less hectic for the one who is cooking. My family says it reminds them of their favorite fast-food breakfast sandwich.
—Amanda Denton, Barre, Vermont

1-1/4	pounds bulk Italian sausage
2	tubes (12 ounces *each)* refrigerated buttermilk biscuits, *divided*
1-1/3	cups chopped sweet red peppers
8	egg, lightly beaten
3/4	cup 2% milk
1/2	cup minced fresh parsley
1-1/2	cups (6 ounces) shredded Monterey Jack cheese
1	tablespoon butter
2	teaspoons dried oregano

In a large skillet, cook sausage over medium heat until no longer pink; drain. Arrange 10 biscuits in a greased 13-in. x 9-in. baking dish. Sprinkle sausage and red peppers over the biscuits. In a large bowl, whisk the eggs, milk and parsley. Pour over sausage. Sprinkle with cheese.

Bake, uncovered, at 350° for 20 minutes. Top with remaining biscuits. Brush biscuits with butter and sprinkle with oregano. Bake 15-20 minutes longer or until biscuits are golden brown and a knife inserted in the egg mixture comes out clean. Let stand for 5 minutes before serving. **yield: 10 servings.**

golden shrimp brunch casserole

prep: 15 min.
bake: 50 min. + standing

During the '40s, Mother had a close group of friends whose husbands or sons were off to war. To ease their worries, the group frequently met for lunch. This was one of my mother's favorite lunch recipes.
—Marilyn Bagshaw
  San Rafael, California

6	eggs, lightly beaten
2-1/2	cups 2% milk
2	tablespoons minced fresh parsley
3/4	teaspoon ground mustard
1/2	teaspoon salt
10	slices bread, crusts removed and cubed
2	cups frozen cooked salad shrimp, thawed
8	ounces sliced process American cheese, cut into thin strips

In a large bowl, whisk the eggs, milk, parsley, mustard and salt. In a greased 11-in. x 7-in. baking dish, layer with bread cubes, shrimp and cheese; pour egg mixture over top.

Bake, uncovered, at 325° for 50-55 minutes or until a knife inserted near the center comes out clean. Let stand for 10 minutes before serving. **yield: 6 servings.**

blueberry blintz souffle

prep: 10 min. • bake: 65 min.

Store-bought blintzes speed up the preparation of this rich blueberry souffle. This delightful brunch entree tastes great with just about any breakfast meat served alongside.
—Iris Katz, Pompano Beach, Florida

- 3 tablespoons butter, melted
- 2 packages (13 ounces *each*) frozen blueberry blintzes
- 4 eggs, lightly beaten
- 1-1/2 cups (12 ounces) sour cream
- 1/4 cup sugar
- 1 tablespoon orange juice
- 1 teaspoon vanilla extract

Confectioners' sugar, optional

Place butter in a 13-in. x 9-in. baking dish. Top with blintzes. In a large bowl, combine the eggs, sour cream, sugar, orange juice and vanilla. Pour over the blintzes.

Cover and bake at 350° for 55 minutes. Uncover; bake 10-15 minutes longer or until lightly browned and a knife inserted in the egg mixture comes out clean. Sprinkle with confectioners' sugar if desired. **yield: 6 servings.**

meatless sausage egg bake

prep: 25 min. • bake: 35 min. + standing

This eye-opener is sure to please every palate at your breakfast table. Crumbled vegetarian patties make the potato casserole a hearty option that doesn't pack on the pounds.
—Taste of Home Test Kitchen

- 1 small onion, chopped
- 1 small green pepper, chopped
- 1 small sweet red pepper, chopped
- 2 teaspoons canola oil
- 12 egg whites
- 6 eggs, lightly beaten
- 1 cup fat-free milk
- 1 package (16 ounces) frozen shredded hash brown potatoes, thawed
- 1 package (8 ounces) frozen vegetarian breakfast sausage patties, thawed and crumbled
- 1 cup (4 ounces) shredded reduced-fat cheddar cheese
- 1 teaspoon salt
- 1/2 teaspoon pepper

In a small nonstick skillet, saute onion and peppers in oil until tender. In a large bowl, beat the egg whites, eggs and milk. Stir in hash browns, crumbled sausage, cheese, salt, pepper and onion mixture.

Transfer to a 13-in. x 9-in. baking dish coated with cooking spray. Bake, uncovered, at 350° for 35-45 minutes or until a knife inserted near the center comes out clean. Let stand for 10 minutes before cutting. **yield: 8 servings.**

french toast strata

prep: 10 min. + chilling • bake: 35 min. + standing

I'm always on the lookout for different breakfast and brunch ideas. I like to serve this easy make-ahead strata when we have out-of-town guests.
—Jill Middleton, Baldwinsville, New York

- 1 loaf (1 pound) cinnamon bread, cubed
- 1 package (8 ounces) cream cheese, cubed
- 8 eggs, lightly beaten
- 2-1/2 cups 2% milk
- 6 tablespoons butter, melted
- 1/4 cup maple syrup

CIDER SYRUP:

- 1/2 cup sugar
- 4 teaspoons cornstarch
- 1/2 teaspoon ground cinnamon
- 1 cup apple cider
- 1 tablespoon lemon juice
- 2 tablespoons butter

Arrange half of the bread cubes in a greased 13-in. x 9-in. baking dish. Layer with cream cheese and remaining bread. In a blender, combine the eggs, milk, butter and maple syrup; cover and process until smooth. Pour over bread. Cover and refrigerate overnight.

Remove from the refrigerator 30 minutes before baking. Bake, uncovered, at 350° for 35-40 minutes or until a knife inserted near the center comes out clean. Let stand for 10 minutes before serving.

For syrup, in a small saucepan, combine the sugar, cornstarch and cinnamon. Gradually whisk in cider and lemon juice. Bring to a boil; cook and stir for 2 minutes or until thickened. Stir in butter until melted. Serve warm with strata. **yield: 8 servings (1 cup syrup).**

KITCHEN TIP

When purchasing maple syrup, read the label to make sure it says pure maple syrup. Some syrups may say "all natural," but they have other ingredients listed besides maple syrup. Once you open the bottle, it should be stored in the refrigerator.

asparagus strata

prep: 20 min. + chilling
bake: 45 min.

This wonderful egg dish originally called for sausage, but I think fresh asparagus is tasty and healthier.
—Amy Grover, Salem, Massachusetts

- 4 cups water
- 1 pound fresh asparagus, trimmed and cut into 1/2-inch pieces
- 2 cups 2% milk
- 6 bread slices, crust removed and cubed
- 6 eggs, lightly beaten
- 1 cup (4 ounces) shredded cheddar cheese
- 1 teaspoon salt

In a large saucepan, bring water to a boil. Add asparagus; boil, uncovered, for 3 minutes. Drain and immediately place asparagus in ice water. Drain and pat dry.

In a large bowl, combine asparagus, milk, bread cubes, eggs, cheese and salt. Transfer to a greased 2-qt. baking dish. Cover and refrigerate overnight.

Remove from refrigerator 30 minutes before baking. Bake, uncovered, at 350° for 45-55 minutes or until a knife inserted near the center comes out clean. Let stand for 10 minutes before serving. **yield: 6 servings.**

zippy egg casserole

prep: 20 min. + chilling • bake: 40 min. + standing

Pepper Jack cheese adds a bit of zip to the eggs in this dish. Instead of plain white bread, it uses seasoned croutons, which give it even more flavor.
—Anita Jones, Raytown, Missouri

- 1 pound bulk pork sausage
- 1 package (5-1/2 ounces) seasoned salad croutons
- 1-1/2 cups (6 ounces) shredded cheddar cheese
- 1 cup (4 ounces) shredded Swiss cheese
- 1 cup (4 ounces) shredded pepper Jack cheese
- 8 eggs, lightly beaten
- 2 cups half-and-half cream
- 1-1/2 cups 2% milk
- 1 tablespoon finely chopped onion
- 1-1/2 teaspoons ground mustard
- 1/4 teaspoon salt
- 1/4 teaspoon pepper

In a large skillet, cook sausage over medium heat until no longer pink; drain. Place the croutons in a greased 13-in. x 9-in. baking dish. Sprinkle with cheeses and sausage.

In a large bowl, whisk the remaining ingredients; pour over the casserole. Cover and refrigerate overnight.

Remove from the refrigerator 30 minutes before baking. Bake, uncovered, at 350° for 40-45 minutes or until a knife inserted near the center comes out clean. Let stand for 10 minutes before serving. **yield: 8-10 servings.**

veggie-packed strata

prep: 15 min. • bake: 1 hour + standing

People are always eager to try this deliciously different casserole featuring eggs, vegetables and cheese. Baked in a springform pan, the colorful strata catches folks' attention no matter where it's served.
—Jennifer Unsell, Vance, Alabama

- 2 medium sweet red peppers, julienned
- 1 medium sweet yellow pepper, julienned
- 1 large red onion, sliced
- 3 tablespoons olive oil, *divided*
- 3 garlic cloves, minced
- 2 medium yellow summer squash, thinly sliced
- 2 medium zucchini, thinly sliced
- 1/2 pound fresh mushrooms, sliced
- 1 package (8 ounces) cream cheese, softened
- 1/4 cup heavy whipping cream
- 2 teaspoons salt
- 1 teaspoon pepper
- 6 eggs
- 8 slices bread, cubed, *divided*
- 2 cups (8 ounces) shredded Swiss cheese

In a large skillet, saute the peppers and onion in 1 tablespoon oil until tender. Add garlic; cook 1 minute longer. Drain; pat dry and set aside. In the same skillet, saute the yellow squash, zucchini and mushrooms in remaining oil until tender. Drain; pat dry and set aside.

In a large bowl, beat the cream cheese, cream, salt and pepper until smooth. Beat in eggs. Stir in vegetables, half of the bread cubes and Swiss cheese. Arrange the remaining bread cubes in a greased 10-in. springform pan. Place on a baking sheet. Pour egg mixture into the pan.

Bake, uncovered, at 325° for 60-70 minutes or until a knife inserted near the center comes out clean. Let stand for 10 minutes before serving. Run a knife around edge of pan to loosen; remove sides. Cut into wedges. **yield: 8-10 servings.**

chili-cheese breakfast bake

prep: 20 min. + chilling
bake: 1 hour

Get everyone out of bed on nippy fall mornings with this savory Southwestern breakfast casserole.
—Kathy Mead, Surprise, Arizona

---

6 slices whole wheat bread, cubed

1/2 cup shredded reduced-fat Mexican cheese blend

1 can (4 ounces) chopped green chilies

4 eggs, lightly beaten

4 egg whites

2 cups fat-free milk

1 teaspoon ground mustard

1/2 teaspoon salt

Dash pepper

In a 1-1/2-qt. baking dish coated with cooking spray, layer half of the bread cubes, cheese and chilies. Repeat the layers.

In a large bowl, whisk the eggs, egg whites, milk, mustard, salt and pepper; pour over top. Cover and refrigerate overnight.

Remove from the refrigerator 30 minutes before baking. Bake, uncovered, at 350° for 60-70 minutes or until a knife inserted near the center comes out clean. Let stand for 5 minutes before cutting. **yield: 4 servings.**

cheese 'n' ham strata

prep: 20 min. + chilling • bake: 40 min. + standing

We love to hold potluck meals at our church, and this is the dish I make for those get-togethers. People always tell me how well they like this strata.
—Ilene Harrington, Nipomo, California

---

5 cups cubed bread, *divided*

2 cups cubed fully cooked ham

1/4 cup chopped green pepper

2 tablespoons chopped onion

2 cups (8 ounces) shredded cheddar cheese

1 cup (4 ounces) shredded pepper Jack cheese

1 can (10-3/4 ounces) condensed cream of chicken soup, undiluted

1-1/3 cups 2% milk

4 eggs, lightly beaten

1 cup mayonnaise

1/2 teaspoon pepper

Dash cayenne pepper

2 tablespoons butter, melted

2 tablespoons minced fresh parsley

Place 3-1/2 cups bread in a greased 13-in. x 9-in. baking dish. Layer with ham, green pepper and onion; sprinkle with cheeses.

In a large bowl, combine soup and milk. Stir in the eggs, mayonnaise, pepper and cayenne. Pour over cheeses. Toss remaining bread cubes with butter. Sprinkle over soup mixture. Cover and refrigerate for 8 hours or overnight.

Remove from the refrigerator 30 minutes before baking. Bake, uncovered, at 350° for 40-45 minutes or until a knife inserted near the center comes out clean. Sprinkle with parsley. Let stand for 5 minutes before serving. **yield: 8-10 servings.**

florentine egg bake

prep: 30 min. • bake: 50 min. + standing

For a flavorful breakfast bake that comes together quickly using handy convenience foods, including refrigerated hash browns, biscuit mix and store-bought pesto, try this recipe. For a seafood variation, replace the ham with crabmeat or shrimp.
—Patricia Harmon, Baden, Pennsylvania

- 1 package (20 ounces) refrigerated shredded hash brown potatoes
- 1 tablespoon olive oil
- 1 package (10 ounces) frozen chopped spinach, thawed and squeezed dry
- 4 ounces Swiss cheese, cubed
- 4 ounces thinly sliced deli ham, coarsely chopped
- 8 eggs, lightly beaten
- 1/2 cup buttermilk
- 1 tablespoon prepared pesto
- 1 cup biscuit/baking mix
- 1/4 teaspoon salt
- 1/8 teaspoon pepper
- 1-1/2 cups shredded Asiago cheese
- 2 tablespoons minced fresh basil

In a large bowl, combine the hash browns and oil. Press into a 13-in. x 9-in. baking dish coated with cooking spray. Bake at 350° for 25-30 minutes or until edges are golden brown.

Combine the spinach and Swiss cheese; sprinkle over crust. Top with ham. In a large bowl, whisk the eggs, buttermilk and pesto. Combine the biscuit mix, salt and pepper; add to egg mixture. Stir in the Asiago cheese. Pour over ham.

Bake, uncovered, for 25-30 minutes or until a knife inserted near the center comes out clean. Let stand for 10-15 minutes before cutting. Sprinkle with basil. **yield: 8 servings.**

KITCHEN TIP

To quickly thaw spinach, remove it from the package and place on a microwave-safe dish. Defrost in the microwave until it starts to break apart. It should still be cold. Place the spinach in a paper towel-lined strainer and press and squeeze the spinach to remove the liquid.

mushroom sausage strata

prep: 15 min. + chilling
bake: 35 min. + standing

This delightful casserole is a filling mainstay for our family's Christmas Day brunch. Being able to assemble the recipe ahead of time is a real plus!
—Julie Sterchi, Harrisburg, Illinois

- 1 pound bulk pork sausage
- 10 slices whole wheat bread, cubed
- 1 can (4 ounces) mushroom stems and pieces, drained
- 1/2 cup shredded cheddar cheese
- 1/2 cup shredded Swiss cheese
- 6 eggs, lightly beaten
- 1 cup 2% milk
- 1 cup half-and-half cream
- 1 teaspoon Worcestershire sauce
- 1/2 teaspoon pepper

In a large skillet, cook sausage over medium heat until no longer pink; drain. Place the bread cubes in a greased 13-in. x 9-in. baking dish. Sprinkle with sausage, mushrooms and cheeses.

In a large bowl, whisk the remaining ingredients; pour over the cheese. Cover and refrigerate overnight.

Remove from the refrigerator 30 minutes before baking. Bake, uncovered, at 350° for 35-45 minutes or until a knife inserted near the center comes out clean. Let stand for 10 minutes before serving. **yield: 8-10 servings.**

artichoke egg casserole

prep: 15 min. • bake: 35 min.

This is a great recipe for a brunch as well as breakfast. I serve it with fresh stir-fried asparagus, a fruit salad and croissants.
—Marilyn Moores
    Indianapolis, Indiana

---

    4 jars (6-1/2 ounces *each*) marinated artichoke hearts
1/2 cup chopped green onions
    1 tablespoon canola oil
    2 to 3 garlic cloves, minced
    8 eggs, lightly beaten
    1 jar (4-1/2 ounces) sliced mushrooms, drained
    3 cups (12 ounces) shredded sharp cheddar cheese
    1 cup butter-flavored cracker crumbs (about 25 crackers)

Drain artichokes, reserving 1/2 cup marinade. Set aside. Cut artichokes into slices; set aside. In a small skillet, saute green onions in oil until tender. Add garlic; cook 1 minute longer. Remove from the heat.

In a large bowl, combine the eggs, artichokes, mushrooms, cheese, cracker crumbs, onion mixture and reserved marinade.

Transfer to a greased 13-in. x 9-in. baking dish. Bake, uncovered, at 350° for 35-40 minutes or until a knife inserted near the center comes out clean. Let stand for 5 minutes before cutting. **yield: 9 servings.**

ham and broccoli bake

prep: 15 min. + chilling • bake: 35 min.

Plan ahead and start this satisfying and comforting casserole the night before you are going to bake it. It's a hearty, warming entree that is also inexpensive to serve.
—Harmony Tardugno, Vernon Center, New York

---

    1 loaf (8 ounces) day-old French bread, cubed
1/2 cup butter, melted
    2 cups (8 ounces) shredded cheddar cheese
    2 cups frozen chopped broccoli, thawed
    2 cups cubed fully cooked ham
    4 eggs, lightly beaten
    2 cups 2% milk
1/4 teaspoon pepper

Toss bread cubes with butter. Place half in a greased 13-in. x 9-in. baking dish. Layer with half of the cheese and broccoli; sprinkle with ham. Layer with remaining broccoli, cheese and bread cubes.

In a large bowl, whisk the eggs, milk and pepper. Pour over casserole. Cover and refrigerate overnight.

Remove from the refrigerator 30 minutes before baking. Bake, uncovered, at 350° for 35-40 minutes or until a knife inserted near the center comes out clean. Let stand for 5 minutes before cutting. **yield: 8 servings.**

breakfast bake

prep: 15 min. • bake: 50 min.

I wanted to have scrambled eggs and hash browns one morning, and this is the dish I created. My wife loved it. Guess who's making breakfast more often?
—Howard Rogers, El Paso, Texas

1-1/2 cups egg substitute
1/2 cup fat-free milk
3-1/2 cups frozen O'Brien potatoes, thawed
1-1/3 cups shredded reduced-fat cheddar cheese, *divided*
1/2 cup chopped sweet onion
4 tablespoons crumbled cooked bacon, *divided*
1/2 teaspoon salt
1/2 teaspoon salt-free seasoning blend
1/4 teaspoon chili powder
4 green onions, chopped

In a large bowl, whisk egg substitute and milk. Stir in the hash browns, 1 cup cheese, onion, 2 tablespoons bacon, salt, seasoning blend and chili powder. Pour into an 8-in. square baking dish coated with cooking spray.

Bake at 350° for 45-50 minutes or until a knife inserted near the center comes out clean. Sprinkle with remaining cheese and bacon. Bake 3-5 minutes longer or until cheese is melted. Sprinkle with the green onions. Let stand for 5 minutes before cutting. **yield: 6 servings.**

savory salami strata

prep: 15 min. + chilling
bake: 55 min. + standing

The mild Italian flavor makes this a fabulous choice for a brunch. I served it at my daughter's First Communion celebration. The wonderful aroma greeted guests as they came into the house.
—Peggy Nelson, Webster, Minnesota

Butter, softened
16 slices bread, crusts removed
1 cup diced fresh tomato
1/4 cup diced green pepper
8 slices salami *or* pepperoni
2 cups (8 ounces) shredded mozzarella cheese
6 egg, lightly beaten
3 cups 2% milk
1 teaspoon dried basil
1/2 teaspoon salt
1/2 teaspoon Italian seasoning

Butter one side of each slice of bread. Place eight slices buttered side up in a greased 13-in. x 9-in. baking dish. Set aside 1 tablespoon each of the tomato and green pepper. Layer with salami, cheese, remaining tomato and green pepper. Top with remaining bread.

In a large bowl, whisk the eggs, milk, basil, salt and Italian seasoning. Pour over bread. Sprinkle with reserved tomatoes and green pepper. Cover and refrigerate for at least 4 hours.

Remove from the refrigerator 30 minutes before baking. Bake, uncovered, at 325° for 55 minutes or until a knife inserted near the center comes out clean. Let stand for 10 minutes before serving. **yield: 8 servings.**

ham 'n' egg tortilla bake

prep: 25 min. • bake: 20 min.

This recipe came about one day when I needed to make my husband's lunch and we were out of bread. It's now one of his favorites and also a great brunch casserole.
—Lauren Budweg, Oberlin, Ohio

- 1 cup sliced fresh mushrooms
- 1 medium onion, chopped
- 1/2 cup chopped green pepper
- 1/4 cup butter, cubed
- 6 eggs, lightly beaten
- 1/4 cup 2% milk
- 1/4 teaspoon pepper
- 1 cup cubed fully cooked ham
- 1 can (10-3/4 ounces) condensed cream of mushroom soup, undiluted
- 10 flour tortillas (8 inches), warmed
- 1-1/2 cups (6 ounces) shredded cheddar cheese

In a large skillet, saute mushrooms, onion and green pepper in butter until tender. Meanwhile, in a large bowl, whisk together the eggs, milk and pepper; add the ham. Pour into skillet. Cook and stir over medium heat until eggs are completely set.

In a greased 13-in. x 9-in. baking dish, spread half of the soup. Place 3 tablespoons egg mixture down the center of each tortilla; sprinkle each with 1 tablespoon cheese. Roll up and place seam side down over soup.

Spread the remaining soup over tortillas. Sprinkle with the remaining cheese. Bake, uncovered, at 350° for 20-25 minutes or until heated through. **yield: 5 servings.**

green chili egg puff

prep: 15 min. • bake: 35 min.

Green chilies add a touch of Southwest flavor to this fluffy egg dish. The cottage cheese offers nice texture, and people always adore the gooey Monterey Jack cheese melted throughout.
—Laurel Leslie, Sonora, California

- 10 eggs
- 1/2 cup all-purpose flour
- 1 teaspoon baking powder
- 1/2 teaspoon salt
- 4 cups (16 ounces) shredded Monterey Jack cheese
- 2 cups (16 ounces) 4% cottage cheese
- 1 can (4 ounces) chopped green chilies

In a large bowl, beat eggs on medium-high speed for 3 minutes or until light and lemon-colored. Combine the flour, baking powder and salt; gradually add to eggs and mix well. Stir in cheeses and chilies.

Pour into a greased 13-in. x 9-in. baking dish. Bake, uncovered, at 350° for 35-40 minutes or until a knife inserted near the center comes out clean. Let stand for 5 minutes before serving. **yield: 12 servings.**

breakfast enchilada bake

prep: 15 min. • bake: 55 min.

My sister gave me the directions for this fuss-free, hearty breakfast, and I can't tell you how many times I've used it for holiday brunch. I'm so pleased with it because it's full of flavor, fast and filling.
—Loree Ellis, Colorado Springs, Colorado

- 2 cups chopped shaved deli ham
- 1/2 cup chopped green onions
- 1/2 cup chopped green pepper
- 1 package (10 ounces) frozen chopped spinach, thawed and squeezed dry
- 1 can (4 ounces) chopped green chilies
- 1-1/4 cups shredded cheddar cheese
- 1-1/4 cups shredded Monterey Jack cheese
- 8 flour tortillas (6 inches)
- 6 eggs, lightly beaten
- 2-1/2 cups half-and-half cream
- 2 tablespoons all-purpose flour
- 1/4 teaspoon garlic powder
- 1/4 teaspoon salt
- 2 to 3 drops hot pepper sauce

In a large bowl, combine the first five ingredients. In another bowl, combine the cheeses. Spoon about 1/4 cup of ham mixture off-center on each tortilla; sprinkle with 2 tablespoons cheese mixture. Fold sides and ends over filling and roll up. Place seam side down in a greased 13-in. x 9-in. baking dish.

In a bowl, whisk eggs, cream, flour, garlic powder, salt and hot pepper sauce. Pour over tortillas. Sprinkle with remaining ham mixture.

Cover and bake at 350° for 50 minutes. Uncover; sprinkle with remaining cheeses. Bake 5-10 minutes longer or until cheese is melted. **yield: 8 servings.**

KITCHEN TIP

Italian sausage links are a great to have on hand in the freezer. They defrost quickly in the microwave, and can be used in place of bulk sausage. Slit the casing lengthwise down the sausage, peel it off and crumble the sausage into the skillet. One average link is about 1/4 pound.

broccoli sausage breakfast bake

prep: 20 min. • bake: 25 min.

I'm very involved in 4-H and raise hogs to show at our county fair. I like to share tasty recipes that help promote the pork industry.
—Kara Cash, Dumont, Texas

- 1/2 pound bulk pork sausage
- 1 cup chopped fresh broccoli
- 2 cups (8 ounces) shredded cheddar cheese
- 3 eggs, lightly beaten
- 1-1/4 cups 2% milk
- 1/2 cup biscuit/baking mix

In a large skillet, cook sausage over medium heat until no longer pink; drain and set aside. Add 1 in. of water and broccoli to a saucepan; bring to a boil. Reduce heat. Cover and simmer for 5-8 minutes or until broccoli is crisp-tender; drain.

In a greased 9-in. pie plate, layer the sausage, cheese and broccoli. In a large bowl, combine the eggs, milk and biscuit mix. Pour over broccoli.

Bake at 350° for 25-30 minutes or until a knife inserted near the center comes out clean. **yield: 6-8 servings.**

blueberry french toast bake

prep: 10 min. + chilling
bake: 35 min. + standing

If you like blueberries and pecans, you'll appreciate this take on a breakfast favorite. I assemble it the night before, then I bake it in the morning to surprise my roommates... who finish it in one sitting.
—Melissa Winona
  Salt Lake City, Utah

- 12 slices day-old French bread (1 inch thick)
- 5 eggs, lightly beaten
- 2-1/2 cups 2% milk
- 1 cup packed brown sugar, *divided*
- 1 teaspoon vanilla extract
- 1/2 teaspoon ground nutmeg
- 1 cup chopped pecans
- 1/4 cup butter, melted
- 2 cups fresh *or* frozen blueberries

Arrange bread in a greased 13-in. x 9-in. baking dish. In a large bowl, combine the eggs, milk, 3/4 cup brown sugar, vanilla and nutmeg; pour over bread. Cover and refrigerate for 8 hours or overnight.

Remove from the refrigerator 30 minutes before baking. Sprinkle pecans over egg mixture. Combine butter and remaining sugar; drizzle over the top.

Bake, uncovered, at 400° for 25 minutes. Sprinkle with blueberries. Bake 10 minutes longer or until a knife inserted near the center comes out clean. **yield: 6-8 servings.**

cinnamon raisin strata

prep: 20 min. + chilling • bake: 40 min.

This delightful rise-and-shine treat is made with day-old raisin bread, and is full of cinnamon flavor. I like to serve it for brunch with sliced bacon and a fruit compote.
—Barbara Tritch, Hope, Idaho

- 1/4 cup butter, softened
- 3 tablespoons ground cinnamon
- 8 slices day-old raisin bread
- 4 tablespoons brown sugar, *divided*
- 6 eggs, lightly beaten
- 1-1/2 cups 2% milk
- 3 tablespoons maple syrup
- 1 teaspoon vanilla extract
Additional maple syrup

In a small bowl, combine butter and cinnamon; spread over one side of each slice of bread. Place four slices, buttered side up, in a greased 8-in. square baking dish (trim to fit if necessary). Sprinkle with 2 tablespoons brown sugar. Repeat with remaining bread and brown sugar.

In a large bowl, whisk the eggs, milk, syrup and vanilla; pour over bread. Cover and refrigerate overnight.

Remove from the refrigerator 30 minutes before baking. Bake, uncovered, at 350° for 40-50 minutes or until a knife inserted near the center comes out clean. Serve with additional syrup. **yield: 4 servings.**

double-cheese ham souffle

prep: 15 min. + chilling • bake: 40 min. + standing

I've made this for holiday breakfasts and shower brunches. It's a big hit. It's also a welcome change at covered-dish dinners at church. There's never another one like it there.

—Aita Gattis, Hawkinsville, Georgia

---

16 slices day-old bread, crust removed and cubed

1 pound cubed fully cooked ham

2 cups (8 ounces) shredded cheddar cheese

1 cup (4 ounces) shredded Swiss cheese

6 eggs, lightly beaten

3 cups 2% milk

1/2 teaspoon onion powder

1/2 teaspoon ground mustard

1/8 teaspoon pepper

Dash to 1/8 teaspoon cayenne pepper

1-1/2 cups finely crushed cornflakes

3 tablespoons butter, melted

Place half of the bread cubes in a greased 13-in. x 9-in. baking dish. Layer with ham, cheeses and remaining bread cubes.

In a large bowl, whisk together the eggs, milk and seasonings; pour over the top. Cover and refrigerate for 8 hours or overnight.

Remove from the refrigerator 30 minutes before baking. Combine the cornflakes and butter; sprinkle over casserole.

Bake, uncovered, at 375° for 40-45 minutes or until a knife inserted near the center comes out clean. Let stand for 10 minutes before serving. **yield: 8-10 servings.**

sausage egg bake

prep: 25 min. • bake: 25 min.

Here's a busy-day breakfast bake that's fast, flavorful and fun to make. As an added bonus, it uses up any hard-cooked eggs you may have in your refrigerator

—Erika Anderson, Wausau, Wisconsin

- 1/2 **pound bulk pork sausage**
- 3 **tablespoons butter, melted, *divided***
- 2 **tablespoons all-purpose flour**
- 1/4 **teaspoon salt**
- 1/4 **teaspoon pepper**
- 1-1/4 **cups 2% milk**
- 2 **cups frozen shredded hash brown potatoes**
- 4 **hard-cooked eggs, sliced**
- 1/2 **cup crushed cornflakes**
- 1/4 **cup sliced green onions**

In a large skillet, cook sausage over medium heat until no longer pink; drain. Stir in 2 tablespoons butter, flour, salt and pepper until blended. Gradually add milk. Bring to a boil; cook and stir for 2 minutes or until thickened. Stir in the hash browns and eggs. Transfer to a greased 1-qt. baking dish.

Toss cornflakes and remaining butter; sprinkle over sausage mixture. Bake, uncovered, at 350° for 25-30 minutes or until heated through. Sprinkle with onions. **yield: 3 servings.**

ham 'n' cheese egg loaf

prep: 10 min. • bake: 55 min. + cooling

My family has enjoyed slices of this moist brunch loaf for many years. Every crumb disappears fast whenever I serve it at potlucks or gatherings.

—Connie Bair, East Wenatchee, Washington

- 6 **eggs**
- 3/4 **cup 2% milk**
- 1 **teaspoon prepared mustard**
- 1-1/2 **cups all-purpose flour**
- 2-1/2 **teaspoons baking powder**
- 1/4 **teaspoon salt**
- 6 **bacon strips, cooked and crumbled**
- 1 **cup cubed fully cooked ham**
- 4 **ounces cheddar cheese, cut into 1/2-inch cubes**
- 4 **ounces Monterey Jack cheese, cut into 1/2-inch cubes**

In a large bowl, beat eggs until frothy, about 1 minute. Add milk and mustard. Combine the flour, baking powder and salt. Add to the egg mixture and beat until smooth. Stir in bacon, ham and cheeses. Transfer to a greased and floured 9-in. x 5-in. loaf pan.

Bake, uncovered, at 350° for 55-60 minutes or until a toothpick inserted near the center comes out clean. Cool for 10-15 minutes. Run a knife around edge of pan to remove. Slice and serve warm. **yield: 6-8 servings**

egg and corn quesadilla

prep: 25 min. • bake: 10 min.

For a deliciously different mid-morning meal, try this excellent quesadilla. It's also great for a light lunch or supper. Corn is a natural in Southwestern cooking and a tasty addition to this zippy egg dish.
—Stacy Joura, Stoneboro, Pennsylvania

- 1 medium onion, chopped
- 1 medium green pepper, chopped
- 2 tablespoons olive oil
- 1 garlic clove, minced
- 3 cups fresh *or* frozen corn
- 1 teaspoon minced chives
- 1/2 teaspoon dried cilantro flakes
- 1/2 teaspoon salt
- 1/4 teaspoon pepper
- 4 eggs, lightly beaten

- 4 flour tortillas (10 inches)
- 1/2 cup salsa
- 1 cup (8 ounces) sour cream
- 1 cup (4 ounces) shredded cheddar cheese
- 1 cup (4 ounces) shredded part-skim mozzarella cheese

Additional salsa and sour cream, optional

In a large skillet, saute onion and green pepper in oil until tender. Add garlic; cook 1 minute longer. Stir in the corn, chives, cilantro, salt and pepper. Cook until heated through, about 3 minutes. Stir in eggs; cook until completely set, stirring occasionally. Remove from the heat.

Place one tortilla on a lightly greased baking sheet or pizza pan; layer with a third of the corn mixture, salsa and sour cream. Sprinkle with a fourth of the cheeses. Repeat layers twice. Top with remaining tortilla and cheeses.

Bake the quesadilla at 350° for 10 minutes or until the cheese is melted. Cut into wedges. Serve with the salsa and sour cream if desired. **yield: 6-8 servings.**

beef

A hearty casserole made with savory beef is sure to satisfy. Beef pairs well with pasta, rice, cheese and vegetables in any combination. You're sure to find a new favorite among these recipes perfect for everyday meals and potluck dinners.

<< pictured left

meatball rigatoni alfredo

prep: 1-1/4 hours • bake: 20 min.

My kids love meatballs with rigatoni or spaghetti. The baked cheese sauce in this recipe just takes it over the top!
—Jennifer Ross, Clinton, Ohio

>   1 egg, lightly beaten
> 3/4 cup seasoned bread crumbs
> 1/3 cup water
> 1/4 cup grated Parmesan cheese
> 4-1/2 teaspoons minced fresh thyme
> 4-1/2 teaspoons minced fresh oregano
> 4-1/2 teaspoons minced fresh basil
> 1-1/2 teaspoons pepper
> 1/2 teaspoon salt
> 1-1/2 pounds ground beef
>   1 tablespoon canola oil
>   1 small onion, chopped
>   3 garlic cloves, minced
> 1/3 cup dry red wine *or* beef broth
>   1 can (28 ounces) crushed tomatoes
>   1 tablespoon minced fresh parsley
>   12 ounces uncooked rigatoni *or* large tube pasta

ALFREDO TOPPING:

> 1/4 cup butter, cubed
>   2 tablespoons all-purpose flour
>   2 cups half-and-half cream
>   1 cup grated Parmesan cheese, *divided*
>   1 teaspoon minced fresh thyme
>   1 teaspoon minced fresh oregano

In a large bowl, combine the first nine ingredients. Crumble beef over mixture and mix well. Shape into 1-1/2-in. balls. In a Dutch oven, brown meatballs in oil in batches; remove and keep warm.

Drain, reserving 1 tablespoon drippings. In the drippings, saute onion until tender. Add garlic; cook 1 minute longer. Add wine; cook and stir for 3 minutes.

Return meatballs to the pan; stir in tomatoes and parsley. Bring to a boil. Reduce heat; cover and simmer for 25-30 minutes or until no pink remains and a meat thermometer reads 160°.

Cook rigatoni according to package directions. Meanwhile, in a small saucepan, melt butter. Stir in flour until smooth; gradually add cream. Bring to a boil; cook and stir for 1-2 minutes or until thickened. Remove from the heat. Stir in 3/4 cup Parmesan cheese.

Drain rigatoni; place in a large bowl. Add meatballs and sauce; stir to coat. Transfer to a greased 13-in. x 9-in. baking dish. Top with Alfredo sauce; sprinkle with thyme, oregano and remaining Parmesan cheese. Bake, uncovered, at 400° for 20-25 minutes or until bubbly. **yield: 6 servings.**

tortilla beef bake

prep: 10 min. • bake: 30 min.

My family enjoys Mexican food, so I came up with this simple, satisfying bake that gets its spark from salsa.
—Kim Osburn, Ligonier, Indiana

> 1-1/2 pounds ground beef
>   1 can (10-3/4 ounces) condensed cream of chicken soup, undiluted
> 2-1/2 cups crushed tortilla chips, *divided*
>   1 jar (16 ounces) salsa
> 1-1/2 cups (6 ounces) shredded cheddar cheese

In a large skillet, cook beef over medium heat until no longer pink; drain. Stir in soup. Sprinkle 1-1/2 cups tortilla chips in a greased shallow 2-1/2-qt. baking dish. Top with beef mixture, salsa and cheese.

Bake, uncovered, at 350° for 25-30 minutes or until bubbly. Sprinkle with the remaining chips. Bake 3 minutes longer or until chips are lightly toasted. **yield: 6 servings.**

beefy tomato rigatoni

prep: 15 min. • bake: 20 min.

Sharing recipes with friends is a favorite pastime of mine, and I get many requests for this wonderful main dish. What is especially nice is that this is a fantastic way to use up leftover roasts.

—Trudy Williams
  Shannonville, Ontario

- 1 large onion, chopped
- 1 tablespoon olive oil
- 2 cans (14-1/2 ounces *each*) Italian diced tomatoes, undrained
- 1 can (8 ounces) tomato sauce
- 3 cups shredded fully cooked beef rump roast
- 1/4 teaspoon salt
- 1/4 teaspoon crushed red pepper flakes
- 4-1/2 cups rigatoni *or* other large tube pasta, cooked and drained
- 2 cups (8 ounces) shredded mozzarella cheese
- 1 cup (4 ounces) shredded provolone cheese

In a large saucepan, saute onion in oil until tender. Stir in the tomatoes and tomato sauce. Bring to a boil. Reduce heat; cover and simmer for 5 minutes. Stir in the beef, salt and pepper flakes. Cover and simmer for 5 minutes. Add pasta; toss to coat.

Transfer to a greased 13-in. x 9-in. baking dish. Sprinkle with cheeses. Bake, uncovered, at 400° for 20-25 minutes or until cheese is melted. **yield: 6-8 servings.**

hamburger noodle bake

prep: 20 min. • bake: 35 min.

I enjoy saving time in the kitchen. This go-to recipe is ideal for busy cooks. You prepare it once and have two casseroles...one to bake now and the other to freeze and use within 3 months.

—Patricia Teller, Lewiston, Idaho

- 5 cups uncooked egg noodles
- 2 pounds ground beef
- 1 cup chopped onion
- 1/2 cup chopped green pepper
- 2 cans (10-3/4 ounces *each*) condensed tomato soup, undiluted
- 2 cups (8 ounces) shredded cheddar cheese
- 1-1/2 cups water
- 1/2 cup chili sauce
- 1-1/2 cups soft bread crumbs
- 3 tablespoons butter, melted

Cook noodles according to package directions until almost tender; drain. In a large skillet, cook the beef, onion and green pepper over medium-high heat for 10-12 minutes or until meat is no longer pink; drain. Stir in the noodles, soup, cheese, water and chili sauce. Transfer to two greased 8-in. square baking dishes.

Toss bread crumbs and butter; sprinkle over casseroles. Bake one casserole, uncovered, at 350° for 35-40 minutes or until bubbly and golden brown. Cover and freeze remaining casserole for up to 3 months.

to use frozen casserole: Remove from the freezer 30 minutes before baking (do not thaw). Cover and bake at 350° for 60 minutes. Uncover; bake 10-15 minutes longer or until heated through. **yield: 2 casseroles (4 servings each).**

creamy corned beef casserole

prep: 15 min. • bake: 45 min. + standing

My gang really loves the flavor of corned beef, so I created this casserole. It is so easy to whip up, and your family will want to dig right in.

—B.M., Overland Park, Kansas

---

    1 can (12 ounces) corned beef, crumbled *or* 1-1/2 cups diced cooked corned beef

    1 can (10-3/4 ounces) condensed cream of chicken soup, undiluted

    8 ounces cheddar cheese, cubed

    1 package (7 ounces) small shell pasta, cooked and drained

    1 cup milk

1/2 cup chopped onion

    2 bread slices, cubed

    2 tablespoons butter, melted

In a large bowl, combine the first six ingredients. Transfer to a greased 2-qt. baking dish. Toss bread cubes with butter; sprinkle over top.

Bake, uncovered, at 350° for 30 minutes. Cover and bake 15 minutes longer or until golden brown. Let stand 10 minutes before serving. **yield: 6-8 servings.**

double-cheese beef pasta

prep: 30 min. • bake: 45 min.

Provolone and mozzarella cheeses star in this rich, comforting pasta casserole. My mother shared the recipe with me years ago when I was a newlywed.
—Marilyn Pearson, Billings, Montana

2-1/2 cups uncooked medium shell pasta
   2 pounds ground beef
   2 medium onions, chopped
   1 jar (14 ounces) spaghetti sauce
   1 can (14-1/2 ounces) stewed tomatoes, undrained and finely chopped
   1 jar (4-1/2 ounces) sliced mushrooms, drained
   1 garlic clove, minced
   1 teaspoon salt
 1/2 teaspoon pepper
   2 cups (16 ounces) sour cream
   1 package (6 ounces) sliced provolone cheese
   1 cup (4 ounces) shredded part-skim mozzarella cheese

Cook pasta according to package directions. Meanwhile, in a large skillet, cook beef and onions over medium heat until meat is no longer pink; drain. Add the spaghetti sauce, tomatoes, mushrooms, garlic, salt and pepper. Bring to a boil. Reduce heat; simmer, uncovered, for 20 minutes, stirring occasionally.

Drain pasta; place half in a greased 3-qt. baking dish. Top with half of the beef mixture. Layer with sour cream and provolone cheese. Top with remaining pasta and beef mixture. Sprinkle with mozzarella cheese.

Cover and bake at 350° for 40 minutes. Uncover; bake 5-10 minutes longer or until cheese is melted. **yield: 6-8 servings.**

beef broccoli supper

prep: 25 min. • bake: 35 min.

When I put together a cookbook for our family reunion, my sister submitted this recipe. It's a great way for me to sneak broccoli into my husband and son's diet.
—*Nita Graffis, Dove Creek, Colorado*

3/4 cup uncooked long grain rice
1 pound ground beef
1-1/2 cups fresh broccoli florets
1 can (10-3/4 ounces) condensed broccoli cheese soup, undiluted
1/2 cup milk
1 teaspoon salt-free seasoning blend
1 teaspoon salt
1/2 teaspoon pepper
1/2 cup dry bread crumbs
2 tablespoons butter, melted

Cook rice according to package directions. Meanwhile, in a large skillet, cook beef over medium heat until no longer pink; drain. Add the rice, broccoli, soup, milk, seasoning blend, salt and pepper; stir until combined. Transfer to a greased 2-qt. baking dish.

Toss bread crumbs and butter; sprinkle over beef mixture. Cover and bake at 350° for 30 minutes. Uncover; bake 5-10 minutes longer or until heated through. **yield: 4-6 servings.**

ground beef shepherd's pie

prep: 10 min. • bake: 30 min.

Bake up an easy, down-home dinner with ground beef, frozen veggies and canned gravy. This hearty supper is ideal for small families.
—*Elaine Williams*
Surrey, British Columbia

1-1/2 pounds ground beef
1 small onion, chopped
2 garlic cloves, minced
1 can (10-1/2 ounces) beef gravy
1 cup frozen mixed vegetables
1/4 teaspoon Worcestershire sauce
Salt and pepper to taste
2-1/2 cups mashed potatoes

In a large skillet, cook beef and onion over medium heat until meat is no longer pink. Add garlic; cook 1 minute longer. Drain. Stir in the gravy, vegetables, Worcestershire sauce, salt and pepper.

Transfer to a greased 1-1/2-qt. baking dish. Spread potatoes over the top. Bake, uncovered, at 350° for 30 minutes or until heated through. **yield: 4 servings.**

cheesy beef macaroni

prep: 25 min. • bake: 20 min.

Little ones will light up the room with smiles when you bring this five-ingredient supper to the table. Corn is an appealing, popular addition to the mild and cheesy combination of ground beef and pasta.

—Dena Evetts, Sentinel, Oklahoma

- 1 **pound ground beef**
- 1 **can (15-1/4 ounces) whole kernel corn, drained**
- 1 **can (10-3/4 ounces) condensed cream of chicken soup, undiluted**
- 8 **ounces process cheese (Velveeta), shredded**
- 2-1/2 **cups cooked elbow macaroni**

In a large skillet, cook beef over medium heat until no longer pink; drain. Add the corn and soup. Set aside 1/2 cup cheese for topping; stir remaining cheese into meat mixture until melted. Gently stir in macaroni until coated.

Transfer to a greased 8-in. square baking dish. Top with reserved cheese. Bake, uncovered, at 350° for 20-25 minutes or until heated through. **yield: 4-6 servings.**

corned beef 'n' sauerkraut bake

prep: 10 min. • bake: 30 min.

I love Reuben sandwiches, so this recipe is a dream come true! We especially like it with my husband's homemade sauerkraut.

—Susan Stahl, Duluth, Minnesota

- 1-3/4 **cups sauerkraut, rinsed and well drained**
- 1/2 **pound thinly sliced deli corned beef, julienned**
- 2 **cups (8 ounces) shredded Swiss cheese**
- 1/4 **cup Thousand Island salad dressing**
- 2 **medium tomatoes, thinly sliced**
- 6 **tablespoons butter,** *divided*
- 1 **cup coarsely crushed seasoned rye crackers**

In a greased 1-1/2 -qt. baking dish, layer half of the sauerkraut, corned beef and cheese. Repeat layers. Drop salad dressing by teaspoonfuls over the cheese. Arrange tomato slices over the top; dot with 2 tablespoons butter.

In a small saucepan, melt the remaining butter. Stir in the crumbs. Sprinkle over top of casserole. Bake, uncovered, at 400° for 30-35 minutes or until heated through. **yield: 6 servings.**

speedy taco feast

prep: 15 min. • bake: 40 min.

I've found that teenagers love the Southwestern taste of this hearty bake. It's not as messy as tacos can be because the ingredients are all combined into an easy-to-eat casserole.
—Janice Steimer, Rochester, New York

---

   2 **pounds ground beef**
   2 **envelopes taco seasoning**
1-1/2 **cups water**
   1 **jar (16 ounces) salsa**
   1 **can (8-3/4 ounces) whole kernel corn, drained**
   2 **cups (8 ounces) shredded Mexican cheese blend**
   2 **packages (8-1/2 ounces *each*) corn bread/muffin mix**
Sour cream, optional

In a large skillet, cook the beef over medium heat until no longer pink; drain. Add the taco seasoning, water, salsa and corn; cook and stir until heated through, about 15 minutes. Transfer to a greased 13-in. x 9-in. baking dish. Sprinkle with cheese.

Prepare corn bread mix according to package directions. Spoon batter evenly over cheese.

Bake, uncovered, at 350° for 40-45 minutes or until a toothpick inserted near the center of the corn bread comes out clean. Serve with sour cream if desired. **yield: 8 servings.**

ground beef noodle bake

prep: 35 min. • bake: 25 min.

This is a dressy recipe that will be a big hit. I think it's nice served with a side of hot vegetables and Texas toast. It's an oldie, but a goody!
—Judy Taylor, Kenna, West Virginia

5	cups uncooked egg noodles
1-1/2	pounds ground beef
1	can (8 ounces) tomato sauce
1	teaspoon salt
1/4	teaspoon garlic salt
1/4	teaspoon pepper
2	teaspoons butter
1	cup (8 ounces) cream-style cottage cheese
1	cup (8 ounces) sour cream
4	green onions, chopped
1/2	cup minced fresh parsley
1	cup (4 ounces) shredded Swiss cheese

Cook noodles according to package directions. Meanwhile, in a large skillet, cook beef over medium heat until no longer pink; drain. Stir in the tomato sauce, salt, garlic salt and pepper. Bring to a boil. Reduce heat; simmer, uncovered, for 5 minutes.

Drain noodles; toss with butter. Set aside. In a blender, process cottage cheese and sour cream until smooth. Transfer to a large bowl; stir in onions and parsley. Add noodles; toss to coat.

In a greased 11-in. x 7-in. baking dish, layer a third of the noodle mixture and half of the meat sauce. Repeat layers. Top with remaining noodle mixture; sprinkle with Swiss cheese.

Bake, uncovered, at 350° for 25-30 minutes or until bubbly and lightly browned.
yield: 6 servings.

unstuffed peppers

prep/total time: 30 min.

If you like stuffed peppers, you'll treasure this speedy version. It offers all the delectable flavor of the original, but takes just half an hour. Instead of cooking the instant rice, you can use 2 cups leftover cooked rice if you have it on hand.
—Beth DeWyer, Du Bois, Pennsylvania

- 1 cup uncooked instant rice
- 1 pound ground beef
- 2 medium green peppers, cut into 1-inch pieces
- 1/2 cup chopped onion
- 1 jar (26 ounces) marinara sauce
- 1-1/2 teaspoons salt-free seasoning blend
- 1/2 cup shredded Italian cheese blend
- 1/2 cup panko (Japanese) bread crumbs
- 1 tablespoon olive oil

Cook rice according to package directions. Meanwhile, in a large skillet, cook the beef, green peppers and onion over medium-high heat for 10-12 minutes or until meat is no longer pink; drain. Stir in the rice, marinara sauce and seasoning blend. Stir in cheese.

Transfer to a greased 2-qt. baking dish. Toss bread crumbs and oil; sprinkle over the top. Bake at 350° for 8-10 minutes or until heated through and topping is golden brown. **yield: 6 servings.**

meatball potato supper

prep: 30 min. • bake: 1 hour

I'm often asked to bring this creamy casserole to potluck suppers. People must enjoy it, because I never have any leftovers to take home!
—Sonya Morton, Molena, Georgia

- 2 eggs
- 1/2 cup dry bread crumbs
- 1 envelope onion soup mix
- 1-1/2 pounds lean ground beef (90% lean)
- 2 tablespoons all-purpose flour
- 6 medium potatoes, peeled and thinly sliced
- 1 can (10-3/4 ounces) condensed cream of celery soup, undiluted
- 1 cup 2% milk

Paprika, optional

In a large bowl, combine the eggs, bread crumbs and soup mix. Crumble beef over mixture and mix well. Shape into 1-in. balls. In a large skillet, brown meatballs in small batches over medium heat; drain. Sprinkle with flour; gently roll to coat.

Place half of the potatoes in a greased 2-1/2-qt. baking dish. Top with meatballs and remaining potatoes. In a small bowl, combine soup and milk until blended; pour over potatoes. Sprinkle with paprika if desired.

Cover and bake at 350° for 60-65 minutes or until the potatoes are tender. **yield: 6-8 servings.**

super supper

prep: 20 min. • bake: 30 min.

My children really like the combination of beef, pasta and cheesy sauce in this tempting dish. I can assemble it in no time.
—Jane Hartery, Sarasota, Florida

- 1 pound ground beef
- 1 small onion, chopped
- 3/4 cup water
- 1 can (6 ounces) tomato paste
- 1 teaspoon salt
- 1/2 teaspoon garlic powder
- 1 package (8 ounces) cream cheese, cubed
- 3/4 cup 2% milk
- 1/2 cup grated Parmesan cheese
- 7 cups cooked egg noodles

In a large skillet, cook beef and onion over medium heat until meat is no longer pink; drain. Add the water, tomato paste, salt and garlic powder. Bring to a boil. Reduce heat; cover and simmer for 5-7 minutes or until heated through.

In a small saucepan, melt cream cheese over low heat, stirring constantly. Gradually stir in milk and Parmesan cheese until blended.

Place noodles in a greased 13-in. x 9-in. baking dish. Spread meat sauce over noodles. Spoon cream cheese mixture evenly over top. Bake the casserole, uncovered, at 350° for 30-35 minutes or until heated through. **yield: 6 servings.**

wagon wheel casserole

prep: 20 min. • bake: 40 min. + standing

Wagon wheel pasta makes my hot dish a fun meal for kids and adults. With spaghetti sauce, mozzarella and Parmesan, it has classic Italian taste.
—Barbara Hopkins, Lusby, Maryland

- 1 pound lean ground beef (90% lean)
- 1 pound sliced fresh mushrooms
- 1 large onion, chopped
- 8 ounces wagon wheel pasta, cooked and drained
- 1/3 cup grated Parmesan cheese
- 1 large green pepper, thinly sliced
- 1 jar (26 ounces) meatless spaghetti sauce
- 1 cup (4 ounces) shredded part-skim mozzarella cheese

In a large nonstick skillet, cook the beef, mushrooms and onion over medium heat until meat is no longer pink; drain. In a shallow 3-qt. baking dish coated with cooking spray, layer the pasta, Parmesan cheese, green pepper, beef mixture and spaghetti sauce.

Cover and bake at 350° for 30 minutes. Uncover; sprinkle with mozzarella cheese. Bake 10 minutes longer or until cheese is melted. Let stand for 10 minutes before serving. **yield: 8 servings.**

grandma's rice dish

prep: 20 min. • bake: 15 min.

My grandmother often made this for supper when I was young. I forgot about it until I found myself adding the same ingredients to leftover rice one day. The memories came flooding back, and I've made this recipe regularly since then.

—Lorna Moore, Glendora, California

- 1 pound ground beef
- 1/3 cup chopped onion
- 1/2 cup chopped green pepper
- 2 cups cooked long grain rice
- 1 can (14-1/2 ounces) diced tomatoes, undrained
- 1 can (11 ounces) whole kernel corn, drained
- 1 can (2-1/4 ounces) sliced ripe olives, drained
- 6 bacon strips, cooked and crumbled
- 2 teaspoons chili powder
- 1 teaspoon garlic powder
- 1/2 teaspoon salt
- 1-1/2 cups (6 ounces) shredded cheddar cheese, *divided*
- 1/2 cup dry bread crumbs
- 1 tablespoon butter, melted

In a large skillet, cook the beef, onion and green pepper over medium heat until meat is no longer pink; drain. Stir in the rice, tomatoes, corn, olives, bacon, chili powder, garlic powder and salt. Bring to a boil; remove from the heat. Add 1 cup of cheese; stir until melted.

Transfer to a greased 11-in. x 7-in. baking dish. Sprinkle with remaining cheese. Toss bread crumbs with butter; sprinkle over top. Bake, uncovered, at 350° for 15-20 minutes or until cheese is melted. **yield: 4 servings.**

KITCHEN TIP

When preparing rice, make extra to have on hand. Packaged in freezer containers or heavy-duty resealable plastic bags, cooked rice will keep in the freezer for up to 6 months. To reheat, add 2 tablespoons of liquid for each cup of rice; microwave until heated through.

taco casserole

prep: 15 min. • bake: 30 min.

My preschooler doesn't eat ground beef unless it's taco flavored, so I came up with this casserole we all like. To make assembly easy, I prepare the taco meat and freeze several bags at a time. I also cook the noodles over the weekend for a timely supper later in the week.

—Kathy Wilson, Romeoville, Illinois

- 3 cups uncooked bow tie pasta
- 1 pound ground beef
- 1/4 cup chopped onion
- 2 cups (8 ounces) shredded cheddar cheese
- 1 jar (16 ounces) salsa
- 1 can (14-1/2 ounces) diced tomatoes, undrained
- 1 envelope taco seasoning
- 2 cups nacho tortilla chips, crushed

Cook pasta according to package directions. Meanwhile, in a large skillet, cook beef and onion over medium heat until meat is no longer pink; drain. Add the cheese, salsa, tomatoes and taco seasoning. Drain pasta; stir into beef mixture.

Transfer to a greased 11-in. x 7-in. baking dish. Cover and bake at 350° for 20 minutes. Uncover; sprinkle with tortilla chips. Bake the casserole 10 minutes longer or until heated through. **yield: 7 servings.**

southwest pasta bake

prep: 20 min. • bake: 35 min. + standing

Fat-free cream cheese and reduced-fat cheddar make this creamy bake lower in fat and calories. It's a good way to get our kids to eat spinach since it is hidden in the cream cheese layer.

—Carol Lepak, Sheboygan, Wisconsin

- 8 ounces uncooked penne pasta
- 1 package (8 ounces) fat-free cream cheese, cubed
- 1/2 cup fat-free milk
- 1 package (10 ounces) frozen chopped spinach, thawed and squeezed dry
- 1 teaspoon dried oregano
- 1 pound lean ground beef (90% lean)
- 2 garlic cloves, minced
- 1 jar (16 ounces) picante sauce
- 1 can (8 ounces) no-salt-added tomato sauce
- 1 can (6 ounces) no-salt-added tomato paste
- 2 teaspoons chili powder
- 1 teaspoon ground cumin
- 1 cup (4 ounces) shredded reduced-fat cheddar cheese
- 1 can (2-1/4 ounces) sliced ripe olives, drained
- 1/4 cup sliced green onions

Cook pasta according to package directions. Meanwhile, in a small bowl, beat cream cheese until smooth. Beat in milk. Stir in spinach and oregano; set aside.

In a nonstick skillet, cook beef over medium heat until meat is no longer pink. Add garlic; cook 1 minute longer. Drain. Stir in the picante sauce, tomato sauce, tomato paste, chili powder and cumin; bring to a boil.

Reduce heat; simmer, uncovered, for 5 minutes. Drain pasta; stir into meat mixture.

In a 13-in. x 9-in. baking dish coated with cooking spray, layer half of the meat mixture and all of the spinach mixture. Top with remaining meat mixture.

Cover and bake at 350° for 30 minutes. Uncover; sprinkle with cheese. Bake 5 minutes longer or until cheese is melted. Sprinkle with olives and onions. Let stand for 10 minutes before serving. **yield: 8 servings.**

two-tater shepherd's pie

prep: 20 min. • bake: 40 min.

Shepherd's pie is one of my favorite dinners, but our oldest son doesn't care for some of the ingredients. So I adjusted my recipe to come up with this Tater Tot version everyone likes.

—Cindy Rebain, Robertsdale, Alabama

1-1/2	pounds ground beef
1	can (10-3/4 ounces) condensed cream of mushroom soup, undiluted
1/2	teaspoon garlic salt
1/4	teaspoon pepper
6	cups frozen Tater Tots
2	cups frozen French-style green beans, thawed
3	cups hot mashed potatoes
1	cup (4 ounces) shredded Colby cheese

In a large skillet, cook beef over medium heat until no longer pink; drain. Stir in the soup, garlic salt and pepper.

Place Tater Tots in a greased 13-in. x 9-in. baking dish. Top with beef mixture and green beans. Spread mashed potatoes over the top; sprinkle with cheese. Bake the casserole, uncovered, at 350° for 40-45 minutes or until heated through. **yield: 8 servings.**

hominy beef bake

prep: 15 min. • bake: 30 min.

I received this recipe from a friend many years ago and have been using it ever since. Corn chips create a tasty topping on a nicely spiced mixture of ground beef, hominy and chili. Even my meat-and-potatoes husband likes it!

—Jean Stokes, Sacramento, California

- 1 pound ground beef
- 1 small onion, chopped
- 2 garlic cloves, minced
- 1 can (15-1/2 ounces) hominy, drained
- 1 can (15 ounces) chili with beans
- 1 can (8 ounces) tomato sauce
- 1/2 cup water
- 3 teaspoons chili powder
- Salt and pepper to taste
- 1 package (10-1/2 ounces) corn chips, crushed

In a large skillet, cook beef and onion over medium heat until meat is no longer pink. Add garlic; cook 1 minute longer. Drain. Stir in the hominy, chili, tomato sauce, water, chili powder, salt and pepper.

Transfer to a greased 13-in. x 9-in. baking dish. Sprinkle with corn chips. Bake, uncovered, at 350° for 30 minutes or until heated through. **yield: 4-6 servings.**

biscuit pizza bake

prep: 15 min. • bake: 25 min.

You'll get all of the flavor of traditional pizza in this convenient casserole. It's chock-full of ground beef, pepperoni, veggies and two kinds of cheese.

—Emma Hageman, Waucoma, Iowa

- 1 pound ground beef
- 2 tubes (12 ounces *each*) refrigerated buttermilk biscuits
- 1 can (15 ounces) pizza sauce
- 1 cup chopped green pepper
- 1/2 cup chopped onion
- 1 can (4 ounces) mushroom stems and pieces, drained
- 1 package (3-1/2 ounces) sliced pepperoni
- 1 cup (4 ounces) shredded part-skim mozzarella cheese
- 1 cup (4 ounces) shredded cheddar cheese

In a large skillet, cook the beef over medium heat until no longer pink. Meanwhile, quarter the biscuits; place in a greased shallow 3-qt. baking dish. Top with pizza sauce. Drain beef; sprinkle over biscuits and sauce.

Layer with the green pepper, onion, mushrooms, pepperoni and cheeses. Bake, uncovered, at 350° for 25-30 minutes or until the cheese is melted. Let stand for 5-10 minutes before serving. **yield: 6-8 servings.**

creamy lasagna casserole

prep: 30 min. • bake: 25 min. + standing

This casserole will satisfy anyone's hunger pangs. A rich combination of cream cheese, sour cream and cheddar cheese is layered with lasagna noodles and a beefy sauce.
—*Shelly Korell, Eaton, Colorado*

- 2 **pounds ground beef**
- 1 **can (29 ounces) tomato sauce**
- 1 **teaspoon salt**
- 1/2 **teaspoon pepper**
- 1/2 **teaspoon garlic powder**
- 2 **packages (3 ounces *each*) cream cheese, softened**
- 2 **cups (16 ounces) sour cream**
- 2 **cups (8 ounces) shredded cheddar cheese, *divided***
- 4 **green onions, chopped**
- 12 **to 14 lasagna noodles, cooked and drained**

In a Dutch oven, cook beef over medium heat until no longer pink; drain. Add the tomato sauce, salt, pepper and garlic powder. Bring to a boil. Reduce heat; simmer, uncovered, for 15 minutes.

In a large bowl, beat cream cheese until smooth. Add the sour cream, 1 cup cheddar cheese and onions; mix well.

Spread about 1/2 cup meat sauce into two greased 8-in. square baking dishes. Place two to three noodles in each dish, trimming to fit if necessary. Top each with about 1/2 cup cream cheese mixture and about 2/3 cup meat sauce. Repeat layers twice. Sprinkle 1/2 cup cheddar cheese over each.

Cover and freeze one casserole for up to 1 month. Bake remaining casserole, uncovered, at 350° for 25-30 minutes or until bubbly and heated through. Let stand for 15 minutes before cutting.

to use frozen casserole: Thaw in the refrigerator for 18 hours. Remove casserole from the refrigerator 30 minutes before baking. Bake the casserole, uncovered, at 350° for 40-50 minutes or until heated through. **yield: 2 casseroles (4-6 servings each).**

editor's note: Reduced-fat or fat-free cream cheese and sour cream are not recommended for this recipe.

corn 'n' beef pasta bake

prep: 15 min. • bake: 65 min.

I call this my "Friendship Casserole" because I often make it for new moms and other folks who need a helping hand. The ingredients are easily assembled for a quick meal.
—Nancy Adams
    Hancock, New Hampshire

- 1 **pound ground beef**
- 1 **medium onion, chopped**
- 1 **medium green** *or* **sweet red pepper, chopped**
- 2 **garlic cloves, minced**
- 2 **cups frozen corn, thawed**
- 1 **can (14-1/2 ounces) diced tomatoes, undrained**
- 1-1/2 **cups uncooked bow tie pasta**
- 1 **cup buttermilk**
- 1 **package (3 ounces) cream cheese, cubed**
- 1 to 2 **teaspoons chili powder**

Salt and pepper to taste

- 1 **cup (4 ounces) shredded Monterey Jack cheese**

In a large skillet, cook the beef, onion, green pepper and garlic over medium heat until meat is no longer pink; drain. Stir in the corn, tomatoes, pasta, buttermilk, cream cheese, chili powder, salt and pepper.

Transfer to a greased 2-1/2-qt. baking dish; sprinkle with cheese. Cover and bake at 375° for 40 minutes. Uncover; bake 25-30 minutes longer or until the pasta is tender. **yield: 6-8 servings.**

au gratin taco bake

prep: 15 min. • bake: 70 min.

This hearty hot dish relies on a package of au gratin potatoes for simple preparation. Brimming with beef, potatoes, corn, tomatoes and cheese, this supper is sure to be a hit in your home.
—Linda Muir, Big Lake, Minnesota

- 1 **pound ground beef**
- 1 **package (4.9 ounces) au gratin potatoes**
- 1 **can (15-1/4 ounces) whole kernel corn, undrained**
- 1 **can (14-1/2 ounces) no-salt-added stewed tomatoes, undrained**
- 3/4 **cup milk**
- 1/2 **cup water**
- 2 **tablespoons taco seasoning**
- 1 **cup (4 ounces) shredded cheddar cheese**

In a large skillet, cook beef over medium heat until no longer pink; drain. Stir in the potatoes and contents of sauce mix, corn, tomatoes, milk, water and taco seasoning. Transfer to a greased 2-qt. baking dish.

Cover and bake at 350° for 65-70 minutes or until potatoes are tender. Sprinkle with cheese. Bake, uncovered, 5 minutes longer or until cheese is melted. **yield: 4-6 servings.**

makeover manicotti crepes

prep: 1-1/2 hours + simmering • bake: 35 min.

This made-lighter main dish will add a special touch to any event. Green pepper and garlic give it a fresh vegetable aroma.
—Christine Rukavena, Milwaukee, Wisconsin

- 1 can (28 ounces) whole tomatoes, undrained
- 1-1/2 cups water
- 1 can (8 ounces) tomato sauce
- 3 teaspoons sugar
- 1 teaspoon dried oregano
- 1/4 teaspoon celery salt

CREPES:
- 2 eggs
- 1 cup egg substitute
- 1-3/4 cups fat-free milk
- 1 teaspoon canola oil
- 1-1/2 cups all-purpose flour
- 1/4 teaspoon salt

FILLING:
- 3 slices whole wheat bread, cubed
- 1/2 cup fat-free milk
- 1/4 cup egg substitute
- 1 cup finely chopped green pepper
- 3 tablespoons minced fresh parsley
- 2 garlic cloves, minced
- 1 teaspoon salt
- 1 teaspoon pepper
- 1 pound lean ground beef (90% lean)

- 1/2 pound Italian turkey sausage links, casings removed
- 1 cup (4 ounces) shredded part-skim mozzarella cheese
- 1/4 cup shredded Parmesan cheese

For sauce, place tomatoes in a blender; cover and process until smooth. Transfer to a large saucepan; add the water, tomato sauce, sugar, oregano and celery salt. Bring to a boil. Reduce heat; gently simmer, uncovered, for 2 hours or until reduced to 4-1/2 cups, stirring occasionally.

Meanwhile, for crepes, beat the eggs, egg substitute, milk and oil in a large bowl. Combine flour and salt; add egg mixture and stir until smooth. Cover and refrigerate for 1 hour.

For filling, in a large bowl, soak bread in milk for 5 minutes. Stir in the egg substitute, green pepper, parsley, garlic, salt and pepper. Crumble beef and sausage over mixture and mix well. Stir in mozzarella. Cover and refrigerate until assembling.

Coat an 8-in. nonstick skillet with cooking spray; heat. Stir crepe batter; pour 3 tablespoons into center of skillet. Lift and tilt pan to coat bottom evenly. Cook until top appears dry; turn and cook 15-20 seconds longer. Remove to a wire rack. Repeat with remaining batter, coating skillet with cooking spray as needed. When cool, stack crepes with waxed paper or paper towels in between.

Spread about 1/4 cup filling down the center of each crepe; roll up and place in a 13-in. x 9-in. baking dish and an 11-in. x 7-in. baking dish coated with cooking spray. Spoon sauce over top; sprinkle with Parmesan cheese.

Cover and bake at 350° for 35-45 minutes or until a thermometer reads 160° **yield: 10 servings.**

sloppy joe hot dish

prep: 15 min. • bake: 20 min.

Dinner will be served in no time with this kid-friendly supper. Get little ones involved by letting them stir together the meaty filling and spoon it onto the crust.

—Marlene Harguth
   Maynard, Minnesota

- 1 package (8 ounces) refrigerated crescent rolls
- 1 pound ground beef
- 1 can (15 ounces) tomato sauce
- 1 envelope sloppy joe mix
- 1 cup (4 ounces) shredded part-skim mozzarella cheese

Unroll crescent dough into two rectangles; seal seams and perforations. Roll out each rectangle between two pieces of waxed paper to fit an 11-in. x 7-in. baking dish.

Grease the dish and place one rectangle inside. Bake at 425° for 5 minutes or until golden brown.

Meanwhile, in a large skillet, cook beef over medium heat until no longer pink; drain. Stir in the tomato sauce and sloppy joe mix; spoon over crust. Sprinkle with cheese; top with remaining dough. Bake 15-20 minutes longer or until golden brown. **yield: 6 servings.**

southwestern rice bake

prep: 15 min. • bake: 20 min.

Whenever I'm wondering what to make for dinner, my husband requests his favorite casserole. It's so satisfying, no side dishes are even necessary.

—Sheila Johnson, Red Feather Lakes, Colorado

- 3 cups cooked brown *or* white rice
- 1/2 pound ground beef, cooked and drained
- 1-1/4 cups sour cream
- 1 cup (4 ounces) shredded Monterey Jack cheese, *divided*
- 1 cup (4 ounces) shredded cheddar cheese, *divided*
- 1 can (4 ounces) chopped green chilies
- 1/2 teaspoon salt
- 1/4 teaspoon pepper

Sliced ripe olives, chopped tomatoes and green onions, optional

In a large bowl, combine rice, beef, sour cream, 3/4 cup Monterey Jack cheese, 3/4 cup cheddar cheese, chilies, salt and pepper.

Spoon into a greased 1-1/2-qt. baking dish. Sprinkle with remaining cheeses. Bake, uncovered, at 350° for 20-25 minutes or until heated through. Serve with the olives, tomatoes and onions if desired. **yield: 4 servings.**

italian noodle casserole

prep: 30 min. • bake: 35 min.

Canned beans and other convenience products make it a snap to assemble this cheesy pasta dish. The Italian flavor makes it very appealing.
—Joann Hosbach, Las Cruces, New Mexico

- 1 pound ground beef
- 1 package (8 ounces) wide egg noodles
- 1 tablespoon olive oil
- 2 cups (8 ounces) shredded Colby cheese, *divided*
- 2 cans (15 ounces *each*) tomato sauce
- 1 can (15-1/2 ounces) great northern beans, rinsed and drained
- 1 can (14-1/2 ounces) Italian stewed tomatoes
- 1 can (10-3/4 ounces) condensed tomato soup, undiluted
- 2 teaspoons Italian seasoning
- 2 teaspoons dried parsley flakes
- 1/8 teaspoon *each* onion salt, garlic salt and pepper
- 2 tablespoons grated Parmesan cheese

In a large skillet, cook beef over medium heat until no longer pink; drain. Meanwhile, cook noodles according to package directions; drain. In a large bowl, combine the beef, noodles, oil, 1-1/2 cups Colby cheese, tomato sauce, beans, tomatoes, soup and seasonings.

Transfer to a greased 13-in. x 9-in. baking dish. Cover and bake at 350° for 30 minutes. Sprinkle with the Parmesan cheese and remaining Colby cheese. Bake, uncovered, for 5-10 minutes longer or until the cheese is melted. **yield: 6-8 servings.**

tasty hamburger casserole

prep: 15 min. • bake: 1-1/2 hours

Just a few ingredients to pack a lot of flavor into this hearty ground beef bake. My daughter received this recipe from a missionary when they were both serving in Zambia. It's delicious.

—Faith Richards, Tampa, Florida

- 5 medium potatoes, peeled and sliced
- 1 small onion, chopped
- 1 pound lean ground beef (90% lean)
- 1 can (10-3/4 ounces) condensed cream of mushroom soup, undiluted
- 1 can (10-1/2 ounces) condensed vegetarian vegetable soup, undiluted
- 1 cup crushed potato chips

In a greased 13-in. x 9-in. baking dish, layer with potatoes and onion. Crumble beef over onion. Spread soups over beef.

Cover and bake at 350° for 55 minutes. Uncover; sprinkle with chips. Bake 20 minutes longer or until the meat is no longer pink and vegetables are tender. **yield: 4-6 servings.**

western chili casserole

prep/total time: 25 min.

In our busy household, easy yet tasty meals are a must. This crunchy bake that uses convenient canned chili really fills the bill.
—Terri Mock, American Falls, Idaho

- **1 pound ground beef**
- **1 cup chopped onion**
- **1/2 cup chopped celery**
- **1 can (15 ounces) chili with beans**
- **1-1/2 cups corn chips, coarsely crushed, *divided***
- **3/4 cup shredded cheddar cheese**

In a large skillet, cook the beef, onion and celery over medium heat until meat is no longer pink and vegetables are tender; drain. Stir in chili and 1/2 cup corn chips.

Transfer to a greased 1-1/2-qt. baking dish. Sprinkle remaining chips around edge of dish; fill center with cheese. Bake, uncovered, at 350° for 10 minutes or until heated through. **yield: 4 servings.**

zippy beef supper

prep: 15 min. • bake: 35 min.

I rely on canned soup and canned tomatoes with chilies to make this spicy, satisfying main dish. Shredded cheddar cheese and crushed tortilla chips create the tasty topping.
—Ruth Foster, Crooksville, Ohio

- **2 pounds ground beef**
- **1 medium onion, chopped**
- **1 cup cubed cooked potatoes**
- **1 can (11 ounces) condensed nacho cheese soup, undiluted**
- **1 can (10-3/4 ounces) condensed cream of onion soup, undiluted**
- **1 can (10 ounces) diced tomatoes and green chilies, undrained**
- **2 to 3 teaspoons ground cumin**
- **1/2 to 1 teaspoon garlic powder**
- **3 cups crushed tortilla chips**
- **1 cup (4 ounces) shredded cheddar cheese**

In a large saucepan, cook beef and onion over medium heat until meat is no longer pink; drain. Add potatoes; cook and stir until heated through. Stir in the soups, tomatoes, cumin and garlic powder.

Transfer to a greased 13-in. x 9-in. baking dish. Cover and bake at 350° for 30 minutes. Uncover; sprinkle with tortilla chips and cheese. Bake, uncovered, 5-10 minutes longer or until cheese is melted. **yield: 6-8 servings.**

beefy rice squares

prep: 10 min. • bake: 35 min.

My mother used to make this when I was growing up. Now I serve it to my family. It's one I rely on because it's fast, easy and delicious.

—Barb Block, Tigerton, Wisconsin

- 1 pound lean ground beef (90% lean)
- 1 medium onion, chopped
- 3 cups Italian tomato sauce, *divided*
- 1/2 cup seasoned bread crumbs
- 1/4 teaspoon salt
- 1/8 teaspoon pepper
- 1-1/3 cups uncooked instant rice
- 1 cup (4 ounces) shredded cheddar cheese

In a large bowl, combine the beef, onion, 1/2 cup tomato sauce, bread crumbs, salt and pepper. Press into a greased 8-in. square baking dish.

In another large bowl, combine the rice, cheese and remaining tomato sauce. Pour over meat mixture. Cover and bake at 350° for 25 minutes. Uncover; bake 10-15 minutes longer or until rice is tender. Let the casseroles stand for 5 minutes before cutting. **yield: 4 servings.**

tater taco casserole

prep: 20 min. • bake: 30 min.

Our family lives and works on a ranch, and we build up big appetites by the time dinner rolls around. This nicely seasoned casserole is great with a tossed salad or nacho chips and dip.

—Ronna Lewis, Plains, Kansas

- 2 pounds ground beef
- 1/4 cup chopped onion
- 1 envelope taco seasoning
- 2/3 cup water
- 1 can (11 ounces) whole kernel corn, drained
- 1 can (11 ounces) condensed fiesta nacho cheese soup, undiluted
- 1 package (32 ounces) frozen Tater Tots

In a large skillet, cook beef and onion over medium heat until meat is no longer pink; drain. Stir in taco seasoning and water. Simmer, uncovered, for 5 minutes. Stir in corn and soup.

Transfer to a greased 13-in. x 9-in. baking dish. Arrange Tater Tots in a single layer over the top. Bake, uncovered, at 350° for 30-35 minutes or until the potatoes are crispy and golden brown. **yield: 8 servings.**

meaty macaroni bake

prep: 30 min. • bake: 30 min. + standing

We go to lots of rodeos. This casserole is ideal for days when you'll be out and about. I prepare it in the morning and refrigerate it. When we get back, I just pop it into the oven to bake.
—Connie Helsing, Ashland, Nebraska

1-1/2 pounds ground beef
1 medium onion, chopped
1 garlic clove, minced
1 jar (14 ounces) spaghetti sauce
1 cup water
1 can (8 ounces) tomato sauce
1 can (6 ounces) tomato paste

1/2 teaspoon salt
1/8 teaspoon pepper
2 eggs, lightly beaten
1/4 cup canola oil
1 package (7 ounces) elbow macaroni, cooked and drained
2 cans (4 ounces *each*) mushroom stems and pieces, drained
1 cup (4 ounces) shredded part-skim mozzarella cheese
1/4 cup grated Parmesan cheese
1 cup soft bread crumbs
Additional mozzarella cheese, optional

In a large skillet, cook beef and onion over medium heat until meat is no longer pink. Add garlic; cook 1 minute longer. Drain. Add the spaghetti sauce, water, tomato sauce, tomato paste, salt and pepper. Bring to a boil. Reduce heat; simmer, uncovered, for 10 minutes.

In a large bowl, combine the eggs, oil, macaroni, mushrooms, cheeses and bread crumbs. Spoon into a 3-qt. baking dish. Top with meat mixture.

Bake the casserole, uncovered, at 350° for 30 minutes. Sprinkle with additional mozzarella cheese if desired. Let stand for 10 minutes before serving. **yield: 6-8 servings.**

beef and bean macaroni

prep: 20 min. • bake: 30 min.

This hearty casserole with ground beef, kidney beans, macaroni and more is a full meal in itself. Using reduced-fat ingredients makes it lighter, too.

—Sally Norcutt, Chatham, Virginia

- 1 pound lean ground beef (90% lean)
- 1 package (7 ounces) elbow macaroni, cooked and drained
- 2 cups (8 ounces) shredded reduced-fat cheddar cheese, *divided*
- 1 can (16 ounces) kidney beans, rinsed and drained
- 1 can (14-1/2 ounces) stewed tomatoes
- 1 medium green pepper, diced
- 1 medium onion, finely chopped
- 1/4 teaspoon garlic powder

Crushed red pepper flakes and pepper to taste
- 2 tablespoons grated Parmesan cheese

In a large skillet, cook beef over medium heat until no longer pink; drain. In a large bowl, combine the macaroni, 1-1/2 cups cheddar cheese, beans, tomatoes, green pepper and onion. Stir in the beef, garlic powder, pepper flakes and pepper.

Spoon into a 13-in. x 9-in. baking dish coated with cooking spray. Sprinkle with Parmesan cheese and remaining cheddar cheese. Cover and bake at 375° for 30 minutes or until heated through. **yield: 10 servings.**

ground beef 'n' rice pie

prep: 15 min. • bake: 35 min.

Seasoned ground beef is pressed into a pie plate to form the crust of this satisfying dish. It's a terrific time-saver because you don't brown the beef separately.

—Rhonda Van Gelderen, Menomonee Falls, Wisconsin

- 1 pound lean ground beef (90% lean)
- 1 can (15 ounces) tomato sauce, *divided*
- 1/2 cup dry bread crumbs
- 1/4 cup chopped onion
- 1/4 cup chopped green pepper, optional
- 1/2 teaspoon salt
- 1/2 teaspoon Italian seasoning
- 1/8 teaspoon dried oregano
- 1/8 teaspoon pepper
- 1 can (6 ounces) tomato paste
- 2-1/2 cups cooked rice
- 1 cup (4 ounces) shredded cheddar cheese, *divided*

In a large bowl, combine the beef, 3/4 cup tomato sauce, bread crumbs, onion, green pepper if desired and seasonings. Press evenly onto the bottom and up the sides of an ungreased 9-in. pie plate, forming a crust.

In another large bowl, combine the tomato paste and remaining tomato sauce. Stir in the rice and 3/4 cup cheese; pour into crust. Place pie plate on a baking sheet.

Cover and bake at 350° for 25 minutes or until the meat is no longer pink. Uncover; drain. Sprinkle with remaining cheese. Bake 10-15 minutes longer or until the cheese is melted. Let stand for 5 minutes before cutting. **yield: 6-8 servings.**

KITCHEN TIP

A 4-ounce serving of lean ground beef has about 60 calories less and 7 grams less fat than the same serving size of 70% ground beef. A 4-ounce serving of lean ground turkey versus lean ground beef will save about 5 calories and 1 gram of fat.

biscuit-topped italian casserole

prep: 20 min. • bake: 25 min.

A saucy beef and vegetable mixture is topped with herb biscuits to create a comforting one-dish dinner.
—*Kathy Ravis, Vermilion, Ohio*

- 1 pound ground beef
- 1 can (8 ounces) tomato sauce
- 3/4 cup water
- 1/4 teaspoon pepper
- 1 package (10 ounces) frozen mixed vegetables
- 2 cups (8 ounces) shredded cheddar cheese, *divided*
- 1 tube (12 ounces) refrigerated buttermilk biscuits
- 1 tablespoon butter, melted
- 1/2 teaspoon dried oregano

In a large skillet, cook beef over medium heat until no longer pink; drain. Stir in the tomato sauce, water and pepper. Bring to a boil. Reduce heat; cover and simmer for 15 minutes. Remove from the heat. Stir in vegetables and 1-1/2 cups cheese. Transfer to a greased 13-in. x 9-in. baking dish.

Split each biscuit in half. Arrange biscuits around edge of dish, overlapping slightly; brush with butter and sprinkle with oregano. Sprinkle remaining cheese over the meat mixture. Bake, uncovered, at 375° for 25-30 minutes or until the biscuits are golden brown.
yield: 6-8 servings.

reuben crescent bake

prep: 20 min. • bake: 15 min.

This bake has all the wonderful taste of a Reuben sandwich, and it's easy to make. I serve it with homemade soup.
—*Kathy Kittell, Lenexa, Kansas*

- 2 tubes (8 ounces each) refrigerated crescent rolls
- 1 pound sliced Swiss cheese
- 1-1/4 pounds sliced deli corned beef
- 1 can (14 ounces) sauerkraut, rinsed and well drained
- 2/3 cup Thousand Island salad dressing
- 1 egg white, lightly beaten
- 3 teaspoons caraway seeds

Unroll one tube of crescent dough into one long rectangle; seal seams and perforations. Press onto the bottom of a greased 13-in. x 9-in. baking dish. Bake at 375° for 8-10 minutes or until golden brown.

Layer with half of the cheese and all of the corned beef. Combine sauerkraut and salad dressing; spread over beef. Top with remaining cheese.

On a lightly floured surface, press or roll second tube of crescent dough into a 13-in. x 9-in. rectangle, sealing seams and perforations. Place over cheese. Brush with egg white; sprinkle with caraway seeds.

Bake for 12-16 minutes or until heated through and crust is golden brown. Let stand for 5 minutes before cutting.
yield: 8 servings.

beans and biscuits

prep/total time: 30 min.

When there's a chill in the air, you can't beat a big helping of this stick-to-your-ribs casserole. It's also great on days when you don't have a lot of time to cook.

—Sandra McKenzie
  Braham, Minnesota

- **1 pound ground beef**
- **2 green onions, chopped**
- **1 garlic clove, minced**
- **1 can (28 ounces) baked beans, drained**
- **1/2 cup barbecue sauce**
- **1/4 cup packed brown sugar**
- **1/4 cup ketchup**
- **1 tablespoon prepared mustard**
- **1 tube (4-1/2 ounces) refrigerated buttermilk biscuits**
- **1/2 cup shredded cheddar cheese**

In a large skillet, cook ground beef and onions over medium heat until meat is no longer pink. Add garlic; cook 1 minute longer. Drain. Add the beans, barbecue sauce, brown sugar, ketchup and mustard. Simmer for 5 minutes or until heated through.

Transfer to a greased 11-in. x 7-in. baking dish. Separate biscuits and cut in half; arrange over beef mixture. Bake, uncovered, at 400° for 18 minutes or until biscuits are golden brown. Sprinkle with cheese; bake 2-3 minutes longer or until cheese is melted. **yield: 4-6 servings.**

editor's note: This recipe was tested with Pillsbury buttermilk biscuits, which has six biscuits in a 4-1/2 ounce tube.

aunt may's lasagna

prep: 1 hour • bake: 35 min. + standing

Some people don't like the ricotta cheese traditionally found in lasagna. My aunt's recipe does not use ricotta or cottage cheese, and the dish is fantastic.

—Angie Estes, Elko, Nevada

- **1 pound ground beef**
- **1 large onion, chopped**
- **2 garlic cloves, minced**
- **1 can (28 ounces) stewed tomatoes**
- **2 cans (6 ounces *each*) tomato paste**
- **1 teaspoon dried basil**
- **1/2 teaspoon dried oregano**
- **1/4 teaspoon pepper**
- **1 bay leaf**
- **9 lasagna noodles**
- **1 can (6 ounces) pitted ripe olives, drained and coarsely chopped**
- **2 cups (8 ounces) shredded part-skim mozzarella cheese**
- **1/2 cup grated Parmesan cheese**

In a large saucepan, cook the beef, onion and garlic over medium heat until meat is no longer pink; drain. Stir in the tomatoes, tomato paste, basil, oregano, pepper and bay leaf. Bring to a boil. Reduce heat; cover and simmer for 40-50 minutes or until thickened.

Meanwhile, cook noodles according to package directions; drain. Discard bay leaf from meat sauce. Stir in olives.

Spread a fourth of the sauce in a greased 13-in. x 9-in. baking dish. Top with three noodles and a third of the mozzarella and Parmesan cheese. Repeat the layers. Top with the remaining noodles, sauce and cheese.

Bake, uncovered, at 350° for 35-40 minutes or until bubbly. Let stand for 15 minutes before cutting. **yield: 12 servings.**

chili mac casserole

prep: 20 min. • bake: 25 min.

With wagon wheel pasta and popular Tex-Mex ingredients, this beefy main dish is a sure to be a hit with adults and kids. Simply add a mixed green salad with any light dressing you like for a complete dinner.

—Janet Kanzler, Yakima, Washington

- 1 cup uncooked wagon wheel pasta
- 1 pound lean ground beef (90% lean)
- 1/2 cup chopped onion
- 1/2 cup chopped green pepper
- 1 can (15 ounces) turkey chili with beans
- 1 can (14-1/2 ounces) stewed tomatoes, undrained
- 1 cup crushed baked tortilla chip scoops
- 1 cup (4 ounces) shredded reduced-fat cheddar cheese, *divided*
- 1/4 cup uncooked instant rice
- 1 teaspoon chili powder
- 1/4 teaspoon salt
- 1/8 teaspoon pepper

Cook pasta according to package directions. Meanwhile, in a large nonstick skillet, cook the beef, onion and green pepper over medium heat until meat is no longer pink; drain. Stir in the chili, tomatoes, chips, 1/2 cup cheese, rice, chili powder, salt and pepper. Drain pasta; add to beef mixture.

Transfer to a 2-qt. baking dish coated with cooking spray. Sprinkle with the remaining cheese. Bake, uncovered, at 350° for 25-30 minutes or until cheese is melted. **yield: 6 servings.**

hamburger hot dish

prep: 15 min. • bake: 50 min.

My dad was particularly fond of this casserole, which has been dinnertime fare in my family for over 60 years. It's a simple, filling combination of ground beef, potatoes and kidney beans.

—Kathleen Larson
  Cooperstown, North Dakota

- 1 pound ground beef
- 1 small onion, chopped
- 5 medium potatoes, peeled and diced
- 1 can (16 ounces) kidney beans, rinsed and drained
- 1 can (10-3/4 ounces) condensed tomato soup, undiluted
- 2 tablespoons minced fresh parsley
- 1 teaspoon chili powder, optional
- 3/4 teaspoon salt
- 1/4 to 1/2 teaspoon pepper

In a large skillet, cook the beef and onion over medium heat until meat is no longer pink; drain. Stir in the potatoes, beans, soup, parsley, chili powder if desired, salt and pepper.

Spoon into a greased 2-qt. baking dish. Cover and bake at 350° for 45 minutes. Uncover; bake 5-10 minutes longer or until potatoes are tender. **yield: 6 servings.**

italian cabbage casserole

prep: 35 min. • bake: 15 min.

If your gang likes stuffed cabbage, they'll love this filling, beefy recipe. And you'll love that it has all the flavor but with a lot less work than stuffed cabbage!

—Debra Sanders, Brevard, North Carolina

- 1 medium head cabbage, coarsely shredded
- 1 pound lean ground beef (90% lean)
- 1 large green pepper, chopped
- 1 medium onion, chopped
- 1 can (14-1/2 ounces) diced tomatoes, undrained
- 1 can (8 ounces) tomato sauce
- 3 tablespoons tomato paste
- 1-1/2 teaspoons dried oregano
- 1/2 teaspoon garlic powder
- 1/2 teaspoon pepper
- 1/8 teaspoon salt
- 1/2 cup shredded part-skim mozzarella cheese

Place cabbage in a steamer basket; place in a large saucepan over 1 in. of water. Bring to a boil; cover and steam for 6-8 minutes or until tender. Drain and set aside.

In a large nonstick skillet over medium heat, cook and stir the beef, green pepper and onion until meat is no longer pink; drain. Stir in the tomatoes, tomato sauce, tomato paste and seasonings. Bring to a boil. Reduce heat; simmer, uncovered, for 10 minutes.

Place half of the cabbage in an 11-in. x 7-in. baking dish coated with cooking spray; top with half of beef mixture. Repeat layers (dish will be full). Sprinkle with cheese. Bake, uncovered, at 350° for 15-20 minutes or until heated through. **yield: 6 servings.**

mashed potato beef casserole

prep: 30 min. • bake: 25 min.

My mother's old cookbook is the source for this dish. The smudges and splatters on the page show that Mom used it extensively to feed our large family. Now I prepare it for our children and grandchildren.
—Helen McGeorge, Abbotsford, British Columbia

- 2 bacon strips, diced
- 1 pound ground beef
- 1 large onion, finely chopped
- 1/4 pound fresh mushrooms, sliced
- 1 large carrot, finely chopped
- 1 celery rib, finely chopped
- 3 tablespoons all-purpose flour
- 1 cup beef broth
- 1 tablespoon Worcestershire sauce
- 1 teaspoon dried tarragon
- 1/4 teaspoon pepper
- 3 cups hot mashed potatoes
- 3/4 cup shredded cheddar cheese, divided

Paprika

In a large skillet, cook bacon until crisp; drain, reserving 1 teaspoon drippings. Set bacon aside. Cook beef in drippings over medium heat until no longer pink; drain.

Toss onion, mushrooms, carrot and celery in flour; add to skillet with the broth, Worcestershire sauce, tarragon and pepper. Bring to a boil; reduce heat. Simmer, uncovered, 15-20 minutes or until the vegetables are tender.

Add bacon; transfer to a greased 2-qt. baking dish. Combine potatoes and 1/2 cup of cheese; spread over beef mixture. Sprinkle with paprika and remaining cheese.

Bake, uncovered, at 350° for 20-25 minutes or until heated through. Broil 4 in. from the heat for 5 minutes or until bubbly. **yield: 4-6 servings.**

meatball sub casserole

prep: 40 min. • bake: 30 min.

You can easily substitute frozen meatballs to make this hearty, homey casserole even faster.

—Gina Harris, Seneca, South Carolina

- 1/3 cup chopped green onions
- 1/4 cup seasoned bread crumbs
- 3 tablespoons grated Parmesan cheese
- 1 pound ground beef
- 1 loaf (1 pound) Italian bread, cut into 1-inch slices
- 1 package (8 ounces) cream cheese, softened
- 1/2 cup mayonnaise
- 1 teaspoon Italian seasoning
- 1/4 teaspoon pepper
- 2 cups (8 ounces) shredded part-skim mozzarella cheese
- 1 jar (28 ounces) spaghetti sauce
- 1 cup water
- 2 garlic cloves, minced

In a bowl, combine the onions, bread crumbs and Parmesan cheese. Crumble beef over mixture and mix well. Shape into 1-in. balls; place on a greased rack in a shallow baking pan. Bake at 400° for 15-20 minutes or until no longer pink.

Meanwhile, arrange bread in a single layer in an ungreased 13-in. x 9-in. baking dish (all of the bread might not be used). Combine the cream cheese, mayonnaise, Italian seasoning and pepper; spread over the bread. Sprinkle with 1/2 cup mozzarella.

Combine the spaghetti sauce, water and garlic; add meatballs. Pour over cheese mixture; sprinkle with remaining mozzarella. Bake, uncovered, at 350° for 30 minutes or until heated through. **yield: 6 servings.**

two-cheese tortilla beef casserole

prep: 30 min. • bake: 25 min. + standing

When I first started making this dish, I wrapped up the tortillas like enchiladas, but this way is much easier and just as good. I've also make it with ground turkey instead of beef.
—Janice Wedemeyer, Holland, Michigan

- 2 pounds ground beef
- 1 can (26 ounces) condensed chicken with rice soup, undiluted
- 1 jar (16 ounces) picante sauce
- 6 flour tortillas (8 inches)
- 2 cups (8 ounces) shredded Colby/Monterey Jack cheese
- 2 cups (8 ounces) shredded Mexican cheese blend

Sour cream, tomatoes, chopped lettuce, ripe olives, onions and/or additional picante sauce, optional

In a Dutch oven, cook the beef over medium heat until no longer pink; drain. Drain broth from soup, reserving rice mixture (discard broth or refrigerate for another use). Stir rice mixture and picante sauce into beef. Bring to a boil. Reduce heat; simmer, uncovered, for 5 minutes.

Place four tortillas on the bottom and up the sides of a greased 13-in. x 9-in. baking dish. Spread with half of the beef mixture. Combine cheeses; sprinkle half over the beef. Top with remaining tortillas, beef mixture and cheese.

Bake, uncovered, at 350° for 25-30 minutes or until heated through and cheese is melted. Let stand for 10 minutes before serving. Serve with sour cream, tomatoes, lettuce, olives, onions and/or picante sauce if desired. **yield: 8-10 servings.**

beefy kraut and rice

prep: 15 min. • bake: 55 min.

My husband and I are both police officers, and after a long workday, I rely on meals that come together easily. This hearty hot dish is easy to make and has a tangy twist that even our kids enjoy.
—Kristi Baker, Sioux City, Iowa

- 1 pound ground beef
- 1 can (14 ounces) sauerkraut, rinsed and drained
- 1-1/2 cups water
- 1 can (10-3/4 ounces) condensed cream of mushroom soup, undiluted
- 1 cup uncooked long grain rice
- 1 envelope beefy mushroom soup mix
- 1/2 cup shredded Swiss cheese, optional

In a large skillet, cook the beef over medium heat until no longer pink; drain. In a large bowl, combine the beef, sauerkraut, water, soup, rice and soup mix.

Transfer to a greased 2-qt. baking dish. Cover and bake at 350° for 50-60 minutes or until rice is tender. Sprinkle with Swiss cheese if desired. Bake 5 minutes longer or until cheese is melted. **yield: 4-6 servings.**

KITCHEN TIP

Casseroles are a favorite dish to take to potlucks. To keep them hot, wrap the dish in one of the new insulated carrying cases that keep foods warm for short periods of time. Be sure to follow directions for recommended maximum holding times for these carriers to ensure food safety.

firecracker casserole

prep: 15 min. • bake: 25 min.

Growing up, I couldn't get enough of this Southwestern casserole my mother frequently placed on the dinner table. Now I fix it for my husband and me. The flavor reminds us of enchiladas.

—Teressa Eastman, El Dorado, Kansas

- **2 pounds ground beef**
- **1 medium onion, chopped**
- **1 can (15 ounces) black beans, rinsed and drained**
- **1 to 2 tablespoons chili powder**
- **2 to 3 teaspoons ground cumin**
- **1/2 teaspoon salt**
- **4 flour tortillas (6 inches)**
- **1 can (10-3/4 ounces) condensed cream of mushroom soup, undiluted**
- **1 can (10 ounces) diced tomatoes and green chilies, undrained**
- **1 cup (4 ounces) shredded cheddar cheese**

In a large skillet, cook beef and onion until the meat is no longer pink; drain. Add the beans, chili powder, cumin and salt.

Transfer to a greased 13-in. x 9-in. baking dish. Arrange tortillas over the top. Combine soup and tomatoes; pour over tortillas. Sprinkle with the cheese.

Bake, uncovered, at 350° for 25-30 minutes or until heated through. **yield: 8 servings.**

taco pasta shells

prep: 25 min. • bake: 25 min.

Here's a kid-friendly dish so flavorful and fun, nobody is likely to guess that it's also lower in fat. A great family supper for busy weeknights!

—Anne Thomsen, Westchester, Ohio

- **18 uncooked jumbo pasta shells**
- **1-1/2 pounds lean ground beef (90% lean)**
- **1 bottle (16 ounces) taco sauce, *divided***
- **3 ounces fat-free cream cheese, cubed**
- **2 teaspoons chili powder**
- **3/4 cup shredded reduced-fat Mexican cheese blend, *divided***
- **20 baked tortilla chip scoops, coarsely crushed**

Cook pasta according to package directions. Meanwhile, in a large nonstick skillet over medium heat, cook beef until no longer pink; drain. Add 1/2 cup taco sauce, cream cheese and chili powder; cook and stir until blended. Stir in 1/4 cup cheese blend.

Drain pasta and rinse in cold water; stuff each shell with about 2 tablespoons beef mixture. Arrange in an 11-in. x 7-in. baking dish coated with cooking spray. Spoon the remaining taco sauce over the top.

Cover and bake at 350° for 20 minutes. Uncover; sprinkle with remaining cheese blend. Bake 5-10 minutes longer or until heated through and the cheese is melted. Sprinkle with the chips. **yield: 6 servings.**

cheeseburger biscuit bake

prep: 15 min. • bake: 20 min.

Popular cheeseburger ingredients create the tasty layers in this family-pleasing casserole. For the "bun," I use refrigerated biscuits to make a golden topping.
—Joy Frasure, Longmont, Colorado

- 1 **pound ground beef**
- 1/4 **cup chopped onion**
- 1 **can (8 ounces) tomato sauce**
- 1/4 **cup ketchup**

Dash pepper

- 2 **cups (8 ounces) shredded cheddar cheese, *divided***
- 1 **tube (12 ounces) refrigerated buttermilk biscuits, separated into 10 biscuits**

In a large skillet, cook beef and onion over medium heat until meat is no longer pink; drain. Stir in the tomato sauce, ketchup and pepper. Spoon half into a greased 8-in. square baking dish; sprinkle with half of the cheese. Repeat layers.

Place biscuits around edges of dish. Bake, uncovered, at 400° for 18-22 minutes or until the meat mixture is bubbly and biscuits are golden brown. **yield: 5 servings.**

ground beef noodle casserole

prep: 25 min. • bake: 30 min.

My mother shared this recipe with me soon after I was married. Most everything I know about cooking, I learned from her. This recipe has always been popular with my group and it's a time-saver as well because it uses spaghetti sauce and gravy mix.
—Christina Takacs
    West Springfield, Massachusetts

- 1 **envelope brown gravy mix**
- 1 **cup cold water**
- 1 **pound ground beef**
- 1 **small onion, diced**
- 3 **garlic cloves, minced**
- 1 **jar (14 ounces) spaghetti sauce**
- 1/2 **cup half-and-half cream**
- 1-1/2 **teaspoons Italian seasoning**
- 1/2 **teaspoon dried rosemary, crushed**

Salt and pepper to taste

- 8 **ounces wide egg noodles, cooked and drained**
- 2/3 **cup grated Parmesan cheese, *divided***

In a small bowl, combine gravy mix and water until smooth; set aside. In a large skillet, cook the beef and onion over medium heat until meat is no longer pink. Add garlic; cook 1 minute longer. Drain.

Add the spaghetti sauce, cream, seasonings and gravy; bring to a boil. Reduce heat; cover and simmer 15 minutes. Stir in the noodles and 1/3 cup cheese.

Transfer to a greased 3-qt. baking dish; sprinkle with remaining cheese. Cover and bake at 350° for 30 minutes or until heated through. **yield: 6 servings.**

beef and corn casserole

prep: 20 min. • bake: 1 hour

This recipe was passed down from my mother. It's now a standby for me as well as our three grown daughters. It's a great dish to pass at potlucks.
—Ruth Jost, Clear Lake, Iowa

- 1 package (10 ounces) fine egg noodles
- 1 pound ground beef
- 1 medium onion, chopped
- 1 can (15-1/4 ounces) whole kernel corn, drained
- 1 can (10-3/4 ounces) condensed tomato soup, undiluted
- 1 cup water
- 1 cup diced process cheese (Velveeta)
- 1/2 medium green pepper, chopped
- 1 medium carrot, thinly sliced
- 1 teaspoon salt
- 1/2 teaspoon pepper

Cook the noodles according to the package directions; drain. In a large skillet, cook the beef and onion over medium heat until the meat is no longer pink; drain. Add the noodles and remaining ingredients.

Transfer to a greased 13-in. x 9-in. baking dish. Cover and bake at 325° for 30 minutes. Uncover; bake 30-35 minutes longer or until bubbly. **yield: 8-10 servings.**

layered macaroni casserole

prep: 70 min. • bake: 40 min. + standing

With this recipe in my files, I never wonder what to fix for a potluck dinner or other get-together. The cheesy macaroni bake goes over big every time.
—Virginia Cherry, Salinas, California

- 1 pound lean ground beef (90% lean)
- 1/2 cup chopped onion
- 1 garlic clove, minced
- 1 can (28 ounces) crushed tomatoes
- 1 can (6 ounces) tomato paste
- 2 teaspoons sugar
- 1 teaspoon salt
- 1 teaspoon chili powder
- 1/2 teaspoon dried basil
- 1/2 teaspoon dried oregano
- 1/8 teaspoon pepper
- 8 ounces uncooked elbow macaroni
- 2 cups (16 ounces) fat-free cottage cheese
- 1-1/2 cups (6 ounces) shredded reduced-fat cheddar cheese

TOPPING:
- 1/4 cup dry bread crumbs
- 1/4 cup grated Parmesan cheese
- 1 tablespoon butter, melted

In a nonstick skillet, cook beef and onion over medium heat until meat is no longer pink. Add garlic; cook 1 minute longer. Drain. Add the tomatoes, tomato paste, sugar and seasonings. Bring to a boil. Reduce heat; cover and simmer for 1 hour.

Meanwhile, cook macaroni according to package directions; drain. Add cottage cheese.

In a 13-in. x 9-in. baking dish coated with cooking spray, layer 1 cup meat sauce, a third of the macaroni mixture and a third of the cheddar cheese. Repeat layers twice. Top with remaining meat sauce.

Combine topping ingredients; sprinkle over sauce. Bake, uncovered, at 325° for 40-45 minutes. Let stand for 10 minutes before serving. **yield: 8 servings.**

zucchini beef bake

prep: 20 min. • bake: 25 min.

Zucchini is a favorite vegetable for cooks because it can be used in countless ways. Here it's teamed up with ground beef, rice and cheese for a pretty, palate-pleasing meal.

—Christy Saniga, Tacoma, Washington

    6 cups water
    4 cups sliced zucchini
    1 pound ground beef
    1 large onion, chopped
    1 garlic clove, minced
    2 cups cooked rice
    1 can (8 ounces) tomato sauce
    1 cup (8 ounces) 4% cottage cheese
    1 egg, lightly beaten
1-1/2 teaspoons minced fresh oregano *or* 1/2 teaspoon dried oregano
    1 teaspoon minced fresh basil *or* 1/4 teaspoon dried basil
1/2 teaspoon salt
    1 cup (4 ounces) shredded cheddar cheese

In a large saucepan, bring water to a boil. Add zucchini. Return to a boil. Reduce heat; cover and simmer for 3 minutes or just until tender. Drain and immediately place zucchini in ice water. Drain and pat dry.

In a large skillet, cook beef and onion over medium heat until meat is no longer pink. Add garlic; cook 1 minute longer. Drain. Stir in the rice, tomato sauce, cottage cheese, egg, oregano, basil and salt.

Arrange half of the zucchini in a greased 13-in. x 9-in. baking dish. Layer with meat mixture and remaining zucchini; sprinkle with cheddar cheese. Bake, uncovered, at 350° for 25-30 minutes or until bubbly and cheese is melted. **yield: 6-8 servings.**

poultry

There are so many delectable uses for leftover cooked chicken and turkey in casseroles and bakes. Fresh poultry also has a place in this home-style fare. Just take a look at all the scrumptious choices in this chapter!

≪ pictured left

chicken asparagus bake

prep: 20 min. • bake: 30 min.

Layers of crunchy Triscuits sandwich a chicken and vegetable filling in this down-home casserole. A friend served this deliciously different dish for an evening meal and I couldn't resist asking for the recipe.
—Margaret Carlson, Amery, Wisconsin

- 1 package (9-1/2 ounces) Triscuits
- 2 cups cubed cooked chicken
- 2 cans (10-3/4 ounces *each*) condensed cream of chicken soup, undiluted
- 1 package (10 ounces) frozen chopped asparagus, thawed and drained
- 1 can (8 ounces) sliced water chestnuts, drained
- 1 can (4 ounces) mushroom stems and pieces, drained
- 1/2 cup mayonnaise

Break two-thirds of the crackers into bite-size pieces; place in a greased 2-1/2-qt. baking dish. Top with the chicken; spread soup over chicken.

In a large bowl, combine asparagus, water chestnuts, mushrooms and mayonnaise; spoon over soup. Crush remaining crackers; sprinkle over the top.

Bake, uncovered, at 350° for 30-40 minutes or until heated through. **yield: 4 servings.**

lattice-topped turkey casserole

prep: 45 min. • bake: 20 min. + standing

My friends tell me this is the best potpie ever. Hearty and full-flavored, this meal in one never lets on that it's lower in fat.
—Agnes Ward, Stratford, Ontario

- 1 can (14-1/2 ounces) reduced-sodium chicken broth
- 2 cups diced red potatoes
- 2 celery ribs, chopped
- 1 large onion, finely chopped
- 1/2 cup water
- 2 teaspoons chicken bouillon granules
- 1/2 teaspoon dried rosemary, crushed
- 1/4 teaspoon garlic powder
- 1/4 teaspoon dried thyme
- 1/8 teaspoon pepper
- 3 tablespoons all-purpose flour
- 2/3 cup fat-free evaporated milk
- 3 cups frozen mixed vegetables, thawed and drained
- 2 cups cubed cooked turkey breast

CRUST:
- 1/4 cup all-purpose flour
- 1/4 cup whole wheat flour
- 1/2 teaspoon baking powder
- 1/8 teaspoon salt
- 4 tablespoons fat-free milk, *divided*
- 1 tablespoon canola oil

Paprika

In a large saucepan, combine the first 10 ingredients. Bring to a boil. Reduce heat; cover and simmer for 15-20 minutes or until potatoes are tender.

In a small bowl, whisk flour and evaporated milk until smooth; stir into broth mixture. Bring to a boil; cook and stir for 2 minutes or until thickened. Stir in vegetables and turkey; heat through. Transfer to an ungreased 8-in. square baking dish.

For crust, combine the flours, baking powder and salt in a small bowl. Stir in 3 tablespoons milk and oil just until combined. Roll out and cut into strips; make a lattice crust over filling. Trim and seal edges. Brush lattice top with remaining milk; sprinkle with paprika.

Bake, uncovered, at 400° for 20-25 minutes or until filling is bubbly. Let stand for 10 minutes before serving. **yield: 6 servings.**

mexican chicken bake

prep: 15 min. • bake: 30 min.

Since my kids, grandkids and guests of all ages request this casserole often, and it takes only about 30 minutes to bake, I have it at least once every other month!
—Linda Humphrey
 Buchanan, Michigan

----

     1 medium onion, chopped
     1 small green pepper, chopped
     2 large jalapeno peppers,
        seeded and chopped
   1/4 cup butter, cubed
     2 cans (10-3/4 ounces *each*)
        condensed cream of chicken
        soup, undiluted
     1 can (12 ounces) evaporated
        milk
     4 cups cooked long grain rice
     3 to 4 cups cubed cooked
        chicken
     3 cups (12 ounces) Colby-
        Monterey Jack cheese,
        divided

In a large skillet, saute the onion, green pepper and jalapeno peppers in butter until tender. In a large bowl, combine soup and milk. Stir in the rice, chicken, 2 cups cheese and onion mixture.

Transfer to a greased 13-in. x 9-in. baking dish. Bake, uncovered, at 350° for 25 minutes. Sprinkle with the remaining cheese. Bake 5-10 minutes longer or until heated through and the cheese is melted. **yield: 8-10 servings.**

----

editor's note: Wear disposable gloves when cutting hot peppers. Avoid touching your face.

chicken stuffing bake

prep: 5 min. • bake: 45 min.

At my bridal shower, each guest brought a recipe card of her best dish. We've tried all the recipes, but this one is a favorite.
—Nicole Vogl Harding, Spokane, Washington

----

     6 boneless skinless chicken breast halves (6 ounces *each*)
     6 slices Swiss cheese
     1 can (10-3/4 ounces) condensed cream of chicken soup,
        undiluted
   1/3 cup white wine *or* chicken broth
     3 cups seasoned stuffing cubes
   1/2 cup butter, melted

Place the chicken in a greased 13-in. x 9-in. baking dish; top with the cheese. In a small bowl, combine the soup and wine; spoon over cheese.

In a small bowl, combine the croutons and butter; sprinkle over soup. Bake, uncovered, at 350° for 45-55 minutes or until a meat thermometer reads 170°. **yield: 6 servings.**

southwest creamy pasta bake

prep: 20 min. • bake: 30 min.

I keep meal-size packages of diced, cooked chicken breast in my freezer. On hectic nights, I just pull one out and defrost it in the microwave while I'm prepping the rest of the meal, such as this pasta dish. I find having the cooked chicken at my fingertips is a real time-saver.

—Patty Putter, Marion, Kansas

12 ounces uncooked spiral pasta

3 cups cubed cooked chicken breast

2 cups (16 ounces) sour cream

2 cups (8 ounces) shredded Colby-Monterey Jack cheese

1 can (10-3/4 ounces) condensed cream of mushroom soup, undiluted

1 can (10-3/4 ounces) condensed cream of celery soup, undiluted

1 can (10 ounces) green chili salsa

1 cup chopped green onions

1 can (4-1/4 ounces) chopped ripe olives

Cook pasta according to package directions. Meanwhile, in a large bowl, combine the remaining ingredients. Drain pasta; stir into chicken mixture.

Transfer to a greased 13-in. x 9-in. baking dish. Bake, uncovered, at 350° for 30-35 minutes or until heated through. **yield: 8 servings.**

chicken tortilla bake

prep: 25 min. • bake: 25 min.

You get two for the price of one in this combo enchilada/lasagna casserole. The dish combines all the flavors of the Mexican staple with the ease of layered lasagna.
—Taste of Home Test Kitchen

---

   1 **pound boneless skinless chicken breasts, cut into 1-inch cubes**

1/2 **teaspoon ground cumin**

1/4 **teaspoon salt**

   1 **tablespoon plus 1 teaspoon olive oil, *divided***

   1 **can (16 ounces) refried beans**

   1 **can (14-1/2 ounces) diced tomatoes with mild green chilies, drained**

   8 **flour tortillas (8 inches), cut into 1-inch strips**

   1 **can (11 ounces) Mexicorn, drained**

   2 **cups (8 ounces) shredded cheddar cheese**

In a large skillet, saute the chicken, cumin and salt in 1 tablespoon oil until chicken is no longer pink.

Combine the refried beans and tomatoes; spread 1 cup into a greased 11-in. x 7-in. baking dish. Top with 24 tortilla strips; layer with half of the corn, bean mixture, chicken and cheese. Repeat layers.

Using remaining tortilla strips, make a lattice crust over filling; brush with remaining oil. Bake, uncovered, at 350° for 25-30 minutes or until heated through and cheese is melted. **yield: 6 servings.**

chicken nugget casserole

prep: 5 min. • bake: 30 min.

It's so easy and uses only five ingredients, so even youngsters can help prepare this entree. Our kids love to eat chicken nuggets this way. It's a filling supper when served with spaghetti and a salad.
—Tylene Loar, Mesa, Arizona

- 1 package (13-1/2 ounces) frozen chicken nuggets
- 1/3 cup grated Parmesan cheese
- 1 can (26-1/2 ounces) spaghetti sauce
- 1 cup (4 ounces) shredded part-skim mozzarella cheese
- 1 teaspoon Italian seasoning

Place chicken nuggets in a greased 11-in. x 7-in. baking dish. Sprinkle with Parmesan cheese. Layer with spaghetti sauce, mozzarella cheese and Italian seasoning.

Cover and bake at 350° for 30-35 minutes or until chicken is heated through and cheese is melted. **yield: 4-6 servings.**

turkey spinach casserole

prep: 20 min. • bake: 40 min.

I lightened up a family recipe to come up with this turkey and rice combination. Accompanied by fresh tomato slices and hot corn bread, this quick meal is one of my gang's absolute favorites.
—Becca Bransfield, Burns, Tennessee

- 1 can (10-3/4 ounces) reduced-fat reduced-sodium condensed cream of chicken soup, undiluted
- 1/2 cup reduced-fat mayonnaise
- 1/2 cup water
- 2 cups cubed cooked turkey breast
- 1 package (10 ounces) frozen chopped spinach, thawed and squeezed dry
- 3/4 cup uncooked instant brown rice
- 1 medium yellow summer squash, cubed
- 1/4 cup chopped red onion
- 1 teaspoon ground mustard
- 1/2 teaspoon dried parsley flakes
- 1/2 teaspoon garlic powder
- 1/8 teaspoon pepper
- 1/4 cup fat-free Parmesan cheese topping
- 1/8 teaspoon paprika

In a large bowl, combine the soup, mayonnaise and water. Stir in the next nine ingredients. Transfer to a shallow 2-1/2-qt. baking dish coated with cooking spray.

Cover and bake at 350° for 35-40 minutes or until the rice is tender. Uncover; sprinkle with the cheese topping and paprika. Bake 5 minutes longer or until cheese is melted. **yield: 6 servings.**

summer squash chicken casserole

prep: 20 min. • bake: 30 min.

This rich and saucy casserole features tender pattypans in a delectable chicken and rice combination. Pair it with a salad for a family-friendly supper that you can feel good about.
—Taste of Home Test Kitchen

- 1/2 cup uncooked instant rice
- 1 can (10-3/4 ounces) condensed cream of chicken soup, undiluted
- 1/3 cup reduced-fat mayonnaise
- 1/3 cup fat-free milk
- 4 cups cubed cooked chicken breast
- 2 cups pattypan squash, halved
- 1 small onion, finely chopped
- 1 jar (2 ounces) diced pimientos, drained
- 1 teaspoon dried thyme
- 1/4 teaspoon garlic powder
- 1/4 teaspoon pepper
- 1/3 cup shredded Parmesan cheese

Cook rice according to the package directions. In a large bowl, combine the soup, mayonnaise and milk. Stir in the chicken, squash, onion, pimientos, thyme, garlic powder, pepper and cooked rice.

Spoon into a 2-qt. baking dish coated with cooking spray. Sprinkle with the cheese. Bake, uncovered, at 350° for 30-40 minutes or until the edges are bubbly and the center is set. **yield: 6 servings.**

crunchy turkey casserole

prep: 15 min. • bake: 30 min.

I call this a plan-over. I plan to make it with the leftovers after I cook a turkey. With its appealing crunch from water chestnuts, almonds and chow mein noodles, this main dish is enjoyed by all.
—Lois Koogler, Sidney, Ohio

- 2 cans (10-3/4 ounces *each*) condensed cream of mushroom soup, undiluted
- 1/2 cup 2% milk *or* chicken broth
- 4 cups cubed cooked turkey
- 2 celery ribs, thinly sliced
- 1 small onion, chopped
- 1 can (8 ounces) sliced water chestnuts, drained and halved
- 1 tablespoon reduced-sodium soy sauce
- 1 can (3 ounces) chow mein noodles
- 1/2 cup slivered almonds

In a large bowl, combine soup and milk. Stir in the turkey, celery, onion, water chestnuts and soy sauce.

Transfer to a greased shallow 2-qt. baking dish. Sprinkle with noodles and almonds. Bake, uncovered, at 350° for 30 minutes or until heated through. **yield: 6-8 servings.**

Cook pasta according to package directions. Meanwhile, crumble beef and sausage into a large skillet; add onion. Cook and stir over medium heat until meat is no longer pink. Add garlic; cook 1 minute longer. Drain. Stir in the tomatoes, tomato paste and seasonings. Bring to a boil. Reduce heat; simmer, uncovered, for 5 minutes.

Drain pasta; stir in meat mixture and pepperoni. Transfer half of the pasta mixture to a 2-qt. baking dish coated with cooking spray. Sprinkle with half of the cheese; repeat layers.

Cover the casserole and bake at 350° for 20-25 minutes or until bubbly. **yield: 6 servings.**

italian pasta casserole

prep: 30 min. • bake: 20 min.

All the traditional Italian flavors are found in this dish. It is reminiscent of lasagna. This is a zippy and hearty recipe that our family and guests really like.
—Denise Rasmussen, Salina, Kansas

- 2 cups uncooked spiral pasta
- 1/2 pound lean ground beef (90% lean)
- 1/2 pound Italian turkey sausage links, casings removed
- 1 small onion, finely chopped
- 1 garlic clove, minced
- 2 cans (14-1/2 ounces *each*) diced tomatoes, undrained
- 1/3 cup tomato paste
- 3/4 teaspoon Italian seasoning
- 1/2 teaspoon chili powder
- 1/4 teaspoon dried oregano
- 1/8 teaspoon salt
- 1/8 teaspoon garlic powder
- 1/8 teaspoon dried thyme
- 1/8 teaspoon pepper
- 2 ounces sliced turkey pepperoni
- 1 cup (4 ounces) shredded part-skim mozzarella cheese

golden chicken casserole

prep: 5 min. • bake: 30 min.

Apricot preserves give a different twist to this saucy sweet-and-sour chicken. With just five ingredients, it's a snap to stir up and serve over rice.
—Melanie May, Fishers, Indiana

- 2 cups cubed cooked chicken
- 1 can (20 ounces) unsweetened pineapple chunks, drained
- 1 jar (12 ounces) apricot preserves *or* spreadable fruit
- 1 can (10-3/4 ounces) condensed cream of chicken soup, undiluted
- 1 can (8 ounces) water chestnuts, drained

Hot cooked rice

In a large bowl, combine the first five ingredients. Transfer to a greased 2-qt. baking dish.

Bake, uncovered, at 350° for 30 minutes or until heated through. Serve with rice. **yield: 6 servings.**

wild rice chicken casserole

prep: 15 min. • bake: 30 min.

My husband of over 50 years loves to eat and I love to cook, so we're both happy when I make this. It's nice and creamy with a little crunch from almonds. The chicken is canned, but you'd never know it from the taste.

—Darrell Plinsky, Wichita, Kansas

- 1 package (6 ounces) long grain and wild rice
- 1/3 cup chopped onion
- 3 tablespoons chopped almonds
- 2 tablespoons dried parsley flakes
- 1/4 cup butter, cubed
- 1/3 cup all-purpose flour
- 2 cups 2% milk
- 1-1/2 cups chicken broth
- 1/2 to 1 teaspoon salt
- 1/4 teaspoon pepper
- 1 can (10 ounces) chunk white chicken, drained

Prepare the rice according to package directions. Meanwhile, in a small skillet, saute the onion, almonds and parsley in butter for 4-5 minutes or until onion is tender and almonds are lightly toasted.

In a large bowl, combine the flour, milk, broth, salt and pepper until smooth. Stir in the chicken, rice and vegetables.

Pour into a greased 13-in. x 9-in. baking dish (mixture will be thin). Bake, uncovered, at 425° for 30-35 minutes or until bubbly and golden brown. **yield: 4-6 servings.**

potato chip-topped hot chicken salad

prep: 15 min. • bake: 30 min.

A creamy mix of crunchy veggies and hot chicken is topped with crispy potato chips. The whole family will look forward to having this delicious meal, and you'll be happy with the quick and easy prep!

—Bernice Knutson, Danbury, Iowa

- 1 package (9 ounces) frozen diced cooked chicken breast, thawed
- 2 cups thinly sliced celery
- 1 can (8 ounces) sliced water chestnuts, drained
- 1/2 cup chopped almonds
- 1/3 cup chopped green pepper
- 1 jar (2 ounces) diced pimientos, drained
- 2 tablespoons finely chopped onion
- 2/3 cup shredded Swiss cheese, *divided*
- 1 cup mayonnaise
- 2 tablespoons lemon juice
- 1/2 teaspoon salt
- 2 cups crushed potato chips

In a large bowl, combine the chicken, celery, water chestnuts, almonds, green pepper, pimientos, onion and 1/3 cup cheese. In a small bowl, combine the mayonnaise, lemon juice and salt. Stir into chicken mixture and toss to coat.

Transfer to a greased 8-in. square baking dish. Bake, uncovered, at 350° for 20 minutes. Sprinkle with potato chips and remaining cheese. Bake 10-15 minutes longer or until heated through and cheese is melted. **yield: 4 servings.**

makeover chicken noodle delight

prep: 25 min. • bake: 40 min.

A neighbor made this dish for us when we had our second child. It was so good that I made a lightened version and my family never knew it was healthier!
—Gail Schumacher, Berthoud, Colorado

- 4 cups uncooked yolk-free noodles
- 1 can (10-3/4 ounces) reduced-fat reduced-sodium condensed cream of chicken soup, undiluted
- 4 ounces reduced-fat cream cheese, cubed
- 1 cup (8 ounces) reduced-fat sour cream
- 1 cup (8 ounces) plain yogurt
- 1/4 cup fat-free milk
- 3 tablespoons minced fresh parsley *or* 1 tablespoon dried parsley flakes
- 1 teaspoon onion powder
- 1/4 teaspoon salt
- 2 cups cubed cooked chicken breast
- 1 cup crushed reduced-fat butter-flavored crackers (about 25 crackers)
- 3 tablespoons reduced-fat butter, melted

Cook noodles according to package directions. Meanwhile, in a large bowl, combine the soup, cream cheese, sour cream, yogurt, milk, parsley, onion powder and salt. Stir in chicken.

Drain noodles; toss with chicken mixture. Transfer to a 2-qt. baking dish coated with cooking spray.

Combine cracker crumbs and butter; sprinkle over casserole. Bake, uncovered, at 350° for 40-45 minutes or until heated through. **yield: 6 servings.**

editor's note: This recipe was tested with Land O'Lakes light stick butter.

baked mostaccioli

prep: 35 min. • bake: 30 min.

I often serve this lower-in-calories version of mostaccioli for dinner parties and always get tons of compliments.
—Donna Ebert, Richfield, Wisconsin

- 8 ounces uncooked mostaccioli
- 1/2 pound lean ground turkey
- 1 small onion, chopped
- 1 can (14-1/2 ounces) diced tomatoes, undrained
- 1 can (6 ounces) tomato paste
- 1/3 cup water
- 1 teaspoon dried oregano
- 1/2 teaspoon salt
- 1/8 teaspoon pepper
- 2 cups (16 ounces) fat-free cottage cheese
- 1 teaspoon dried marjoram
- 1-1/2 cups (6 ounces) shredded part-skim mozzarella cheese
- 1/4 cup grated Parmesan cheese

Cook mostaccioli according to package directions. Meanwhile, in a large saucepan, cook turkey and onion over medium heat until meat is no longer pink; drain if necessary.

Stir in the tomatoes, tomato paste, water, oregano, salt and pepper. Bring to a boil. Reduce heat; cover and simmer for 15 minutes.

In a small bowl, combine cottage cheese and marjoram; set aside. Drain mostaccioli.

Spread 1/2 cup meat sauce into an 11-in. x 7-in. baking dish coated with cooking spray. Layer with half of the mostaccioli, meat sauce and mozzarella cheese. Top with cottage cheese mixture. Layer with remaining mostaccioli, meat sauce and mozzarella cheese. Sprinkle with Parmesan cheese (dish will be full).

Bake, uncovered, at 350° for 30-40 minutes or until bubbly and heated through. **yield: 6 servings.**

ranch chicken 'n' rice

prep: 10 min. • bake: 35 min.

When I clipped this recipe from a neighborhood shopper a few years ago, I couldn't wait to try it. Just as I expected, my family enjoyed it so much that they ask for it time and again.
—Erlene Crusoe, Litchfield, Minnesota

- 2 cups uncooked instant rice
- 1-1/2 cups 2% milk
- 1 cup water
- 1 envelope ranch salad dressing mix
- 1 pound boneless skinless chicken breasts, cut into 1/2-inch strips
- 1/4 cup butter, melted

Paprika

Place rice in a greased shallow 2-qt. baking dish. In a small bowl, combine the milk, water and salad dressing mix; set aside 1/4 cup. Pour remaining mixture over rice. Top with chicken strips. Drizzle with butter and reserved milk mixture.

Cover and bake at 350° for 35-40 minutes or until rice is tender and chicken is no longer pink. Sprinkle with paprika. **yield: 4 servings.**

KITCHEN TIP

For a change of pace, try instant brown rice instead of white rice. The brown rice will add a nutty taste and more fiber to the casserole. Plus, it has less calories per serving!

spaghetti squash supreme

prep: 45 min. • bake: 20 min.

While dreaming up a healthier pasta dish, I decided to experiment with spaghetti squash. After a few tries, I settled on this delicious one that is bursting with flavor but not fat.
—Christina Morris, Calabasas, California

  1 medium spaghetti squash (4 pounds)
  1 can (14-1/2 ounces) diced tomatoes, undrained
  2 tablespoons prepared pesto
1/2 teaspoon garlic powder
1/2 teaspoon Italian seasoning
1/4 cup dry bread crumbs
1/4 cup shredded Parmesan cheese
  1 pound boneless skinless chicken breasts, cut into 1/2-inch cubes
  1 tablespoon plus 1 teaspoon olive oil, *divided*
1/2 pound sliced fresh mushrooms
  1 medium onion, chopped
  1 garlic clove, minced
1/2 cup chicken broth
1/3 cup shredded cheddar cheese

Cut squash in half lengthwise; discard seeds. Place squash cut side down on a microwave-safe plate. Microwave, uncovered, on high for 14-16 minutes or until tender.

Meanwhile, in a blender, combine tomatoes, pesto, garlic powder and Italian seasoning. Cover and process until blended; set aside. In a small bowl, combine bread crumbs and Parmesan cheese; set aside.

In a large skillet, cook chicken in 1 tablespoon oil until no longer pink; remove and keep warm. In the same skillet, saute mushrooms and onion in remaining oil until tender. Add garlic; cook 1 minute longer. Stir in the broth, chicken and reserved tomato mixture. Bring to a boil. Reduce heat; simmer, uncovered, for 5 minutes.

When squash is cool enough to handle, use a fork to separate the strands. In a large ovenproof skillet, layer with half of the squash, chicken mixture and reserved crumb mixture. Repeat layers.

Bake, uncovered, at 350° for 15 minutes or until heated through. Sprinkle with cheddar cheese. Broil 3-4 in. from the heat for 5-6 minutes or until cheese is melted and golden brown. **yield: 5 servings.**

editor's note: This recipe was tested in a 1,100-watt microwave.

chicken broccoli shells

prep: 15 min. • bake: 30 min.

This cheesy entree can be assembled ahead of time and popped in the oven when company arrives. I round out the meal with a tossed salad and warm bread.
—Karen Jagger
  Columbia City, Indiana

  1 jar (16 ounces) Alfredo sauce
  2 cups frozen chopped broccoli, thawed
  2 cups diced cooked chicken
  1 cup (4 ounces) shredded cheddar cheese
1/4 cup shredded Parmesan cheese
 21 jumbo pasta shells, cooked and drained

In a large bowl, combine the Alfredo sauce, broccoli, chicken and cheeses. Spoon into pasta shells. Place in a greased 13-in. x 9-in. baking dish.

Cover and bake at 350° for 30-35 minutes or until heated through. **yield: 7 servings.**

secondhand turkey

prep: 30 min. • bake: 20 min.

Turkey leftovers take on a fresh appeal in this saucy noodle bake. Mushrooms, celery and thyme give it wonderful flavor.

—Dixie Terry, Goreville, Illinois

  1/2 **pound sliced fresh mushrooms**
  1/2 **cup chopped celery**
    5 **tablespoons butter,** *divided*
    2 **tablespoons cornstarch**
    2 **cups 2% milk**
    2 **cups cubed cooked turkey**
    2 **cups cooked egg noodles**
  1/4 **cup chicken broth**
    1 **teaspoon salt**
  1/2 **teaspoon dried thyme**
  1/8 **teaspoon white pepper**
  1/2 **cup dry bread crumbs**

In a large skillet, saute the mushrooms and celery in 3 tablespoons butter until tender. Combine cornstarch and milk until smooth; stir into the mushroom mixture. Bring to a boil over medium heat, stirring constantly. Cook for 1 minute or until thickened.

Stir in the turkey, noodles, broth, salt, thyme and pepper. Pour into a greased 2-qt. baking dish. Melt the remaining butter; toss with bread crumbs. Sprinkle over casserole.

Bake, uncovered, at 375° for 20-25 minutes or until heated through. **yield: 4 servings.**

butternut turkey bake

prep: 70 min. • bake: 25 min.

Butternut squash adds a little sweetness to this satisfying turkey entree. You can use leftover meat and even replace the croutons with leftover stuffing, if you wish.
—Mary Ann Dell, Phoenixville, Pennsylvania

- 1 medium butternut squash (about 2-1/2 pounds)
- 3/4 cup finely chopped onion
- 2 tablespoons butter
- 2 cups seasoned salad croutons
- 1/2 teaspoon salt
- 1/2 teaspoon poultry seasoning
- 1/2 teaspoon pepper
- 2 cups cubed cooked turkey
- 1 cup chicken broth
- 1/2 cup shredded cheddar cheese

Cut squash in half; discard seeds. Place cut side down in a 15-in. x 10-in. x 1-in. baking pan; add 1/2 in. of hot water. Bake, uncovered, at 350° for 45 minutes.

Drain water from pan; turn squash cut side up. Bake 10-15 minutes longer or until tender. Scoop out pulp; mash and set aside.

In a large skillet, saute onion in butter until tender. Stir in the croutons, salt, poultry seasoning and pepper. Cook 2-3 minutes longer or until croutons are toasted. Stir in the squash, turkey and broth; heat through.

Transfer to a greased 1-1/2-qt. baking dish. Bake, uncovered, at 350° for 20 minutes. Sprinkle with cheese. Bake 5-10 minutes longer or until edges are bubbly and cheese is melted. **yield: 4 servings.**

comforting chicken

prep: 15 min. • bake: 55 min.

When you don't need to cook for a whole crew, try this smaller-sized casserole that feeds just a few. The saucy combination of chicken and rice is one of our go-to suppers.
—Edna Thomas, Warsaw, Indiana

- 1 pound boneless skinless chicken breasts, cut into cubes
- 1/2 cup finely chopped onion
- 1/2 cup finely chopped green pepper
- 1 tablespoon canola oil
- 1 tablespoon butter
- 1 can (10-3/4 ounces) condensed cream of mushroom soup, undiluted
- 1 cup water
- 3/4 cup uncooked long grain rice
- 1/2 teaspoon salt
- 1/2 teaspoon chili powder
- 1/4 teaspoon pepper
- 1/4 teaspoon paprika

In a large skillet, cook the chicken, onion and green pepper in oil and butter until chicken is no longer pink and vegetables are tender. Stir in the remaining ingredients.

Transfer to a lightly greased 1-1/2-qt. baking dish. Cover and bake at 375° for 55-60 minutes or until bubbly and rice is tender. **yield: 4 servings.**

alfredo chicken 'n' biscuits

prep: 20 min. • bake: 20 min.

Chock-full of veggies and topped off with golden-brown biscuits and Alfredo sauce, this is a complete meal. It's fun to prepare and has excellent flavor.
—Cheryl Miller, Fort Collins, Colorado

- 2 cups chopped fresh broccoli
- 1-1/2 cups sliced fresh carrots
- 1 cup chopped onion
- 2 tablespoons olive oil
- 2 cups cubed cooked chicken
- 1 carton (10 ounces) refrigerated Alfredo sauce
- 1 cup biscuit/baking mix
- 1/3 cup 2% milk
- 1/4 teaspoon dill weed

In a large skillet, saute the broccoli, carrots and onion in oil until crisp-tender. Stir in chicken and Alfredo sauce; heat through. Transfer to a lightly greased 8-in. square baking dish.

In a small bowl, combine the baking mix, milk and dill just until moistened. Drop by rounded tablespoonfuls onto chicken mixture.

Bake, uncovered, at 400° for 18-22 minutes or until bubbly and biscuits are golden brown. **yield: 4 servings.**

chicken corn bread stuffing casserole

prep: 15 min. • bake: 35 min.

I am frequently asked to make this casserole for the monthly potluck dinners in our retirement complex. There are never any leftovers. It's so moist, comforting, simple and flavorful!
—Carmelia Saxon, Chapel Hill, North Carolina

- 2 eggs, lightly beaten
- 1 package (14 ounces) crushed corn bread stuffing
- 4 cups cubed cooked chicken breast
- 3 cups reduced-sodium chicken broth, warmed
- 1 can (10-3/4 ounces) reduced-fat reduced-sodium condensed cream of chicken soup, undiluted
- 1 small onion, chopped
- 1/4 cup chopped celery
- 1 teaspoon rubbed sage

In a large bowl, combine all the ingredients. Transfer to a 13-in. x 9-in. baking dish coated with cooking spray.

Cover and bake at 375° for 25 minutes. Uncover; bake 10-15 minutes longer or until a thermometer reads 160°. **yield: 8 servings.**

chicken rice casserole

prep: 20 min. • bake: 20 min.

This heartwarming main course with lots of chicken, cheese and rice makes a quick and comforting weeknight meal. It's a great recipe for people with full-time jobs.

—Donna Burnett, Baileyton, Alabama

- 1 package (5.6 ounces) instant rice and chicken-flavored sauce mix
- 2 cups cubed cooked chicken
- 1 can (10-3/4 ounces) condensed cream of celery soup, undiluted
- 1/2 cup mayonnaise
- 1/2 teaspoon Worcestershire sauce
- 1/4 teaspoon pepper
- 1 cup (4 ounces) shredded cheddar cheese

Cook rice mix according to package directions. In a large bowl, combine the chicken, soup, mayonnaise, Worcestershire sauce and pepper. Stir in the rice.

Transfer to a greased 1-1/2-qt. baking dish. Sprinkle with the cheese. Bake the casserole, uncovered, at 350° for 20-25 minutes or until heated through. **yield: 4 servings.**

mexicali casserole

prep: 15 min. • bake: 55 min.

Kids will love this hearty yet mild-tasting Mexican-style supper. It's also popular at potluck dinners.

—Gertrudis Miller, Evansville, Indiana

- 1 pound lean ground turkey
- 1-1/2 cups chopped onions
- 1/2 cup chopped green pepper
- 1 garlic clove, minced
- 1 teaspoon chili powder
- 1/2 teaspoon salt
- 1 can (16 ounces) kidney beans, rinsed and drained
- 1 can (14-1/2 ounces) diced tomatoes, undrained
- 1 cup water
- 2/3 cup uncooked long grain rice
- 1/3 cup sliced ripe olives
- 1/2 cup shredded reduced-fat cheddar cheese

In a large skillet coated with cooking spray, cook the turkey, onions and green pepper over medium heat until meat is no longer pink and vegetables are tender. Add garlic; cook 1 minute longer. Drain. Sprinkle with chili powder and salt. Stir in the beans, tomatoes, water, rice and olives.

Transfer to a 2-1/2-qt. baking dish coated with cooking spray. Cover and bake at 375° for 50-55 minutes or until rice is tender. Uncover; sprinkle with cheese. Bake 5 minutes longer or until cheese is melted. **yield: 6 servings.**

sausage 'n' chicken casserole

prep: 10 min. • bake: 55 min.

Meat-and-potato fans will fall for this recipe because simple seasonings really bring out the flavors.
—Alice Ceresa, Rochester, New York

---

  5 medium potatoes (about 3 pounds), peeled and quartered

  1 teaspoon salt

  1 teaspoon dried oregano

  1 teaspoon paprika

1/2 teaspoon garlic salt

1/2 pound Italian sausage links, cooked and cut into 1-inch pieces

  4 bone-in chicken breast halves, skin removed (7 ounces *each*)

  2 tablespoons canola oil

Place potatoes in a greased 13-in. x 9-in. baking dish. In a small bowl, combine the salt, oregano, paprika and garlic salt; sprinkle half over potatoes.

Arrange sausage and chicken over the potatoes. Drizzle with oil; sprinkle with remaining seasonings.

Cover and bake at 400° for 55-60 minutes or until a meat thermometer inserted in the chicken reads 170°. **yield: 4 servings.**

enchilada stuffed shells

prep: 20 min. • bake: 30 min.

I served this entree to my husband, my sister and my brother-in-law, who is a hard-to-please eater. He said he liked it and even took leftovers for lunch the next day. I was thrilled!
—Rebecca Stout, Conroe, Texas

---

15 uncooked jumbo pasta shells

1 pound lean ground turkey

1 can (10 ounces) enchilada sauce

1/2 teaspoon dried minced onion

1/4 teaspoon dried basil

1/4 teaspoon dried oregano

1/4 teaspoon ground cumin

1/2 cup fat-free refried beans

1 cup (4 ounces) shredded reduced-fat cheddar cheese

Cook pasta according to package directions; drain and rinse in cold water. In a nonstick skillet, cook turkey over medium heat until no longer pink; drain. Stir in enchilada sauce and seasonings; set aside.

Place a rounded teaspoonful of refried beans in each pasta shell, then fill with turkey mixture. Place in an 11-in. x 7-in. baking dish coated with cooking spray.

Cover and bake at 350° for 25 minutes. Uncover; sprinkle with cheese. Bake 5 minutes longer or until cheese is melted. **yield: 5 servings.**

mushroom turkey tetrazzini

prep: 35 min. • bake: 25 min.

This creamy, heartwarming bake is a fantastic way to use up leftover holiday turkey. And it's a real family pleaser!
—Linda Howe, Lisle, Illinois

- 12 ounces uncooked spaghetti, broken into 2-inch pieces
- 2 teaspoons chicken bouillon granules
- 1/2 pound sliced fresh mushrooms
- 2 tablespoons butter
- 2 tablespoons all-purpose flour
- 1/4 cup sherry *or* reduced-sodium chicken broth
- 3/4 teaspoon salt-free lemon-pepper seasoning
- 1/2 teaspoon salt
- 1/8 teaspoon ground nutmeg
- 1 cup fat-free evaporated milk
- 2/3 cup grated Parmesan cheese, *divided*
- 4 cups cubed cooked turkey breast
- 1/4 teaspoon paprika

Cook spaghetti according to package directions. Drain, reserving 2-1/2 cups cooking liquid. Stir bouillon into cooking liquid and set aside. Place spaghetti in a 13-in. x 9-in. baking dish coated with cooking spray; set aside.

In a large nonstick skillet, saute mushrooms in butter until tender. Stir in flour until blended. Gradually stir in sherry and reserved cooking liquid. Add the lemon-pepper, salt and nutmeg. Bring to a boil; cook and stir for 2 minutes or until thickened.

Reduce heat to low; stir in milk and 1/3 cup Parmesan cheese until blended. Add turkey; cook and stir until heated through. Pour turkey mixture over spaghetti and toss to combine. Sprinkle with paprika and remaining Parmesan cheese.

Cover and bake at 375° for 25-30 minutes or until bubbly. **yield: 8 servings.**

easy chicken divan

prep: 15 min. • bake: 20 min.

I got this recipe from a coworker and then made a few changes to it to suit my family's tastes. It's excellent with corn bread.
—Violet Englert, Leicester, New York

- 3 cups cubed cooked chicken
- 1/2 teaspoon salt
- 1/4 teaspoon pepper
- 6 cups frozen broccoli florets, thawed
- 2 cans (10-3/4 ounces *each*) condensed cream of chicken soup, undiluted
- 1/3 cup mayonnaise
- 1/4 cup 2% milk
- 2 cups (8 ounces) shredded Mexican cheese blend *or* cheddar cheese, *divided*

In a greased shallow 2-1/2-qt. baking dish, combine chicken, salt and pepper. Top with the broccoli. In a large bowl, combine soup, mayonnaise, milk and 1-1/2 cups cheese; pour over broccoli. Sprinkle with remaining cheese.

Bake, uncovered, at 375° for 20-25 minutes or until heated through. **yield: 4-6 servings.**

turkey casserole

prep: 20 min. • bake: 30 min.

Turkey teams up temptingly with pretty green peas and crunchy water chestnuts in this yummy dish. Its creamy sauce combined with melted cheese and a golden crouton topping is sure to win you compliments.
—Beth Struble, Bryan, Ohio

- 2 cups cubed cooked turkey breast
- 1 package (10 ounces) frozen peas, thawed
- 1 cup chopped celery
- 1 can (8 ounces) sliced water chestnuts, drained
- 2 tablespoons chopped green pepper
- 1 tablespoon chopped onion
- 1 can (10-3/4 ounces) reduced-fat reduced sodium condensed cream of chicken soup, undiluted
- 1/2 cup fat-free milk
- 1 cup (4 ounces) shredded reduced-fat cheddar cheese, *divided*
- 2 tablespoons white wine *or* chicken broth
- 1 tablespoon lemon juice
- 1/2 teaspoon salt
- 2 slices white bread, cubed

In a large bowl, combine the first six ingredients; set aside.

In a small saucepan, combine the soup, milk, 1/2 cup cheese, wine, lemon juice and salt. Cook and stir over low heat until smooth and heated through. Pour over turkey mixture; toss to coat.

Transfer to a 2-qt. baking dish coated with cooking spray. Top with bread cubes.

Bake, uncovered, at 375° for 25 minutes. Sprinkle with remaining cheese; bake 5 minutes longer or until cheese is melted. **yield: 6 servings.**

chicken brown rice bake

prep: 20 min. • bake: 25 min.

Corn and red pepper bring color to this nicely seasoned chicken and rice bake. The crunch from toasted almonds sprinkled on top also sets it apart from classic versions of this casserole.
—*Mary Louise Chubb, Perkasie, Pennsylvania*

---

  6 boneless skinless chicken breast halves (1-1/2 pounds)
  1 tablespoon canola oil
3/4 cup chopped sweet red pepper
3/4 cup chopped green pepper
1/2 cup chopped onion
1/2 cup chopped fresh mushrooms
  1 garlic clove, minced
  2 cups uncooked instant brown rice
  2 cups chicken broth
1-1/2 cups frozen corn, thawed
1/4 teaspoon salt
1/8 teaspoon pepper
1/4 cup slivered almonds, toasted
  2 tablespoons minced parsley

In a large skillet, brown chicken in oil for 4 minutes on each side or until a meat thermometer reads 170°. Remove and keep warm. In the same skillet, saute the peppers, onion and mushrooms until tender. Add garlic; cook 1 minute longer. Stir in the rice, broth, corn, salt and pepper; bring to a boil.

Transfer to an 11-in. x 7-in. baking dish coated with cooking spray. Top with the chicken. Cover and bake at 350° for 20 minutes. Uncover; bake 5 minutes longer or until heated through. Sprinkle with the almonds and parsley. **yield: 6 servings.**

california chicken casserole

prep: 10 min. • bake: 45 min.

I think it is fun to try new recipes, and this chicken and vegetable combo passed my family's taste test. If there are leftovers, I package them for my husband's lunch. They easily reheat in the microwave.

—Debbie Kokes, Tabor, South Dakota

1 can (10-3/4 ounces) condensed cream of mushroom soup, undiluted
1/3 cup 2% milk
1 package (16 ounces) frozen California-blend vegetables, thawed
1-1/2 cups cubed cooked chicken
1-1/2 cups (6 ounces) shredded Swiss cheese, *divided*
1 jar (2 ounces) diced pimientos, drained
Salt and pepper to taste
Hot cooked rice

In a large bowl, combine the soup and milk. Stir in the vegetables, chicken, 1-1/4 cups cheese, pimientos, salt and pepper. Transfer mixture to a greased 9-in. square baking dish.

Cover and bake at 350° for 40 minutes. Uncover; top with remaining cheese. Bake 5-10 minutes longer or until bubbly. Let stand for 5 minutes. Serve with rice. **yield: 4 servings.**

old-fashioned chicken 'n' biscuits

prep: 25 min. • bake: 30 min.

This chicken with biscuits is a home-style meal that has a colorful medley of vegetables and chunky chicken. The golden homemade biscuits on top make it a good choice when the weather turns cool.
—Marilyn Minnick, Hillsboro, Indiana

- 1 medium onion, chopped
- 2 teaspoons canola oil
- 1/4 cup all-purpose flour
- 1/2 teaspoon dried basil
- 1/2 teaspoon dried thyme
- 1/4 teaspoon pepper
- 2-1/2 cups fat-free milk
- 1 tablespoon Worcestershire sauce
- 1 package (16 ounces) frozen mixed vegetables
- 2 cups cubed cooked chicken
- 2 tablespoons grated Parmesan cheese

BISCUITS:
- 1 cup all-purpose flour
- 1 tablespoon sugar
- 1-1/2 teaspoons baking powder
- 1/4 teaspoon salt
- 1/3 cup fat-free milk
- 3 tablespoons canola oil
- 1 tablespoon minced fresh parsley

In a large saucepan, saute onion in oil until tender. Stir in the flour, basil, thyme and pepper until blended. Gradually stir in milk and Worcestershire sauce until smooth. Bring to a boil; cook and stir for 2 minutes or until thickened. Stir in the vegetables, chicken and cheese; reduce heat to low.

Meanwhile, in a large bowl, combine the flour, sugar, baking powder and salt. In a small bowl, combine the milk, oil and parsley; stir into dry ingredients just until combined.

Transfer hot chicken mixture to a greased 2-1/2-qt. baking dish. Drop biscuit batter by rounded tablespoonfuls onto chicken mixture.

Bake, uncovered, at 375° for 30-40 minutes or until biscuits are lightly browned. **yield: 8 servings.**

chicken broccoli bake

prep: 25 min. • bake: 35 min.

Get the benefits of broccoli while enjoying a guilt-free dish. This recipe makes a satisfying and simple-to-prepare supper.
—Phyllis Schmalz
  Kansas City, Kansas

- 4 cups uncooked egg noodles
- 1 medium onion, chopped
- 4 teaspoons butter
- 5 tablespoons all-purpose flour
- 1/2 teaspoon salt
- 1/2 teaspoon pepper
- 1 can (14-1/2 ounces) reduced-sodium chicken broth
- 1 cup fat-free milk
- 3 cups cubed cooked chicken breast
- 3 cups frozen chopped broccoli, thawed and drained
- 1 cup (4 ounces) shredded reduced-fat cheddar cheese

Cook noodles according to package directions. Meanwhile, in a large nonstick saucepan over medium heat, cook onion in butter until tender. Stir in the flour, salt and pepper until blended. Gradually stir in broth and milk. Bring to a boil; cook and stir for 1-2 minutes or until thickened.

Remove from the heat. Drain noodles; place in a 2-qt. baking dish coated with cooking spray. Stir in 1 cup sauce. Layer with the chicken, broccoli and remaining sauce.

Cover and bake at 350° for 30 minutes. Uncover; sprinkle with cheese. Bake 5-10 minutes longer or until heated through and cheese is melted. **yield: 6 servings.**

cashew chicken bake

prep/total time: 30 min.

I first tasted this easy chicken dish at the home of a good friend years ago. I've made it many times since for my husband, who likes it as much as I do.
—Ruth Olson, Brooklyn Park, Minnesota

- 3 cups cubed cooked chicken
- 1-1/2 cups chopped celery
- 1-1/2 cups cooked small pasta
- 1 cup mayonnaise
- 1/2 cup shredded cheddar cheese
- 1 jar (2 ounces) diced pimientos, drained
- 1 tablespoon grated onion
- 1/2 teaspoons salt

Dash pepper

- 1 cup salted cashew halves

In a large bowl, combine the chicken, celery, pasta, mayonnaise, cheese, pimientos, onion, salt and pepper. Chop 1/4 cup cashews; set aside. Stir the remaining cashews into chicken mixture.

Transfer to a greased 8-in. square baking dish. Sprinkle with chopped cashews. Bake, uncovered, at 375° for 20-25 minutes or until heated through. **yield: 4-6 servings.**

KITCHEN TIP

When making a hot dish to bring for large potluck, make it in two casserole dishes. Place one on the food line and keep the other one warm. Once the first dish is empty, bring the warm second dish out.

chicken lasagna

prep: 25 min. • bake: 30 min. + standing

A friend served this to us one night and I just had to try it at home. It's quick, easy and so delicious! I love to serve it to guests with a Caesar salad and warm rolls. Also, it can be frozen and saved for a busy weeknight.

—Janelle Rutrough, Rocky Mount, Virginia

- 2 cups (16 ounces) 2% cottage cheese
- 1 package (3 ounces) cream cheese, softened
- 4 cups cubed cooked chicken
- 1 can (10-3/4 ounces) condensed cream of chicken soup, undiluted
- 1 can (10-3/4 ounces) condensed cream of celery soup, undiluted
- 2/3 cup 2% milk
- 1/2 cup chopped onion
- 1/2 teaspoon salt
- 6 lasagna noodles, cooked and drained
- 1 package (6 ounces) stuffing mix
- 1/2 cup butter, melted

In a small bowl, combine cottage cheese and cream cheese. In a large bowl, combine the chicken, soups, milk, onion and salt.

Spread half of the chicken mixture into a greased 13-in. x 9-in. baking dish. Top with three noodles. Spread with half of the cheese mixture. Repeat layers. Toss stuffing mix with butter; sprinkle over casserole.

Bake, uncovered, at 350° for 30-40 minutes or bubbly and until golden brown. Let stand for 10 minutes. **yield: 8 servings.**

avocado chicken casserole

prep: 25 min. • bake: 20 min.

Avocados look luscious in this fantastic layered casserole. It has a rich cream sauce, chicken and noodles.
—*Martha Sue Stroud*
  Clarksville, Texas

- 1/4 cup butter, cubed
- 1/4 cup all-purpose flour
- 1/2 teaspoon salt
- 1/4 teaspoon *each* garlic powder, onion powder, dried basil, marjoram and thyme
- 1-1/2 cups 2% milk
- 1 cup half-and-half cream
- 8 ounces medium egg noodles, cooked and drained
- 3 medium ripe avocados, peeled and sliced
- 3 cups cubed cooked chicken
- 2 cups (8 ounces) shredded cheddar cheese

In a large saucepan, melt the butter; stir in the flour and seasonings until smooth. Gradually add the milk and cream. Bring to a boil; cook and stir for 2 minutes or until thickened. Remove from the heat.

In a greased 13-in. x 9-in. baking dish, layer with half of the noodles, avocados, chicken, white sauce and cheese. Repeat layers.

Cover the casserole and bake at 350° for 20-25 minutes. Uncover; bake 5 minutes longer or until bubbly. **yield: 6 servings.**

tastes like thanksgiving casserole

prep: 30 min. • bake: 30 min.

This hearty, rich-tasting main dish is sure to be a hit with your family. It's a wonderful way to use up Thanksgiving turkey, and you can use 5-1/2 cups leftover mashed potatoes for the 6 potatoes.
—*Mary Lou Timpson, Colorado City, Arizona*

- 6 medium potatoes, peeled and cut into chunks
- 1-1/4 cups chopped celery
- 3/4 cup chopped onion
- 1/2 cup butter, cubed
- 6 cups unseasoned stuffing cubes
- 1 teaspoon poultry seasoning
- 1/4 teaspoon rubbed sage
- 1 cup chicken broth
- 4 cups cubed cooked turkey
- 2 cans (10-3/4 ounces *each*) condensed cream of chicken soup, undiluted
- 1 teaspoon garlic powder
- 3/4 cup sour cream, *divided*
- 4 ounces cream cheese, softened
- 1/2 teaspoon pepper
- 1/4 teaspoon salt
- 1-1/2 cups (6 ounces) shredded cheddar cheese

Place potatoes in a Dutch oven and cover with water. Bring to a boil. Reduce heat; cover and cook for 10-15 minutes or until tender.

Meanwhile, in a large skillet, saute celery and onion in butter until tender. Remove from the heat.

In a large bowl, combine the stuffing cubes, poultry seasoning and sage. Stir in broth and celery mixture. Transfer to a greased 13-in. x 9-in. baking dish.

In another large bowl, combine the turkey, soup, garlic powder and 1/4 cup sour cream; spoon over stuffing mixture. Drain the potatoes; mash in a large bowl. Beat in the cream cheese, pepper, salt and remaining sour cream; spread over the turkey mixture. Sprinkle with the cheese.

Bake, uncovered, at 350° for 30-35 minutes or until heated through. **yield: 8 servings.**

chicken pie in a pan

prep: 25 min. • bake: 35 min.

Tasty and filling, this potpie is a perfect way to put leftover chicken or turkey to tasty use. It takes some time to prepare, but luckily, I have five children at home to help me. This dish travels well and is ideal to take to a potluck or family reunion.
—Kristine Conway, Alliance, Ohio

- 2 celery ribs, diced
- 2 medium carrots, diced
- 1 small onion, chopped
- 3 tablespoons butter
- 1/4 cup all-purpose flour
- 1/2 teaspoon salt
- 1 cup 2% milk
- 1 cup chicken broth
- 1 can (10-3/4 ounces) condensed cream of mushroom soup, undiluted
- 4 cups cubed cooked chicken

CRUST:
- 1-1/2 cups all-purpose flour
- 3/4 teaspoon baking powder
- 1 teaspoon salt
- 3 tablespoons cold butter
- 1/2 cup 2% milk
- 2 cups (8 ounces) shredded cheddar cheese

In a large skillet, saute the celery, carrots and onion in butter until tender. Stir in flour and salt until blended; gradually add milk and broth. Bring to a boil; cook and stir for 2 minutes or until thickened. Stir in soup and chicken. Spoon into a greased 13-in. x 9-in. baking dish; set aside.

For crust, combine the flour, baking powder and salt. Cut in butter until crumbly. Add milk, tossing with a fork until mixture forms a soft dough; shape into a ball.

On a lightly floured surface, roll into a 12-in. x 10-in. rectangle. Sprinkle with cheese. Roll up jelly-roll style, starting from a long side. Cut into 12 slices. Place cut side down over chicken mixture. Bake, uncovered, at 350° for 35-40 minutes or until the crust is lightly browned. **yield: 6-8 servings.**

cheddar chicken pie

prep: 20 min. • bake: 30 min.

This speedy main dish uses handy biscuit mix, so there's no need to fuss with a crust. Just add fruit salad and crusty, hot bread for a delicious meal.
—Betty Pierce, Slaterville Springs, New York

3 cups (12 ounces) shredded cheddar cheese, *divided*
3 cups frozen chopped broccoli, thawed and drained
1-1/2 cups cubed cooked chicken
2/3 cup finely chopped onion
1-1/3 cups 2% milk
3 eggs
3/4 cup biscuit/baking mix
3/4 teaspoon salt
1/4 teaspoon pepper

In a large bowl, combine 2 cups cheese, broccoli, chicken and onion; spread into a greased 10-in. pie plate. In a small bowl, beat the milk, eggs, biscuit mix, salt and pepper until smooth. Pour over broccoli mixture (do not stir).

Bake at 400° for 30-35 minutes or until a knife inserted near the center comes out clean. Sprinkle with the remaining cheese. Let stand for 5 minutes or until cheese is melted. **yield: 6 servings.**

corny chicken bake

prep: 15 min. • bake: 25 min.

My mother gave me the directions for this quick glazed chicken and stuffing bake after she received it from a friend. The glaze recipe can be doubled for those who like a tangy taste.
—Barbara Ramstack, Fond du Lac, Wisconsin

- 3 cups crushed corn bread stuffing
- 1 can (14-3/4 ounces) cream-style corn
- 1/3 cup finely chopped onion
- 1 celery rib, chopped
- 4 boneless skinless chicken breast halves (4 ounces *each*)
- 1/4 cup packed brown sugar
- 1/4 cup butter, melted
- 3 tablespoons spicy brown mustard

In a large bowl, combine the stuffing, corn, onion and celery. Spoon into a greased 11-in. x 7-in. baking dish. Top with chicken.

In a small bowl, combine the brown sugar, butter and mustard; spoon over chicken. Bake, uncovered, at 400° for 25-30 minutes or until a meat thermometer reads 170°. **yield: 4 servings.**

wild turkey rice bake

prep: 40 min. • bake: 55 min.

Wild rice, turkey and vegetables are combined in a savory sauce and topped with golden crumbs in this hearty dish. Cooked wild turkey can be a little dry, but not when it's prepared this way.

—Margaret Hill, Roanoke, Virginia

---

1 package (6 ounces) long grain and wild rice mix
1 teaspoon chicken bouillon granules
1 cup hot water
3-1/2 cups cubed cooked wild turkey
1-1/2 cups chopped celery
1 can (10-3/4 ounces) condensed cream of mushroom soup, undiluted
1 can (8 ounces) sliced water chestnuts, drained
1 jar (6 ounces) sliced mushrooms, drained
1/2 cup chopped onion
1/4 cup soy sauce
1 cup soft bread crumbs
2 tablespoons butter, melted

Prepare rice according to package directions; place in a large bowl. Dissolve bouillon in hot water; add to rice. Stir in the turkey, celery, soup, water chestnuts, mushrooms, onion and soy sauce.

Transfer to a greased 3-qt. baking dish. Toss bread crumbs and butter; sprinkle over the top. Bake, uncovered, at 350° for 55-60 minutes or until heated through. **yield: 8 servings.**

chicken artichoke casserole

prep: 20 min. • bake: 25 min.

This creamy chicken dish is so easy to prepare that it's perfect for serving to guests for lunch or supper.
—Diane Hixon, Niceville, Florida

- 1 **pound boneless skinless chicken breasts, cut into 2-inch cubes**
- 4 **tablespoons butter,** *divided*

Salt and pepper to taste

- 1 **package (8 ounces) frozen artichoke hearts** *or* **1 can (14 ounces) water-packed artichoke hearts, rinsed and drained**
- 1/4 **cup all-purpose flour**
- 1/8 **teaspoon ground nutmeg**
- 2 **cups chicken broth**
- 1 **cup (4 ounces) shredded cheddar cheese**
- 1/4 **cup dry bread crumbs**
- 1 **tablespoon minced fresh savory** *or* **1 teaspoon dried savory**
- 1 **tablespoon minced fresh thyme** *or* **1 teaspoon dried thyme**

Hot cooked noodles *or* **rice**

In a large skillet, saute chicken in 1 tablespoon butter until no longer pink. Season with salt and pepper. Place chicken and artichokes in a greased 11-in. x 7-in. baking dish; set aside.

In a large saucepan, melt remaining butter; stir in flour and nutmeg until smooth. Gradually add broth. Bring to a boil; cook and stir for 2 minutes or until thickened and bubbly. Stir in cheese until melted; spoon over chicken.

Combine the bread crumbs, savory and thyme; sprinkle over chicken. Bake, uncovered, at 350° for 25-35 minutes or until golden brown. Serve with noodles or rice. **yield: 4-6 servings.**

turkey spaghetti casserole

prep: 30 min. • bake: 1-1/4 hours

My mom made this creamy spaghetti main dish when I was growing up. Whenever I have any leftover chicken or turkey, I look forward to making this simple yet tasty dinner.
—Casandra Hetrick, Lindsey, Ohio

- 1 **medium onion, chopped**
- 1 **medium carrot, chopped**
- 1 **celery rib, chopped**
- 1/3 **cup sliced fresh mushrooms**
- 1 **tablespoon butter**
- 2-1/2 **cups reduced-sodium chicken broth**
- 1 **can (10-3/4 ounces) reduced-fat reduced-sodium condensed cream of mushroom soup, undiluted**
- 1/4 **teaspoon salt**
- 1/4 **teaspoon pepper**
- 2-1/2 **cups cubed cooked turkey breast**
- 6 **ounces uncooked spaghetti, broken into 2-inch pieces**
- 1/2 **cup shredded reduced-fat Colby-Monterey Jack cheese**
- 1/2 **teaspoon paprika**

In a small skillet, saute the vegetables in butter until tender. In a large bowl, combine broth, soup, salt and pepper.

In a 2-1/2-qt. baking dish coated with cooking spray, layer with turkey, spaghetti and vegetable mixture. Pour broth mixture over the top.

Cover and bake at 350° for 70-80 minutes or until spaghetti is tender, stirring once. Uncover; sprinkle with cheese and paprika. Bake 5-10 minutes longer or until cheese is melted. **yield: 6 servings.**

black bean chicken casserole

prep: 25 min. • bake: 35 min.

I never fail to hear words of appreciation when I serve this Southwestern-inspired supper. The ingredients come together so nicely to give it a unique wonderful flavor.
—*Tracy Kimzey, Blacksburg, Virginia*

- 1 large onion, chopped
- 1 small green pepper, chopped
- 1 tablespoon canola oil
- 2 garlic cloves, minced
- 1 can (14-1/2 ounces) diced tomatoes, undrained
- 1/2 cup salsa
- 1 teaspoon ground cumin
- 1/2 teaspoon salt
- 1/2 teaspoon dried oregano
- 1/4 teaspoon pepper
- 2 cans (15 ounces *each*) black beans, rinsed and drained
- 3 cups cubed cooked chicken breast
- 8 corn tortillas (6 inches)
- 1-1/2 cups (6 ounces) shredded reduced-fat Monterey Jack *or* Mexican cheese blend, *divided*
- Fat-free sour cream, chopped green onions and sliced ripe olives, optional

In a large saucepan, saute onion and green pepper in oil until tender. Add garlic; cook 1 minute longer. Stir in the tomatoes, salsa, cumin, salt, oregano and pepper. Add beans and chicken; heat through.

Spread a third of the mixture into a 13-in. x 9-in. baking dish coated with cooking spray. Layer with four tortillas, a third of the chicken mixture and 1 cup cheese. Repeat with remaining tortillas and chicken mixture.

Cover and bake at 350° for 25-30 minutes or until heated through. Uncover; sprinkle with remaining cheese. Bake 8-10 minutes longer or until cheese is melted. Serve with sour cream, green onions and olives if desired. **yield: 10 servings.**

onion-chicken stuffing bake

prep: 15 min. • bake: 30 min.

A friend shared this savory meal in one with me, and it has since become one of my top choices to serve to guests. It's sure to be a hit at your home, too.
—*Audrey Aldrich, Berlin Heights, Ohio*

- 1 package (6 ounces) seasoned stuffing mix
- 3 cups cubed cooked chicken
- 1 can (10-3/4 ounces) condensed cream of chicken soup, undiluted
- 1 cup (8 ounces) sour cream
- 2 tablespoons onion soup mix
- 1 can (4 ounces) mushroom stems and pieces, drained
- 1 can (8 ounces) sliced water chestnuts, drained
- 1/4 cup grated Parmesan cheese

Prepare stuffing mix according to package directions; set aside. Place chicken in a greased 2-qt. baking dish. Combine the soup, sour cream and soup mix; spread over the chicken.

Sprinkle with mushrooms and water chestnuts. Spread stuffing over top. Sprinkle with cheese. Bake, uncovered, at 350° for 30-35 minutes or until bubbly. **yield: 6-8 servings.**

KITCHEN TIP

If your family likes spicy foods, you can add more zip to the Black Bean Chicken Casserole: Add 1/2 teaspoon chili powder along with the other seasonings; saute a diced jalapeno pepper with the green pepper; or use hot salsa or pepper Jack cheese instead of the Monterey Jack.

curried chicken with asparagus

prep: 20 min. • bake: 25 min.

A mild curry sauce nicely coats tender chicken and asparagus in this must-have recipe. It's a classic I've used for years.

—Miriam Christophel, Battle Creek, Michigan

- 1 can (10-3/4 ounces) condensed cream of chicken soup, undiluted
- 1/3 cup mayonnaise
- 1 teaspoon lemon juice
- 1/2 teaspoon curry powder
- 1/8 teaspoon pepper
- 1 package (10 ounces) frozen asparagus spears, thawed
- 1 pound boneless skinless chicken breasts, cut into 1/2-inch pieces
- 2 tablespoons canola oil
- 1/4 cup shredded cheddar cheese

In a large bowl, combine the soup, mayonnaise, lemon juice, curry and pepper; set aside.

Place half of the asparagus in a greased 8-in. square baking dish. Spread with half of the soup mixture.

In a large skillet, saute chicken in oil until no longer pink. Place chicken over soup mixture. Top with remaining asparagus and soup mixture.

Cover and bake at 375° for 20 minutes. Uncover; sprinkle with cheese. Bake 5-8 minutes longer or until cheese is melted. **yield: 4 servings.**

hearty chicken casserole

prep: 25 min. • bake: 10 min.

I found this recipe in a cookbook we received as a wedding gift and altered it to fit my family's tastes. Now, I always cook enough extra chicken so we can have this casserole the next day. My husband and daughters rush to the table when they know it's on the menu.

—Janet Applin, Gladstone, Michigan

2-1/2 cups frozen mixed vegetables
1/2 cup chopped onion
1/2 cup butter, *divided*
1/3 cup all-purpose flour
1/2 teaspoon dried sage leaves
1/2 teaspoon pepper
1/4 teaspoon salt
2 cups chicken broth
3/4 cup 2% milk
3 cups cubed cooked chicken
1 can (14-1/2 ounces) sliced potatoes, drained and quartered
2 cups seasoned stuffing cubes

Cook vegetables according to package directions; drain.

Meanwhile, in a large saucepan, saute the onion in 1/4 cup butter for 2-3 minutes or until tender. Stir in the flour, sage, pepper and salt until blended. Gradually add broth and milk. Bring to a boil; cook and stir until thickened. Stir in the chicken, potatoes and mixed vegetables; heat through.

Transfer to a greased 13-in. x 9-in. baking dish. Melt the remaining butter; toss with stuffing cubes. Sprinkle over chicken mixture.

Bake, uncovered, at 450° for 10-12 minutes or until the casserole is heated through. **yield: 6 servings.**

bayou chicken

prep: 25 min. • bake: 1-1/4 hours

When I came across this Southern-style recipe many years ago, I knew I had a new recipe to add to my file of keepers. The chicken always turns out moist and tender.
—Fran Dell, Las Vegas, Nevada

- 1/2 cup all-purpose flour
- 1/2 teaspoon salt
- 1/4 teaspoon pepper
- 1/4 teaspoon paprika
- 1 broiler/fryer chicken (3 to 4 pounds), cut up
- 2 tablespoons butter
- 2 tablespoons canola oil
- 1/2 pound sliced fresh mushrooms
- 1/4 cup chopped onion
- 3 cans (15-1/2 ounces *each*) black-eyed peas, drained
- 1/2 teaspoon garlic salt
- 1/4 teaspoon herbes de Provence
- 1/2 cup white wine *or* chicken broth
- 1 medium tomato, chopped

In a large resealable plastic bag, combine the flour, salt, pepper and paprika. Add chicken, a few pieces at a time, and shake to coat. In a large skillet, brown chicken in butter and oil on all sides. Remove and set aside.

In the same skillet, saute mushrooms and onion until onion is crisp-tender, stirring to loosen browned bits from pan. Stir in the peas, garlic salt and herbes de Provence. Transfer to an ungreased 13-in. x 9-in. baking dish.

Arrange chicken over pea mixture. Pour wine over chicken; sprinkle with tomato. Cover and bake at 325° for 1-1/4 to 1-1/2 hours or until chicken juices run clear. **yield: 6 servings.**

editor's note: Look for herbes de Provence in the spice aisle.

greek spaghetti

prep: 25 min. • bake: 25 min.

A comforting dinner is sure to be had when flavorful spaghetti is on the menu. Featuring chicken, spinach and two types of cheese, this will please any crowd.
—Melanie Dalbec, Inver Grove Heights, Minnesota

- 1 package (16 ounces) spaghetti, broken into 2-inch pieces
- 4 cups cubed cooked chicken breast
- 2 packages (10 ounces *each*) frozen chopped spinach, thawed and squeezed dry
- 2 cans (10-3/4 ounces *each*) condensed cream of chicken soup, undiluted
- 1 cup mayonnaise
- 1 cup (8 ounces) sour cream
- 3 celery ribs, chopped
- 1 small onion, chopped
- 1/2 cup chopped green pepper
- 1 jar (2 ounces) diced pimientos, drained
- 1/2 teaspoon lemon-pepper seasoning
- 1 cup (4 ounces) shredded Monterey Jack cheese
- 1/2 cup soft bread crumbs
- 1/2 cup shredded Parmesan cheese

Cook spaghetti according to package directions; drain. Return spaghetti to saucepan. Stir in the chicken, spinach, soup, mayonnaise, sour cream, celery, onion, green pepper, pimientos and lemon-pepper.

Transfer to a greased 13-in. x 9-in. baking dish (dish will be full). Top with the Monterey Jack cheese, bread crumbs and Parmesan cheese. Bake, uncovered, at 350° for 25-30 minutes or until the casserole is heated through. **yield: 10 servings.**

stuffed chicken breasts

prep: 20 min. • bake: 25 min.

Baked in a creamy mushroom sauce, this easy entree is nice for a special family dinner. I serve this dish with rice, asparagus and a tossed salad.
—Dolores Kastello
   Waukesha, Wisconsin

   4 boneless skinless chicken
      breast halves (6 ounces *each*)
Salt and pepper to taste
   1 package (6 ounces) chicken
      stuffing mix
1/2 cup chopped pecans
   2 tablespoons butter
   1 can (10-3/4 ounces)
      condensed cream of
      mushroom soup, undiluted

Flatten chicken to 1/4-in. thickness; sprinkle with salt and pepper. Prepare stuffing mix according to package directions. Meanwhile, in a small skillet, saute pecans in butter until lightly browned; add to the stuffing.

Place 1/2 cup stuffing down the center of each chicken breast half; roll up and secure with a toothpick. Place seam side down in a greased shallow 1-qt. baking dish.

Spoon soup over chicken; sprinkle with remaining stuffing. Cover and bake at 400° for 25-30 minutes or until chicken is no longer pink. Remove toothpicks. **yield: 4 servings.**

zesty chicken casserole

prep: 15 min. • bake: 55 min.

Broccoli, chicken and rice get a little zip from Italian salad dressing. Anyone who favors food with lots of flavor will enjoy this dish.
—Dianne Spurlock, Dayton, Ohio

   2 cups uncooked instant rice
   1 package (16 ounces) frozen broccoli cuts, thawed
   1 medium onion, chopped
   1 celery rib, chopped
   2 tablespoons minced fresh parsley
   1 teaspoon salt
   6 boneless skinless chicken breast halves (4 ounces *each*)
   1 can (10-3/4 ounces) condensed cream of celery soup, undiluted
1-1/4 cups water
   3/4 cup process cheese sauce
   1/2 cup Italian salad dressing
   1/2 cup 2% milk
Fresh red currants, optional

Place rice in a greased 13-in. x 9-in. baking dish. Top with the broccoli, onion, celery, parsley and salt. Arrange chicken over vegetables.

In a large saucepan, combine the soup, water, cheese sauce, salad dressing and milk. Cook and stir until cheese sauce is melted and mixture is smooth. Pour over chicken.

Cover and bake at 375° for 45 minutes. Uncover; bake 10-15 minutes longer or until a meat thermometer reads 170°. Garnish with red currants if desired. **yield: 6 servings.**

2 tablespoons finely
chopped onion

1/2 teaspoon salt

1/4 teaspoon poultry
seasoning

3 cups cubed cooked chicken

1 cup cooked rice

1 cup sliced fresh mushrooms

1/3 cup butter, cubed

3 tablespoons all-purpose
flour

1/2 teaspoon salt

1/4 teaspoon pepper

1-1/2 cups 2% milk

In a large bowl, combine bread
crumbs, broth, eggs, celery,
pimientos, onion, salt and poultry
seasoning. Stir in the chicken
and rice.

Transfer to a greased 8-in. square
baking dish. Bake, uncovered, at 350°
for 55-65 minutes or until bubbly and
golden brown.

Meanwhile, in a large saucepan,
saute mushrooms in butter. Stir in the
flour, salt and pepper until blended.
Gradually add milk. Bring to a boil;
cook and stir for 2 minutes or until
thickened. Cut chicken casserole into
squares. Serve with mushroom sauce.
yield: 6-8 servings.

saucy chicken squares

prep: 10 min. • bake: 55 min.

*When I serve a meal that's considered good by all eight members
of my family, I call that a winner. These chicken squares with
mushroom sauce passed the test.*

—*Irene Burkholder, Leola, Pennsylvania*

2 cups soft bread crumbs

2 cups chicken broth

4 eggs, lightly beaten

1 celery rib, chopped

1 jar (4 ounces) diced pimientos, drained

pork

Warm-from-the-oven casseroles are comforting. These home-style dishes bring families together for dinner. The recipes in this chapter are made with pork chops, ham and sausage, and are combined with pasta, potatoes and all types of delicious sauces.

≪ pictured left

hawaiian ham bake

prep: 15 min. • bake: 30 min.

Take this sweet-and-sour specialty to your next potluck and get ready to hand out the recipe. It's special enough for Sunday dinners, yet simple enough for busy weeknights.

—Judy Reist, Bloomingdale, Ontario

- 3 cups cubed fully cooked ham
- 1 medium onion, thinly sliced
- 1 small green pepper, cut into rings
- 2/3 cup raisins
- 3/4 cup pineapple tidbits, drained
- 3/4 cup packed brown sugar
- 3 tablespoons cornstarch
- 3 teaspoons ground mustard
- 1/4 teaspoon salt
- 1-1/2 cups pineapple juice
- 1/2 cup cider vinegar
- 4-1/2 teaspoons soy sauce
- **Hot cooked rice**

In a greased 2-qt. baking dish, layer with ham, onion, green pepper, raisins and pineapple.

In a saucepan, combine the brown sugar, cornstarch, mustard and salt. Stir in pineapple juice and vinegar until smooth. Bring to a boil; cook and stir for 2 minutes or until thickened.

Remove from the heat; stir in soy sauce. Pour over pineapple. Cover and bake at 350° for 30 minutes or until heated through. Serve with rice. **yield: 4-6 servings.**

florentine spaghetti bake

prep: 30 min. • bake: 1 hour + standing

This plate-filling sausage dish appeals to most every appetite, from basic meat-and-potatoes fans to gourmets. My daughter, a Montana wheat rancher's wife, says she serves it often to satisfy her hardworking family.

—Lorraine Martin, Lincoln, California

- 8 ounces uncooked spaghetti
- 1 pound bulk Italian sausage
- 1 cup chopped onion
- 1 garlic clove, minced
- 1 jar (26 ounces) spaghetti sauce
- 1 can (4 ounces) mushroom stems and pieces, drained
- 1 egg, lightly beaten
- 2 cups (16 ounces) 4% cottage cheese
- 1 package (10 ounces) frozen chopped spinach, thawed and squeezed dry
- 1/4 cup grated Parmesan cheese
- 1/2 teaspoon seasoned salt
- 1/4 teaspoon pepper
- 2 cups (8 ounces) shredded part-skim mozzarella cheese

Cook pasta according to package directions. Meanwhile, in a large skillet, cook sausage and onion over medium heat until sausage is no longer pink. Add garlic; cook 1 minute longer. Drain. Stir in spaghetti sauce and mushrooms. Bring to a boil. Reduce heat; cover and cook for 15 minutes or until heated through.

Drain pasta. In a large bowl, combine the egg, cottage cheese, spinach, Parmesan cheese, salt and pepper. Spread 1 cup sausage mixture in a greased 13-in. x 9-in. baking dish, Top with spaghetti and remaining sausage mixture. Layer with spinach mixture and mozzarella cheese.

Cover casserole and bake at 375° for 45 minutes. Uncover; bake 15 minutes longer or until lightly browned and heated through. Let stand for 15 minutes before cutting. **yield: 9 servings.**

great pork chop bake

prep: 10 min. • bake: 55 min.

A friend brought this hearty and meaty bake to our home when we returned from the hospital after our youngest child was born. Since then, we have enjoyed it many times. It's a snap to throw together on a busy day, then pop in the oven to bake. The tender chops, potato wedges and golden gravy are simple and satisfying.

—Rosie Glenn, Los Alamos, New Mexico

---

6 bone-in pork loin chops (3/4 inch thick and 8 ounces *each*)

1 tablespoon canola oil

1 can (10-3/4 ounces) condensed cream of chicken soup, undiluted

3 tablespoons ketchup

2 tablespoons Worcestershire sauce

1/2 teaspoon salt

1/4 teaspoon pepper

4 medium potatoes, cut into 1/2-inch wedges

1 medium onion, sliced into rings

In a large skillet, brown pork chops in oil. Transfer to a greased 13-in. x 9-in. baking dish. In a large bowl, combine the soup, ketchup, Worcestershire sauce, salt and pepper. Add potatoes and onion; toss to coat. Pour over the chops.

Cover and bake at 350° for 55-60 minutes or until a meat thermometer reads 160° and potatoes are tender. **yield: 6 servings.**

sweet potato sausage casserole

prep: 20 min. • bake: 25 min.

Most people never consider combining sweet potatoes with pasta and kielbasa, but I adapted this recipe from several others and have received several compliments on it. You can add more cheese or sausage to suit your taste.

—Rickey Madden, Clinton, South Carolina

- 8 ounces uncooked spiral pasta
- 8 ounces smoked sausage, cut into 1/4 inch slices
- 2 medium sweet potatoes, peeled and cut into 1/2 inch cubes
- 1 cup chopped green pepper
- 1/2 cup chopped onion
- 2 tablespoons olive oil
- 1 teaspoon minced garlic
- 1 can (14-1/2 ounces) diced tomatoes, undrained
- 1 cup heavy whipping cream
- 1/4 teaspoon salt
- 1/4 teaspoon pepper
- 1 cup (4 ounces) shredded cheddar cheese

Cook pasta according to package directions. Meanwhile, in a large skillet, cook the sausage, sweet potatoes, green pepper, onion in oil over medium heat for 5 minutes or until vegetables are tender. Add garlic; cook 1 minute longer. Drain.

Add the tomatoes, cream, salt and pepper. Bring to a boil; remove from the heat. Drain pasta; stir into sausage mixture. Transfer to a greased 13-in. x 9-in. baking dish. Sprinkle with cheese.

Bake, uncovered, at 350° for 25-30 minutes or until bubbly. Let stand for 5 minutes before serving. **yield: 8 servings.**

reuben dogs

prep/total time: 30 min.

My husband and children enjoy Reuben sandwiches, and this quick casserole is as close as you can get without the mess.

—Colleen Hawkins
  Monrovia, Maryland

- 1 can (27 ounces) sauerkraut, rinsed and drained
- 1 to 2 teaspoons caraway seeds
- 8 hot dogs, halved lengthwise
- 1 cup (4 ounces) shredded Swiss cheese

Thousand Island salad dressing

Place sauerkraut in a greased 2-qt. baking dish. Sprinkle with caraway seeds. Top with hot dogs.

Bake, uncovered, at 350° for 15-20 minutes or until heated through. Sprinkle with cheese. Bake 3-5 minutes longer or until cheese is melted. Serve with salad dressing. **yield: 4-6 servings.**

cheesy franks and potatoes

prep: 20 min. • bake: 30 min.

I came up with this recipe primarily because my husband loves hot dogs and I needed a break from standard fare using franks. It was an instant hit. Even I enjoy the rich taste.
—Shirley Bradley, Wildwood, Florida

- 6 jumbo hot dogs, halved lengthwise and cut into 1/2-inch pieces
- 1 tablespoon canola oil
- 1 medium onion, chopped
- 1/2 cup chopped green pepper
- 1 can (10-3/4 ounces) condensed cheddar cheese soup, undiluted
- 2/3 cup half-and-half cream
- 2 medium potatoes, cooked, peeled and cubed
- 1/4 teaspoon salt

In a large skillet over medium heat, brown hot dogs in oil for 2-3 minutes or until lightly browned. Remove with a slotted spoon. In the same skillet, saute the onion and green pepper until tender.

In a small bowl, combine the soup, cream and onion mixture. Place potatoes in a greased 11-in. x 7-in. baking dish; sprinkle with salt. Top with hot dogs. Pour soup mixture over all. Bake, uncovered, at 350° for 30-35 minutes or until heated through. **yield: 6 servings.**

italian casserole

prep: 25 min. • bake: 30 min.

We usually have toasted garlic bread and a tossed salad with this hearty pizza-flavored dish.
—Lee Sauers, Mifflinburg, Pennsylvania

- 3 ounces uncooked spaghetti
- 1 Italian sausage link, casing removed
- 1 small onion, sliced
- 1 small zucchini, sliced
- Dash pepper
- 1 bacon strip, cooked and crumbled
- 1/4 cup shredded Parmesan cheese
- 1 cup spaghetti sauce, *divided*
- 2 tablespoons chopped sweet red pepper
- 1/2 cup shredded part-skim mozzarella cheese
- 12 slices pepperoni
- Dash *each* dried oregano, thyme and basil

Cook spaghetti according to package directions. Meanwhile, crumble sausage into a small skillet; add onion. Cook over medium heat until meat is no longer pink; drain.

Drain spaghetti. Arrange zucchini in a shallow 1-qt. baking dish coated with cooking spray; sprinkle with pepper. Layer with bacon, Parmesan cheese, 1/2 cup spaghetti sauce, spaghetti, remaining sauce, red pepper, sausage mixture, mozzarella cheese and pepperoni.

Sprinkle with herbs. Bake, uncovered, at 350° for 30-35 minutes or until vegetables are tender. **yield: 3 servings.**

chops 'n' kraut

prep: 25 min. • bake: 20 min.

Diced tomatoes lend color to this hearty entree and brown sugar softens the tang of the sauerkraut.

—Ruth Tamul, Morehead City, North Carolina

- 6 bone-in pork loin chops (3/4 inch thick and 7 ounces *each*)
- 1/4 teaspoon salt
- 1/4 teaspoon pepper
- 3 teaspoons canola oil, *divided*
- 1 medium onion, thinly sliced
- 2 garlic cloves, minced
- 1 can (14-1/2 ounces) petite diced tomatoes, undrained
- 1 can (14 ounces) sauerkraut, rinsed and well drained
- 1/3 cup packed brown sugar
- 1-1/2 teaspoons caraway seeds

Sprinkle both sides of pork chops with salt and pepper. In a large nonstick skillet coated with cooking spray, cook three chops in 1 teaspoon oil for 2-3 minutes on each side or until browned; drain. Repeat with remaining chops and 1 teaspoon oil.

Place pork chops in a 13-in. x 9-in. baking dish coated with cooking spray; set aside. In the same skillet, cook onion in remaining oil until tender. Add garlic; cook 1 minute longer. Stir in the tomatoes, sauerkraut, brown sugar and caraway seeds. Cook and stir until mixture comes to a boil.

Carefully pour over chops. Cover and bake at 350° for 20-25 minutes or until a meat thermometer reads 160°. **yield: 6 servings.**

meaty manicotti

prep: 20 min. • bake: 45 min.

This sausage and ground beef-filled manicotti has been very popular at family gatherings and potlucks. You can assemble it ahead of time.
—Lori Thompson, New London, Texas

14 uncooked manicotti shells
1 pound bulk Italian sausage
3/4 pound ground beef
2 garlic cloves, minced
2 cups (8 ounces) shredded part-skim mozzarella cheese
1 package (3 ounces) cream cheese, cubed
1/4 teaspoon salt
4 cups meatless spaghetti sauce, *divided*
1/4 cup grated Parmesan cheese

Cook manicotti shells according to package directions. Meanwhile, in a large skillet, cook sausage and beef over medium heat until meat is no longer pink. Add garlic; cook 1 minute longer. Drain. Remove from the heat. Cool for 10 minutes.

Drain shells and rinse in cold water. Stir the mozzarella cheese, cream cheese and salt into meat mixture. Spread 2 cups spaghetti sauce in a greased 13-in. x 9-in. baking dish.

Stuff each shell with about 1/4 cupful meat mixture; arrange over sauce. Pour remaining sauce over top. Sprinkle with Parmesan cheese.

Cover and bake at 350° for 40 minutes. Uncover; bake 5-10 minutes longer or until bubbly and heated through. **yield: 7 servings.**

baked spaghetti

prep: 20 min. • bake: 30 min. + standing

This satisfying pasta bake is quick to make and please young and old alike. Add a salad and breadsticks, and you're ready for company.

–Betty Rabe, Mahtomedi, Minnesota

---

    8 ounces uncooked spaghetti, broken into thirds
    1 egg
1/2 cup milk
1/2 teaspoon salt
1/2 pound ground beef
1/2 pound bulk Italian sausage
    1 small onion, chopped
1/4 cup chopped green pepper
    1 jar (14 ounces) meatless spaghetti sauce
    1 can (8 ounces) tomato sauce
    1 to 2 cups (4 to 8 ounces) shredded part-skim mozzarella cheese

---

Cook spaghetti according to package directions; drain. In a large bowl, beat the egg, milk and salt. Add spaghetti; toss to coat. Transfer to a greased 13-in. x 9-in. baking dish.

In a large skillet, cook the beef, sausage, onion and green pepper over medium heat until meat is no longer pink; drain. Stir in spaghetti sauce and tomato sauce. Spoon over the spaghetti mixture.

Bake, uncovered, at 350° for 20 minutes. Sprinkle with the cheese. Bake 10 minutes longer or until cheese is melted. Let stand for 10 minutes before cutting. **yield: 6-8 servings.**

ham 'n' cheese bow ties

prep/total time: 30 min.

Everyone who tries this yummy casserole lists it as a favorite from then on. Bow tie pasta makes it fun; ham makes it hearty.

—Stephanie Moon, Boise, Idaho

- 1 garlic clove, minced
- 1/4 cup butter, cubed
- 1/4 cup all-purpose flour
- 1/2 teaspoon salt
- 1/8 teaspoon pepper
- 2 cups 2% milk
- 1/2 teaspoon prepared mustard
- 2-1/2 cups (10 ounces) shredded Colby cheese
- 2 cups uncooked bow tie pasta, cooked and drained
- 6 to 8 ounces fully cooked ham, julienned
- 1/4 cup grated Parmesan cheese

In a large saucepan, saute garlic in butter for 1 minute. Stir in the flour, salt and pepper until blended. Gradually add milk. Bring to a boil; cook and stir for 2 minutes or until thickened and bubbly. Stir in mustard and Colby cheese; cook and stir until cheese is melted. Add pasta and ham; stir until coated.

Transfer to a greased 2-qt. baking dish. Sprinkle with Parmesan cheese. Bake, uncovered, at 350° for 20-25 minutes or until heated through. **yield: 4-6 servings.**

bavarian casserole

prep: 40 min. • bake: 40 min.

This one-dish meal is a little different from the usual meat-and-potato casseroles. The sauerkraut and tomatoes add a nice tangy flavor to the tender pork chops. I've also used boneless skinless chicken breasts and turkey bacon with good results.

—Barbara LaFlair, Houghton Lake, Michigan

- 4 medium red potatoes
- 6 bacon strips, diced
- 6 bone-in pork loin chops (3/4 inch thick and 7 ounces *each*)
- 1 large onion, chopped
- 1 jar (32 ounces) sauerkraut, rinsed and well drained
- 1 can (28 ounces) stewed tomatoes, drained
- 1 teaspoon caraway seeds
- 1/2 teaspoon salt
- 1/4 teaspoon pepper

Place potatoes in a large saucepan and cover with water. Bring to a boil. Reduce heat; cover and cook for 15-20 minutes or until almost tender. Drain; when cool enough to handle, cut into 1/4-in. slices.

In a large skillet, cook bacon over medium heat until crisp. Using a slotted spoon, remove to paper towels. In the drippings, brown pork chops on both sides. Remove chops; drain, reserving 1 tablespoon drippings. Saute onion in drippings until tender. Stir in sauerkraut and bacon; cook for 3-4 minutes.

Spoon sauerkraut mixture into a greased 13-in. x 9-in. baking dish. Layer with pork chops, potato slices and tomatoes. Sprinkle with caraway seeds, salt and pepper. Cover and bake at 350° for 40-45 minutes or until a meat thermometer reads 160°. **yield: 6 servings.**

KITCHEN TIP

If you don't have bow tie pasta in your pantry, don't run out to the store at the last minute. Just substitute 2 cups of another small pasta, such as medium shells, penne, elbow macaroni or rotini.

corny pork chops

prep: 15 min. • bake: 45 min.

My grandmother began making this recipe in the 1950s, and it has remained in the family's recipe box ever since. As simple as it seems, the corn dressing complements the pork beautifully.
—Ralph Petterson, Salt Lake City, Utah

4 bone-in pork loin chops (3/4 to 1 inch thick and 7 ounces *each*)

1 teaspoon salt, *divided*

1/4 teaspoon pepper, *divided*

1 tablespoon canola oil

1 can (15-1/4 ounces) whole kernel corn, drained

2 celery ribs, diced

1 cup soft bread crumbs

1/3 cup ketchup

1 tablespoon chopped green onion

Season pork chops with 1/2 teaspoon salt and 1/8 teaspoon pepper. In a large skillet, brown pork in oil on both sides.

Combine the corn, celery, bread crumbs, ketchup, onion, and remaining salt and pepper; place in a greased 11-in. x 7-in. baking dish. Top with chops.

Cover and bake at 350° for 45-55 minutes or until a meat thermometer reads 160°. **yield: 4 servings.**

ham ravioli bake

prep: 20 min. • bake: 20 min.

I based this recipe on a dish my husband likes to order when we go out for Italian food. Not only does he love it, my young daughter does, too. She'll grab a whole ravioli and eat it!
—Jennifer Berger
    Eau Claire, Wisconsin

- 1 package (25 ounces) frozen cheese ravioli
- 1-1/2 cups cubed fully cooked ham
- 1-1/3 cups sliced fresh mushrooms
- 1/4 cup chopped onion
- 1/4 cup chopped green pepper
- 1 tablespoon canola oil
- 1 jar (15 ounces) Alfredo sauce

Cook ravioli according to package directions. Meanwhile, in a large skillet, cook the ham, mushrooms, onion and green pepper in oil over medium heat for 4-5 minutes or until vegetables are crisp-tender.

Spread 2 tablespoons Alfredo sauce into a greased 8-in. square baking dish. Stir remaining sauce into ham mixture; cook for 3-4 minutes or until heated through.

Drain ravioli; place half in the prepared baking dish. Top with half of the ham mixture. Repeat layers. Cover and bake at 375° for 20-25 minutes or until bubbly. **yield: 4 servings.**

sausage spinach manicotti

prep: 20 min. • bake: 65 min. + standing

My newly married daughter didn't want to ask her mother-in-law for the recipe for her husband's favorite meal. Instead, she asked me to help her figure out a recipe. Together, we came up with this delicious stick-to-the-ribs casserole.
—Donna Moyer, Grants Pass, Oregon

- 2 cups (8 ounces) shredded mozzarella cheese, *divided*
- 1-1/2 cups (12 ounces) 4% cottage cheese
- 1 package (10 ounces) frozen chopped spinach, thawed and squeezed dry
- 1/2 cup grated Parmesan cheese
- 1 egg, lightly beaten
- 1/4 teaspoon dried oregano
- 1 garlic clove, minced
- 10 uncooked manicotti shells
- 1 pound bulk Italian sausage
- 1 jar (26 ounces) spaghetti sauce
- 3/4 cup water

In a large bowl, combine 1 cup mozzarella cheese, cottage cheese, spinach, Parmesan cheese, egg, oregano and garlic; stuff into uncooked manicotti shells. Place in a greased 13-in. x 9-in. baking dish.

Crumble sausage into a large skillet; cook over medium heat until no longer pink. Drain. Stir in spaghetti sauce; pour over manicotti. Pour water along sides of pan.

Cover and bake at 350° for 1 hour. Uncover; sprinkle with remaining mozzarella. Bake 5-8 minutes longer or until cheese is melted. Let stand for 10 minutes before serving. **yield: 5 servings.**

KITCHEN TIP

To cut down on the prep time for Ham Ravioli Bake, use refrigerated ravioli instead of frozen. Refrigerated ravioli will cook more quickly than the frozen kind.

1 teaspoon salt

1 teaspoon Italian
   seasoning

1/2 teaspoon pepper

1/4 cup grated Parmesan
   cheese, *divided*

2 cups (8 ounces) shredded
   part-skim mozzarella
   cheese

1 tube (11 ounces) refrigerated
   breadsticks

In a large skillet, saute onion and
peppers in oil for 2-3 minutes or until
crisp-tender. Add the zucchini; saute
4-6 minutes longer or until vegetables
are tender. Add the garlic and cook
1 minute longer.

Stir in the tomatoes, sausage, tomato
paste, salt, Italian seasoning, pepper
and 2 tablespoons Parmesan cheese.
Bring to a boil. Reduce heat; simmer,
uncovered, for 8-10 minutes or until
heated through.

Spoon half of the sausage mixture into
a greased 13-in. x 9-in. baking dish.
Sprinkle with mozzarella cheese; top
with remaining sausage mixture.
Separate breadsticks; arrange in a
lattice pattern over the top. Sprinkle
with remaining Parmesan cheese.

Bake, uncovered, at 375° for 25-30
minutes or until topping is golden
brown and filling is bubbly. Let stand
for 10 minutes before serving. **yield:
6-8 servings.**

pizza casserole

prep: 25 min. • bake: 25 min. + standing

*Looking for a healthy dinner the whole family will love? This fast
and flavorful pizza entree fills my home with a wonderful aroma.
Refrigerated breadsticks make the crust fuss-free, and any leftovers
freeze well for another busy day.*

—Nancy Zimmerman, Cape May Court House, New Jersey

3/4 cup chopped onion

1 medium sweet yellow pepper, diced

1 medium sweet red pepper, diced

1 tablespoon olive oil

1 medium zucchini, halved lengthwise and sliced

1 teaspoon minced garlic

2 cans (14-1/2 ounces *each*) diced tomatoes, drained

3/4 pound smoked sausage, sliced

1 can (6 ounces) tomato paste

sausage macaroni bake

prep: 20 min. • bake: 20 min.

Because we have children who keep us busy, casseroles have been life-savers for me. This one especially appeals to me because it has a rich Italian flavor.
—Amber Zurbrugg, Alliance, Ohio

1-1/2 **cups uncooked elbow macaroni**
3/4 **pound bulk Italian sausage**
1 **small onion, chopped**
1/4 **cup chopped green pepper**
1 **can (8 ounces) tomato sauce**
1 **cup (4 ounces) shredded part-skim mozzarella cheese**
1/2 **cup grated Parmesan cheese, *divided***
2 **tablespoons minced fresh parsley**
1 **garlic clove, minced**
1/2 **teaspoon dried oregano**
1/4 **teaspoon salt**
1/4 **teaspoon dried basil**
1/4 **teaspoon pepper**

Cook macaroni according to package directions. Meanwhile, in a large skillet, cook the sausage, onion and green pepper over medium heat until meat is no longer pink; drain. Drain the macaroni.

In a large bowl, combine the macaroni, sausage mixture, tomato sauce, mozzarella cheese, 1/4 cup Parmesan cheese, parsley, garlic, oregano, salt, basil and pepper.

Transfer to a greased 2-qt. baking dish. Sprinkle with remaining Parmesan cheese. Bake, uncovered at 350° for 20-25 minutes or until heated through. **yield: 4 servings.**

one-pot pork and rice

prep: 20 min. • bake: 1 hour

No one will guess that this filling entree goes easy on fat and calories. Green pepper and onion enhance the Spanish-style rice and tender chops, which are covered with diced tomatoes and gravy.
—Duna Stephens, Palisade, Colorado

6 **boneless pork loin chops (5 ounces *each*)**
2 **teaspoons canola oil**
1 **cup uncooked long grain rice**
1 **large onion, sliced**
1 **large green pepper, sliced**
1 **envelope pork gravy mix**
1 **can (28 ounces) diced tomatoes, undrained**
1-1/2 **cups water**

In a Dutch oven, brown pork chops in oil on both sides; drain. Remove chops from pan and keep warm. Layer rice, onion and green pepper in Dutch oven; top with pork chops.

Combine the gravy mix, tomatoes and water; pour over chops. Cover; bake at 350° for 1 hour or until a meat thermometer reads 160°. **yield: 6 servings.**

ham broccoli pasta bake

prep: 15 min. • bake: 20 min.

Trying to come up with a way to use leftover cooked broccoli, I adapted this recipe from a friend. My husband and brother-in-law thought it was great. The three of us had no trouble finishing the entire pan!
—Jennifer Shiew, Jetmore, Kansas

1-1/4 cups uncooked elbow macaroni

1-1/2 cups chopped fresh broccoli

1 can (10-3/4 ounces) condensed cream of mushroom soup, undiluted

1 cup cubed fully cooked ham

1 cup (4 ounces) shredded cheddar cheese

1/2 cup shredded part-skim mozzarella cheese

1/2 cup 2% milk

1 tablespoon dried minced onion

1/4 teaspoon pepper

1 cup crushed potato chips

Cook macaroni according to package directions. Meanwhile, in a large bowl, combine the broccoli, soup, ham, cheeses, milk, onion and pepper. Drain macaroni; add to ham mixture.

Transfer to a greased 8-in. square baking dish; sprinkle with potato chips. Bake, uncovered, at 350° for 20-25 minutes or until bubbly. **yield: 4 servings.**

scalloped potatoes 'n' franks

prep: 25 min. • bake: 1 hour 40 min.

This kid-pleasing combination was requested often when our children were young. Now that they're grown, they like to make it for their families because it doesn't require any fancy ingredients.
—Sandra Scheirer
  Mertztown, Pennsylvania

---

  2 tablespoons chopped onion
  3 tablespoons butter
  1/4 cup all-purpose flour
1-1/2 teaspoons salt
  1/8 teaspoon pepper
  2 cups 2% milk
  1 cup (4 ounces) shredded Swiss cheese
  2 tablespoons minced fresh parsley
  5 medium potatoes, peeled and thinly sliced
  8 hot dogs, halved and sliced

In a large saucepan, saute onion in butter until tender. Stir in the flour, salt and pepper until blended. Gradually add milk. Bring to a boil over medium heat; cook and stir for 2 minutes or until thickened. Remove from the heat; stir in cheese until melted. Add the parsley.

Place half of the potatoes in a greased 2-qt. baking dish; top with half of the sauce. Arrange hot dogs over the sauce. Top with remaining potatoes and sauce.

Cover and bake at 350° for 1-1/2 hours or until bubbly and potatoes are tender. Uncover and bake 10 minutes longer or until lightly browned. **yield: 4-6 servings.**

autumn sausage casserole

prep: 20 min. • bake: 25 min.

Apple, raisins and spices give this tasty sausage-rice casserole a taste of autumn. We enjoy it with a green salad on a cool fall day. It would be a nice potluck dish, too.
—Diane Brunell
  Washington, Massachusetts

---

  1 pound bulk pork sausage
  1 medium apple, peeled and chopped
  1 medium onion, chopped
  1/2 cup chopped celery
  3 cups cooked long grain rice
  1/2 cup raisins
  1/3 cup minced fresh parsley
  1 tablespoon brown sugar
  1/2 teaspoon salt
  1/4 teaspoon ground allspice
  1/4 teaspoon ground cinnamon
  1/8 teaspoon pepper

In a large skillet, cook the sausage, apple, onion and celery over medium heat until the sausage is no longer pink; drain. Stir in the remaining ingredients.

Transfer to a greased 2-qt. baking dish. Cover and bake at 350° for 25-30 minutes or until heated through. **yield: 4-6 servings.**

2 minutes or until thickened. Remove from the heat. Stir in the cheese and sour cream until melted.

Drain cauliflower. In a large bowl, combine the cauliflower, ham and mushrooms. Add cheese sauce and toss to coat. Transfer to a greased 2-qt. baking dish.

Combine topping ingredients; sprinkle over casserole. Bake, uncovered, at 350° for 40-45 minutes or until heated through. **yield: 6 servings.**

busy day ham bake

prep: 15 min. • bake: 30 min.

It only takes a few everyday ingredients to make this eye-catching dish. It's great with crusty rolls and fruit salad. Sometimes I replace the ham with cooked turkey for a change of pace.
—Brenda Daugherty
 Lake City, Florida

1 can (10-3/4 ounces) condensed cheddar cheese soup, undiluted
3 cups frozen chopped broccoli, thawed
1 cup cooked rice
1 cup cubed fully cooked ham
1/4 cup sour cream
1/4 cup mayonnaise
1/4 cup dry bread crumbs
1 tablespoon butter

In a large bowl, combine the first six ingredients. Transfer to a greased 1-1/2-qt. baking dish. Toss bread crumbs and butter; sprinkle over the top.

Bake, uncovered, at 350° for 30 minutes or until heated through. **yield: 4 servings.**

cauliflower ham casserole

prep: 20 min. • bake: 40 min.

Cauliflower replaces the potatoes in this homey supper, which I've been making for quite a few years. Whenever we have leftover ham, my husband asks me to make this casserole.
—Sue Herlund, White Bear Lake, Minnesota

4 cups chopped fresh cauliflower
1/4 cup butter, cubed
1/3 cup all-purpose flour
2 cups 2% milk
1 cup (4 ounces) shredded cheddar cheese
1/2 cup sour cream
2 cups cubed fully cooked ham
1 jar (4-1/2 ounces) sliced mushrooms, drained
TOPPING:
1 cup soft bread crumbs
1 tablespoon butter, melted

Place cauliflower in a large saucepan; cover with 1 in. water. Bring to a boil. Reduce heat; cover and simmer for 5-10 minutes or until tender.

Meanwhile, in another large saucepan, melt butter. Stir in flour until smooth; gradually add milk. Bring to a boil; cook and stir for

smoked pork chops with sweet potatoes

prep: 20 min. • **bake:** 40 min.

Apple and sweet potato flavors combine so nicely with pork. My family enjoys simple dinners like this one.
—Helen Sanders, Fort Myers, Florida

6 smoked boneless pork chops (7 ounces *each*)
1 tablespoon canola oil
4 large sweet potatoes, cooked, peeled and cut lengthwise into thirds
1/2 cup packed brown sugar
1/8 teaspoon pepper
2 large tart apples, peeled and thinly sliced
1/4 cup apple juice *or* water

In a large skillet, brown pork chops in oil on each side. Transfer to a greased 13-in. x 9-in. baking dish. Top with sweet potatoes. Combine brown sugar and pepper; sprinkle over sweet potatoes. Top with apples; drizzle with apple juice.

Cover and bake at 375° for 30 minutes. Uncover; bake 10-15 minutes longer or until a meat thermometer reads 160°. **yield: 6 servings.**

mac 'n' cheese with ham

prep: 25 min. • bake: 25 min.

Homemade mac 'n' cheese becomes a filling and well-rounded supper with the addition of asparagus and ham. It has a satisfying homemade flavor.
—Anita Durst, Madison, Wisconsin

1 package (7 ounces) elbow macaroni
2 tablespoons butter
3 tablespoons all-purpose flour
1 teaspoon dried parsley flakes
3/4 teaspoon ground mustard
1/4 teaspoon pepper
2 cups 2% milk
1 package (16 ounces) process cheese (Velveeta), cubed
2 cups cubed fully cooked ham
1 package (10 ounces) frozen cut asparagus, thawed
1 jar (6 ounces) sliced mushrooms, drained
3 tablespoons dry bread crumbs

Cook macaroni according to package directions. Meanwhile, in a large saucepan, melt butter. Stir in the flour, parsley, mustard and pepper until blended. Gradually stir in milk. Bring to a boil; cook and stir for 2 minutes or until thickened. Stir in cheese until melted.

Drain macaroni; add to cheese sauce. Stir in the ham, asparagus and mushrooms.

Transfer to a greased 2-1/2-qt. baking dish. Sprinkle with bread crumbs. Bake, uncovered, at 350° for 25-30 minutes or until bubbly. **yield: 6 servings.**

ham & peas noodle dinner

prep: 15 min. • bake: 50 min.

Whether I'm cooking for company or my own gang, this delicious casserole is always well-received.
—Eileen Nilsson, Plymouth, Massachusetts

2-1/2 cups uncooked egg noodles
1 celery rib, chopped
1 medium onion, chopped
1 tablespoon canola oil
2 cups cubed fully cooked ham
1 can (10-3/4 ounces) condensed cream of mushroom soup, undiluted
1 package (10 ounces) frozen peas, thawed
1 cup (4 ounces) shredded cheddar cheese
3/4 cup 2% milk
1 teaspoon ground mustard

Cook noodles according to package directions; drain. Meanwhile, in a large skillet, saute the celery and onion in oil until tender. Stir in noodles and remaining ingredients.

Transfer to a greased 2-qt. baking dish. Cover and bake at 350° for 50-60 minutes or until heated through. **yield: 4-6 servings.**

ham-stuffed jumbo shells

prep: 20 min. • bake: 30 min.

This is a good way to use up leftover ham. I made it for a family reunion, and the dish came back empty. I am often asked for the recipe.
—Leona Reuer, Medina, North Dakota

24 jumbo pasta shells
3 tablespoons all-purpose flour
2 cups 1% milk
1/2 pound fresh mushrooms, halved and sliced
1/2 cup chopped onion
1/2 cup chopped green pepper
1 tablespoon canola oil
3 cups cubed fully cooked lean ham
1 cup (4 ounces) shredded reduced-fat Swiss cheese, *divided*
3 tablespoons grated Parmesan cheese
2 tablespoons minced fresh parsley
1/4 teaspoon paprika

Cook pasta according to package directions. Meanwhile, in a small saucepan, combine flour and milk until smooth. Bring to a boil; cook and stir for 2 minutes or until thickened. Remove from heat; set aside.

In a large nonstick skillet, saute the mushrooms, onion and green pepper in oil until tender. Reduce heat; add ham, 1/2 cup Swiss cheese and Parmesan cheese. Cook and stir until cheese is melted. Remove from the heat. Stir in 1/2 cup of the reserved sauce.

Drain pasta; stuff each shell with about 3 tablespoons of filing. Place in a 13-in. x 9-in. baking dish coated with cooking spray. Top with the remaining sauce. Cover and bake at 350° for 30 minutes or until heated through. Sprinkle with the parsley, paprika and remaining Swiss cheese. **yield: 8 servings.**

pork chop casserole

prep: 10 min. • bake: 40 min.

Orange juice and canned soup boost the flavor of this tender pork chop and rice bake. It's tasty and a little different from your usual fare.
—Wanda Plinsky, Wichita, Kansas

4 bone-in pork loin chops (1/2 inch thick and 8 ounces *each*)
1 tablespoon canola oil
1-1/3 cups uncooked long grain rice
1 cup orange juice
1 can (10-1/2 ounces) condensed chicken with rice soup, undiluted

In a large skillet, brown pork chops in oil; drain. Place the rice in an ungreased shallow 3-qt. baking dish; pour orange juice over rice. Top with pork chops and soup.

Cover and bake at 350° for 40-45 minutes or until a meat thermometer reads 160°. **yield: 4 servings.**

meaty sauerkraut supper

prep: 10 min. • bake: 65 min.

When I was growing up, this was a supper that would grace our table in autumn. My mother served it with made-from-scratch rolls and custard raisin pie.

—Carol Ann Cassaday
St. Louis, Missouri

- 2/3 **cup finely chopped fully cooked ham**
- 2 **cups cooked long grain rice**
- 1-1/4 **cups finely chopped onions, *divided***
- 1-1/4 **teaspoons salt, *divided***
- 1/4 **teaspoon pepper, *divided***
- 1 **pound lean ground beef (90% lean)**
- 1 **can (14 ounces) sauerkraut, rinsed and drained**
- 1/2 **teaspoon sugar**
- 1 **bacon strip, diced**

In a large bowl, combine the ham, rice, 3/4 cup onions, 1 teaspoon salt and 1/8 teaspoon pepper; crumble beef over mixture and mix gently.

In a greased 2-1/2-qt. baking dish, place half of the sauerkraut; sprinkle with half of the remaining onions. Top with meat mixture, remaining sauerkraut and onions. Sprinkle with sugar and remaining salt and pepper. Top with bacon.

Cover and bake at 375° for 65-70 minutes or until hot and bubbly. **yield: 6 servings.**

baked chops and fries

prep: 20 min. • bake: 55 min.

Convenience items like frozen vegetables and a jar of cheese sauce make it a snap to assemble this comforting pork chop supper. It's an easy meal-in-one.

—Gregg Voss, Emerson, Nebraska

- 6 **bone-in pork loin chops (1 inch thick and 7 ounces *each*)**
- 1 **tablespoon olive oil**
- 1/2 **teaspoon seasoned salt**
- 1 **jar (8 ounces) process cheese sauce**
- 1/2 **cup 2% milk**
- 4 **cups frozen cottage fries**
- 1 **can (2.8 ounces) french-fried onions, *divided***
- 4 **cups frozen broccoli florets**

In a large skillet, brown pork chops in oil; sprinkle with seasoned salt. In a small bowl, combine cheese sauce and milk until blended.

Spread into a greased 13-in. x 9-in. baking dish. Top with cottage fries and half of the onions. Layer with broccoli and pork chops.

Cover and bake at 350° for 45 minutes. Sprinkle with remaining onions. Bake 10 minutes longer or until a meat thermometer reads 160°. **yield: 6 servings.**

pork chop barley bake

prep: 65 min. • bake: 1 hour

Orange marmalade and orange juice are the key ingredients behind this dinner's lovely glaze. Barley bakes right with the pork for a complete meal.
—Mary Sullivan, Spokane, Washington

- 1 cup medium pearl barley
- 1/2 cup chopped onion
- 1/2 cup chopped celery
- 4 tablespoons butter, *divided*
- 1 garlic clove, minced
- 2 cups chicken broth
- 1 cup orange juice
- 1 teaspoon grated orange peel
- 1/2 teaspoon dried rosemary, crushed
- 1/2 cup chopped pecans, toasted
- 6 bone-in pork loin chops (1 inch thick and 7 ounces *each*)

Salt and pepper to taste

GLAZE:

- 1 cup orange marmalade
- 2 tablespoons orange juice
- 1 tablespoon prepared mustard
- 1/2 teaspoon ground ginger

Orange slices and fresh rosemary, optional

In a large saucepan, saute the barley, onion and celery in 3 tablespoons butter until barley is golden brown and vegetables are tender. Add garlic; cook 1 minuet longer. Stir in the broth, orange juice, peel and rosemary; bring to a boil. Reduce heat; cover and simmer for 35 minutes or until barley is partially cooked. Add pecans.

Transfer to a greased 13-in. x 9-in. baking dish. In a large skillet, brown pork chops on both sides in remaining butter. Sprinkle with salt and pepper. Arrange over barley mixture.

Combine glaze ingredients; brush half over chops. Cover and bake at 350° for 45 minutes. Uncover; brush with remaining glaze. Bake 15 minutes longer or until a meat thermometer reads 160°. Garnish with orange and rosemary if desired. **yield: 6 servings.**

sweet potato ham bake

prep: 10 min. • bake: 30 min.

Three ingredients are all you need for this colorful hot dish, sized perfectly for two. It's a good way to use up ham from the holidays.
—Jennette Fourne, Detroit, Michigan

- 1 can (15 ounces) cut sweet potatoes, drained and quartered lengthwise
- 2 cups cubed fully cooked ham
- 1 cup (4 ounces) shredded cheddar cheese

In a greased 1-qt. baking dish, layer half of the sweet potatoes, ham and cheese. Repeat the layers. Cover and bake at 350° for 20 minutes. Uncover; bake 8-10 minutes longer or until cheese is melted. **yield: 2-3 servings.**

corn tortilla quiche

prep: 15 min. • bake: 45 min.

A corn tortilla crust makes this tasty quiche a snap to assemble. Cheesy wedges are great for breakfast, lunch or dinner.
—Leicha Welton, Fairbanks, Alaska

3/4	pound bulk pork sausage
5	corn tortillas (6 inches)
1	cup (4 ounces) shredded Monterey Jack cheese
1	cup (4 ounces) shredded cheddar cheese
1/4	cup chopped canned green chilies
6	eggs, lightly beaten
1/2	cup heavy whipping cream
1/2	cup 4% cottage cheese
1/2	teaspoon chili powder
1/4	cup minced fresh cilantro

In a large skillet, cook the sausage until no longer pink; drain.

Place four tortillas in a greased 9-in. pie plate, overlapping and extending 1/2 in. beyond rim. Place remaining tortilla in the center. Layer with sausage, Monterey Jack and cheddar cheeses and chilies.

In a large bowl, combine the eggs, cream, cottage cheese and chili powder; slowly pour over chilies. Bake at 350° for 45 minutes or until a knife inserted near the center comes out clean. Sprinkle with cilantro. Cut into wedges. **yield: 6 servings.**

Cook pasta according to package directions. Drain and set aside. In a large skillet, saute onion in oil until tender. Add garlic; cook 1 minute longer. Stir in the tomatoes, tomato paste, green and sweet red peppers, salami, olives, salt and pepper. Simmer, uncovered, for 5 minutes.

Remove from the heat; stir in pasta. Combine cheeses. Spoon half of pasta mixture into a greased 2-qt. baking dish. Sprinkle with 1-1/3 cups cheese. Layer with remaining pasta and cheese.

Bake, uncovered, at 350° for 15-20 minutes or until bubbly and cheese is melted. **yield: 4-6 servings.**

ham and rice bake

prep: 10 min. • bake: 25 min.

A can of soup, some rice, a few convenience items plus leftover ham create a flavorful, no-fuss casserole.
—*Sharol Binger, Tulare, South Dakota*

- 1 can (10-3/4 ounces) condensed cream of chicken soup, undiluted
- 1 cup (4 ounces) shredded cheddar cheese, *divided*
- 1 package (16 ounces) frozen California-blend vegetables, thawed
- 1 cup cooked rice
- 1 cup cubed fully cooked ham

In a large saucepan, combine the soup and 1/2 cup cheese; cook and stir until cheese is melted. Stir in the vegetables, rice and ham.

Transfer to a greased 1-1/2-qt. baking dish. Sprinkle with remaining cheese. Bake, uncovered, at 350° for 25-30 minutes or until heated through. **yield: 4 servings.**

penne salami bake

prep: 20 min. • bake: 15 min.

This entree is so versatile that you can add whatever veggies you have on hand. I've tossed in a variety of produce, including mushrooms, peas, broccoli, zucchini and pattypan squash. Just saute them right along with the onion and garlic.
—*Tanya Murray, Olympia, Washington*

- 2 cups uncooked penne pasta
- 1 small onion, diced
- 3 tablespoons olive oil
- 1 garlic clove, minced
- 2 cups canned diced tomatoes, drained
- 1 tablespoon tomato paste
- 1 medium green pepper, chopped
- 1 medium sweet red pepper, chopped
- 1/3 pound salami, cubed
- 10 pitted ripe olives, halved

Salt and pepper
- 1 cup (4 ounces) shredded part-skim mozzarella cheese
- 1 cup (4 ounces) shredded cheddar cheese

pork tetrazzini

prep: 20 min. • bake: 30 min.

My mom always made this with leftover turkey or ham. You can also use chicken or tuna instead of pork.
—Doreen Kelly, Rosyln, Pennsylvania

- 1 small onion, diced
- 1 celery rib, diced
- 1 tablespoon butter
- 5 tablespoons all-purpose flour
- 1 can (14-1/2 ounces) chicken broth
- 1 cup 2% milk
- 1 bay leaf
- 1/2 teaspoon onion salt
- 1/4 teaspoon pepper
- 2 tablespoons sour cream
- 1 tablespoon dried parsley flakes
- 1 tablespoon lemon juice
- 2 cups cooked spaghetti
- 2 cups diced cooked pork
- 2 tablespoons seasoned bread crumbs

In a small saucepan, saute onion and celery in butter until tender. Combine flour and broth until smooth; stir into the pan. Add the milk, bay leaf, onion salt and pepper. Bring to a boil; cook and stir for 2 minutes or until thickened. Remove from the heat. Discard bay leaf. Whisk in the sour cream, parsley and lemon juice.

Place the spaghetti in a greased 11-in. x 7-in. baking dish; top with pork and white sauce. Sprinkle with bread crumbs. Bake, uncovered, at 350° for 30-35 minutes or until bubbly. Let stand for 5 minutes before serving.
yield: 4 servings.

hot dog casserole

prep: 10 min. • bake: 70 min.

When our children were small and I was busy trying to get all those extra things done that are part of a mom's normal schedule, I would make this quick hot dish. My kids love it.
—JoAnn Gunio, Franklin, North Carolina

- 3 tablespoons butter
- 2 tablespoons all-purpose flour
- 1 to 1-1/2 teaspoons salt
- 1/4 to 1/2 teaspoon pepper
- 1-1/2 cups 2% milk
- 5 medium red potatoes, thinly sliced
- 1 package (1 pound) hot dogs, halved lengthwise and cut into 1/2-inch slices
- 1 medium onion, chopped
- 1/3 cup shredded cheddar cheese

In a small saucepan, melt butter. Stir in the flour, salt and pepper until smooth. Gradually add milk. Bring to a boil; cook and stir for 2 minutes or until thickened and bubbly.

In a greased 2-1/2-qt. baking dish, layer with a third of the potatoes, half of the hot dogs and half of the onion. Repeat layers. Top with remaining potatoes. Pour white sauce over all.

Cover and bake at 350° for 1 hour. Uncover; sprinkle with the cheese. Bake 10-15 minutes longer or until potatoes are tender.
yield: 8 servings.

baked ziti and sausage

prep: 25 min. • bake: 30 min.

This is my husband's favorite casserole, and he requests it often. He loves the combination of zesty Italian sausage and three types of cheese: Parmesan, cottage and mozzarella.
—Christina Ingalls, Manhattan, Kansas

- 3 cups uncooked ziti *or* other small tube pasta
- 1/2 pound Italian sausage links
- 1/4 cup butter, cubed
- 1/4 cup all-purpose flour

- 1-1/2 teaspoons salt, *divided*
- 1/4 teaspoon plus 1/8 teaspoon pepper, *divided*
- 2 cups 2% milk
- 1/2 cup grated Parmesan cheese, *divided*
- 1 egg, lightly beaten
- 2 cups (16 ounces) 4% cottage cheese
- 1 tablespoon minced fresh parsley
- 1 cup (4 ounces) shredded part-skim mozzarella cheese

Paprika

Cook pasta according to package directions. Drain; place in a large bowl. In a small skillet, cook sausage over medium heat until no longer pink; drain and cut into 1/2-in. slices.

In a large saucepan, melt butter. Stir in the flour, 1 teaspoon salt and 1/4 teaspoon pepper until smooth; gradually add milk. Bring to a boil; cook and stir for 2 minutes or until thickened. Remove from the heat; stir in 1/4 cup Parmesan cheese. Pour over pasta; toss to coat.

In a small bowl, combine the egg, cottage cheese, parsley, and remaining Parmesan cheese, salt and pepper. Spoon half of the pasta mixture into a greased 2-1/2-qt. baking dish. Top with cottage cheese mixture. Add sausage to the remaining pasta mixture; spoon over the top. Sprinkle with the mozzarella cheese and paprika.

Bake, uncovered, at 350° for 30-35 minutes or until a thermometer reads 160°. **yield: 6 servings.**

ham noodle casserole

prep: 15 min. • bake: 20 min.

My mom used to make the original version of this mild curry casserole, which I enjoyed. It didn't fit my healthier eating habits until I made a few changes. Now our whole family can enjoy it without the guilt.
—Sheri Switzer
    Crawfordville, Indiana

- 6 cups uncooked no-yolk medium noodles
- 1 can (10-3/4 ounces) reduced-fat reduced-sodium condensed cream of celery soup, undiluted
- 1 cup cubed fully cooked lean ham
- 2/3 cup cubed reduced-fat process American cheese
- 1/2 cup fat-free milk
- 1/4 cup thinly sliced green onions
- 1/2 teaspoon curry powder

Cook noodles according to package directions; drain and place in a large bowl. Stir in the remaining ingredients.

Transfer to a 2-1/2-qt. baking dish coated with cooking spray. Cover and bake at 375° for 20-30 minutes or until heated through. **yield: 6 servings.**

smoked pork chop casserole

prep: 25 min. • bake: 1 hour

I found this recipe several years ago. The taste of the smoked pork chops with the apples and potatoes is amazing!
—Patricia Sue Kopecky, Lake Arrowhead, California

- 8 medium potatoes, peeled and cut into 1/4-inch slices
- 1 large tart apple, peeled and cut into 1/4-inch slices
- 1 tablespoon chopped onion
- 1 cup (4 ounces) shredded Swiss cheese
- 6 smoked pork chops (6 ounces *each*)

SAUCE:
- 2 tablespoons butter
- 2 tablespoons all-purpose flour
- 1 cup 2% milk
- 4 teaspoons Dijon mustard

Salt and pepper to taste

Place potatoes in a Dutch oven and cover with water. Bring to a boil. Reduce heat; cover and cook for 10-15 minutes or until tender. Drain. Stir in apple and onion.

Transfer to a greased 13-in. x 9-in. baking dish. Sprinkle with the cheese; top with the pork chops. Cover and bake at 350° for 30 minutes.

In a small saucepan, melt butter over medium heat. Stir in flour until smooth; gradually add milk. Bring to a boil; cook and stir for 1-2 minutes or until thickened. Stir in the mustard, salt and pepper.

Pour over pork chops. Bake, uncovered, for 30 minutes or until heated through. **yield: 6 servings.**

KITCHEN TIP

Most smoked pork chops are fully cooked and only need to be reheated. Smoking gives the meat a distinctive flavor. If you like Canadian bacon or ham, you will most likely enjoy smoked pork chops.

mother's ham casserole

prep: 35 min. • bake: 25 min.

One of my mother's favorite dishes, this casserole always brings back fond memories of her when I prepare it. It's a terrific use of leftover ham from a holiday dinner.

—Linda Childers, Murfreesboro, Tennessee

- 2 cups cubed peeled potatoes
- 1 large carrot, sliced
- 2 celery ribs, chopped
- 3 cups water
- 2 cups cubed fully cooked ham
- 2 tablespoons chopped green pepper
- 2 teaspoons finely chopped onion
- 7 tablespoons butter, *divided*
- 3 tablespoons all-purpose flour
- 1-1/2 cups milk
- 3/4 teaspoon salt
- 1/8 teaspoon pepper
- 1 cup (4 ounces) shredded cheddar cheese
- 1/2 cup soft bread crumbs

In a saucepan, bring the potatoes, carrot, celery and water to a boil. Reduce heat; cover and cook about 15 minutes or until tender. Drain.

In a large skillet, saute the ham, green pepper and onion in 3 tablespoons butter until tender. Add to the potato mixture. Transfer to a greased 1-1/2-qt. baking dish.

In a large saucepan, melt the remaining butter; stir in flour until smooth. Gradually add the milk, salt and pepper. Bring to a boil; cook and stir for 2 minutes or until thickened. Reduce heat; add cheese and stir until melted.

Pour over the ham mixture. Sprinkle with bread crumbs. Bake, uncovered, at 375° for 25-30 minutes or until heated through. **yield: 4-6 servings.**

seafood

Cook up a special dinner treat for your family with shrimp, scallops, crab, fish and even canned tuna. Stretch your dollar by combining seafood with pasta and other ingredients to create a number of delectable entrees.

<< pictured left

special seafood casserole
prep: 25 min. • bake: 25 min. + standing

I first sampled this casserole at a baby shower and found myself going back for more! It has a delectable assortment of shellfish combined with artichokes and water chestnuts in a velvety sauce.
—Angela Schwartz, Marietta, Georgia

- 1/2 **pound sea scallops**
- 1 **small onion, finely chopped**
- 1 **celery rib, finely chopped**
- 6 **tablespoons butter, cubed**
- 7 **tablespoons all-purpose flour**
- 1-1/2 **cups half-and-half cream**
- 1 **cup (4 ounces) shredded sharp cheddar cheese**
- 6 **tablespoons sherry *or* apple juice**
- 3/4 **teaspoon salt**
- 1/4 **teaspoon cayenne pepper**
- 1 **pound cooked medium shrimp, peeled and deveined**
- 1 **can (6 ounces) crabmeat, drained, flaked and cartilage removed**
- 1 **can (14 ounces) water-packed artichoke hearts, drained, rinsed, chopped and patted dry**
- 1 **can (8 ounces) sliced water chestnuts, drained**
- 1/2 **cup sliced almonds**
- 1/4 **cup grated Parmesan cheese**

In a Dutch oven, saute the scallops, onion and celery in butter. Stir in the flour until blended. Add cream. Bring to a boil; cook and stir for 2 minutes or until thickened. Reduce heat; add the cheddar cheese, sherry, salt and cayenne, stirring until cheese is melted. Remove from the heat; set aside.

In a greased 11-in. x 7-in. baking dish, layer with shrimp, crab, artichokes and water chestnuts. Top with sauce. Sprinkle with almonds and Parmesan cheese.

Bake, uncovered, at 350° for 25-30 minutes or until heated through. Let stand for 10 minutes before serving. **yield: 6 servings.**

salmon stroganoff
prep: 15 min. • bake: 30 min.

A golden-brown crumb topping is the finishing touch on this rich noodle casserole that takes advantage of canned salmon from the pantry. It's so good that I'm always asked for the recipe.
—Joan Sherlock
Belle Plaine, Minnesota

- 4 **cups cooked wide egg noodles**
- 1 **can (14-3/4 ounces) salmon, drained, bones and skin removed**
- 1 **jar (4-1/2 ounces) sliced mushrooms, drained**
- 1 **jar (2 ounces) diced pimientos, drained**
- 1-1/2 **cups (12 ounces) 4% cottage cheese**
- 1-1/2 **cups (12 ounces) sour cream**
- 1/2 **cup mayonnaise**
- 3 **tablespoons grated onion**
- 1 **garlic clove, minced**
- 1-1/2 **teaspoons Worcestershire sauce**
- 1 **teaspoon salt**
- 1 **cup (4 ounces) shredded cheddar cheese**
- 1/3 **cup dry bread crumbs**
- 2 **tablespoons butter, melted**

In a large bowl, combine the noodles, salmon, mushrooms and pimientos. In another large bowl, combine the cottage cheese, sour cream, mayonnaise, onion, garlic, Worcestershire sauce and salt; add to noodle mixture. Stir in cheddar cheese.

Transfer to a greased 2-qt. baking dish. Toss bread crumbs and butter; sprinkle over the casserole. Bake, uncovered, at 350° for 30-35 minutes or until bubbly and golden brown. **yield: 4-6 servings.**

salmon broccoli bake

prep: 15 min. • bake: 35 min.

A good friend gave me this quick-and-easy recipe that uses canned salmon, wild rice and frozen broccoli. I often serve this bake with a wilted spinach salad for a complete meal.
—Brigitte Schaller
    Flemington, Missouri

- 1 cup chopped onion
- 1 tablespoon butter
- 1-1/2 cups cooked wild rice
- 1 can (7-1/2 ounces) salmon, drained, bones and skin removed
- 1 egg
- 1/2 cup mayonnaise
- 1/2 cup grated Parmesan cheese
- 3 cups frozen chopped broccoli, thawed and drained
- 1-1/2 cups (6 ounces) shredded cheddar cheese, *divided*

In a large skillet, saute onion in butter until tender. Remove from the heat; stir in the rice and salmon. Combine the egg and mayonnaise; add to the salmon mixture.

Spoon half into a greased 2-qt. baking dish; top with half of the Parmesan cheese and broccoli. Sprinkle with 1 cup cheddar cheese. Top with the remaining salmon mixture, Parmesan cheese and broccoli.

Bake, uncovered, at 350° for 30 minutes. Sprinkle with remaining cheddar cheese. Bake 5 minutes longer or until cheese is melted. **yield: 4 servings.**

cheesy tuna mac

prep: 15 min. • bake: 25 min.

What could be easier than dressing up a boxed macaroni and cheese mix with tuna and canned soup? This tasty casserole is a snap to fix, and my two boys gobble it up. You can vary the soup and veggies to suit your family's preferences.
—Stephanie Martin, Macomb, Michigan

- 1 package (7-1/2 ounces) macaroni and cheese mix
- 1/2 cup 2% milk
- 1 tablespoon butter
- 1 can (10-3/4 ounces) condensed cream of broccoli soup, undiluted
- 1 can (5 ounces) tuna, drained and flaked
- 3/4 cup frozen peas
- 2 tablespoons finely chopped onion
- 1 tablespoon process cheese sauce

Cook macaroni according to package directions; drain. Stir in the milk, butter and contents of cheese packet. Add the soup, tuna, peas, onion and cheese sauce.

Spoon into a greased 1-1/2-qt. baking dish. Cover and bake at 350° for 20 minutes. Uncover; bake 5-10 minutes longer or until heated through. **yield: 4 servings.**

sunday shrimp pasta bake

prep: 30 min. • bake: 25 min.

Pasta is popular in our home, so most of my favorite meals have it in the main course. In this sensational dish, pasta complements the shrimp our local fishermen bring in.
—Sundra Hauck, Bogalusa, Louisiana

- 12 **ounces uncooked vermicelli**
- 1 **medium green pepper, chopped**
- 5 **green onions, chopped**
- 6 **tablespoons butter, cubed**
- 6 **garlic cloves, minced**
- 2 **tablespoons all-purpose flour**
- 2 **pounds cooked medium shrimp, peeled and deveined**
- 1 **teaspoon celery salt**
- 1/8 **teaspoon pepper**
- 1 **pound process cheese (Velveeta), cubed**
- 1 **can (10 ounces) diced tomatoes and green chilies, drained**
- 1 **can (4 ounces) mushroom stems and pieces, drained**
- 1 **tablespoon grated Parmesan cheese**

Cook vermicelli according to package directions. Meanwhile, in a large skillet, saute green pepper and onions in butter until tender. Add garlic; cook 1 minute longer. Gradually stir in flour until blended. Stir in the shrimp, celery salt and pepper; cook, uncovered, over medium heat for 5-6 minutes or until heated through.

In a microwave-safe bowl, combine the process cheese, tomatoes and mushrooms. Microwave, uncovered, on high for 3-4 minutes or until cheese is melted, stirring occasionally. Add to shrimp mixture. Drain vermicelli; stir into skillet.

Pour into a greased 13-in. x 9-in. baking dish. Sprinkle with the Parmesan cheese. Bake, uncovered, at 350° for 25-30 minutes or until heated through. **yield: 8 servings.**

editor's note: This recipe was tested in a 1,100-watt microwave.

hearty tuna casserole

prep: 30 min. • bake: 35 min.

Here's a jazzed-up version of my mom's tuna casserole that's sure to be a home-style dish the whole family will enjoy! I add pizzazz to the traditional dish with mustard, sour cream, thyme and zucchini.

—Jan Heshelman, Bloomfield, Indiana

- 3 cups uncooked yolk-free wide noodles
- 1 can (12ounces) light water-packed tuna, drained and flaked
- 1 cup shredded zucchini
- 3/4 cup reduced-fat sour cream
- 1 celery rib with leaves, thinly sliced
- 1/4 cup chopped onion
- 1/4 cup reduced-fat mayonnaise
- 2 teaspoons prepared mustard
- 1/2 teaspoon dried thyme
- 1/4 teaspoon salt
- 1 cup (4 ounces) shredded part-skim mozzarella cheese
- 1 medium tomato, chopped

Cook noodles according to package directions; drain. In a large bowl, combine the noodles, tuna, zucchini, sour cream, celery, onion, mayonnaise, mustard, thyme and salt.

Spoon half into a 2-qt. baking dish coated with cooking spray. Sprinkle with half of the cheese. Repeat layers. Top with tomato.

Cover and bake at 350° for 30-35 minutes. Uncover; bake 5 minutes longer. **yield: 6 servings**

cheddar shrimp and penne

prep: 15 min. • bake: 35 min.

My wife and I take turns in the kitchen. When I created this creamy dish, it quickly became one of our favorites.

—Brad Walker, Holt, Michigan

- 2 cups uncooked penne pasta
- 2 garlic cloves, minced
- 2 tablespoons butter
- 2 tablespoons all-purpose flour
- 1/2 teaspoon salt
- 1/4 teaspoon pepper
- 2 cups 2% milk
- 1-1/2 cups (6 ounces) shredded cheddar cheese, *divided*
- 1 pound cooked medium shrimp, peeled and deveined
- 1 can (15-1/4 ounces) whole kernel corn, drained

Cook pasta according to package directions. Meanwhile, in a large saucepan, cook the garlic in butter over medium heat for 1 minute. Stir in flour, salt and pepper until blended. Gradually add milk. Bring to a boil; cook and stir for 2 minutes or until thickened. Reduce heat; stir in 1 cup of cheese until melted. Remove from the heat.

Drain pasta; add the pasta, shrimp and corn to cheese sauce. Transfer to a greased 2-qt. baking dish.

Cover and bake at 350° for 25 minutes. Uncover; sprinkle with remaining cheese. Bake 10-15 minutes longer or until bubbly. **yield: 4-6 servings.**

seafood 'n' shells casserole

prep: 25 min. • bake: 25 min.

Poaching the cod before baking prevents it from watering out in this wonderful bake. With pasta and vegetables, this dish will warm you up on chilly nights.
—Taste of Home Test Kitchen

6	cups water
1	teaspoon lemon-pepper seasoning
1	bay leaf
2	pounds cod fillets, cut into 1-inch pieces
1	cup uncooked small pasta shells
1	medium sweet red pepper, chopped
1	medium green pepper, chopped
1	medium onion, chopped
1	tablespoon butter
3	tablespoons all-purpose flour
2-1/2	cups fat-free evaporated milk
3/4	teaspoon salt
1/2	teaspoon dried thyme
1/4	teaspoon pepper
1	cup (4 ounces) shredded Mexican cheese blend

In a large skillet, bring the water, lemon-pepper and bay leaf to a boil. Reduce heat; carefully add cod. Cover and simmer for 5-8 minutes or until fish flakes easily with a fork; drain and set aside. Discard bay leaf.

Cook pasta according to package directions. In a saucepan, saute peppers and onion in butter over medium heat until tender. Stir in flour until blended. Gradually stir in milk. Bring to a boil; cook and stir for 2 minutes or until thickened. Stir in salt, thyme and pepper. Remove from the heat; add the cheese, stirring until melted.

Drain pasta. Stir fish and pasta into sauce. Transfer to a 2-qt. baking dish coated with cooking spray. Cover and bake at 350° for 25-30 minutes or until heated through. **yield: 6 servings.**

artichoke shrimp bake

prep: 20 min. • bake: 20 min.

I usually serve this dish with rice or baking powder biscuits. You can substitute frozen asparagus cuts for the artichokes and cream of asparagus soup for cream of shrimp.

—Jeanne Holt
  Mendota Heights, Minnesota

- 1 **pound cooked medium shrimp, peeled and deveined**
- 1 **can (14 ounces) water-packed quartered artichoke hearts, rinsed, drained and quartered**
- 2/3 **cup frozen pearl onions, thawed**
- 2 **cups sliced fresh mushrooms**
- 1 **small sweet red pepper, chopped**
- 2 **tablespoons butter**
- 1 **can (10-3/4 ounces) condensed cream of shrimp soup, undiluted**
- 1/2 **cup sour cream**
- 1/4 **cup sherry *or* chicken broth**
- 2 **teaspoons Worcestershire sauce**
- 1 **teaspoon grated lemon peel**
- 1/8 **teaspoon white pepper**

TOPPING:
- 1/2 **cup soft bread crumbs**
- 1/3 **cup grated Parmesan cheese**
- 1 **tablespoon minced fresh parsley**
- 1 **tablespoon butter, melted**

Hot cooked rice, optional

Place the shrimp, artichokes and onions in a greased 11-in. x 7-in. baking dish; set aside.

In a large skillet, saute the mushrooms and red pepper in butter until tender. Stir in the soup, sour cream, sherry, Worcestershire sauce, lemon peel and white pepper; heat through. Pour over the shrimp mixture.

In a small bowl, combine the bread crumbs, cheese, parsley and butter; sprinkle over top.

Bake, uncovered, at 375° for 20-25 minutes or until bubbly and the topping is golden brown. Serve with rice if desired. **yield: 4 servings.**

favorite halibut casserole

prep/total time: 30 min.

I've been using this recipe since my college days. I even took it to Western Samoa when I was teaching school there. You can substitute any whitefish for the halibut.
—*Gayle Brown, Millville, Utah*

- 5 tablespoons butter, *divided*
- 1/4 cup all-purpose flour
- 1/2 teaspoon salt
- 1/8 to 1/4 teaspoon white pepper
- 1-1/2 cups 2% milk
- 1 small green pepper, chopped
- 1 small onion, chopped
- 2 cups cubed cooked halibut (about 1 pound)
- 3 hard-cooked eggs, chopped
- 1 jar (2 ounces) diced pimientos, drained
- 1/3 cup shredded cheddar cheese

In a large saucepan, melt 4 tablespoons butter. Stir in the flour, salt and pepper until smooth. Gradually add milk. Bring to a boil; cook and stir for 2 minutes or until thickened. Remove from heat; cover and set aside.

In a small skillet, saute the green pepper and onion in remaining butter until tender. Stir into the white sauce. Add the halibut, eggs and pimientos.

Transfer to a greased 1-1/2-qt. baking dish. Sprinkle with cheese. Bake, uncovered, at 375° for 15-20 minutes or until bubbly. **yield: 4 servings.**

oyster fricassee

prep: 20 min. • bake: 25 min. + standing

The colonists had a ready source of oysters from Chesapeake Bay and used them in many dishes. I enjoy this rich, creamy casserole, a special dish from Colonial Williamsburg's holiday recipe collection.
—*Susan Dippre, Williamsburg, Virginia*

- 1 quart shucked oysters
- 2 medium onions, chopped
- 1-1/2 cups chopped celery
- 3/4 cup butter, *divided*
- 1/2 cup all-purpose flour
- 2 cups half-and-half cream
- 2 teaspoons minced fresh parsley
- 1 teaspoon salt
- 1 teaspoon minced fresh thyme *or* 1/2 teaspoon dried thyme
- 1/4 teaspoon pepper
- 1/8 teaspoon cayenne pepper
- 4 egg yolks, lightly beaten
- 2 cups crushed butter-flavored crackers (about 50 crackers)

Lemon slices and fresh thyme sprigs for garnish

Drain oysters, reserving oyster liquor; set aside. In a large saucepan, saute onions and celery in 1/2 cup butter for 4-6 minutes or until tender. Stir in flour until blended; gradually add cream. Bring to a boil; cook and stir for 2 minutes or until thickened.

Reduce heat; add the parsley, salt, thyme, pepper, cayenne and reserved oyster liquor. Cook and stir for 2 minutes or until smooth. Remove from the heat. Stir a small amount of hot liquid into egg yolks; return all to the pan, stirring constantly.

Pour half of the sauce into a greased 13-in. x 9-in. baking dish. Top with half of the oysters; sprinkle with half of the cracker crumbs. Repeat layers. Melt remaining butter; drizzle over the top.

Bake, uncovered, at 400° for 23-28 minutes or until golden brown. Let stand for 10 minutes before serving. Garnish with lemon slices and thyme sprigs. **yield: 6 servings.**

alfredo shrimp shells

prep: 15 min. • bake: 20 min.

Prepared Alfredo sauce streamlines the preparation of these tasty stuffed shells. They're filled with shrimp, mushrooms and green onion. Serve with sauteed zucchini and follow with cubed melon for dessert.
—Gertrude Peischl
    Allentown, Pennsylvania

- 1/2 cup chopped fresh mushrooms
- 1 teaspoon butter
- 1 green onion, sliced
- 1 package (5 ounces) frozen cooked salad shrimp, thawed
- 2 tablespoons plus 1/2 cup Alfredo sauce, *divided*
- 6 jumbo pasta shells, cooked and drained

Lemon wedges and fresh parsley

In a small skillet, saute mushrooms in butter until almost tender. Add onion; cook until tender. Stir in the shrimp and 2 tablespoons Alfredo sauce. Pour 1/4 cup of the remaining sauce into a greased 8-in. square baking dish.

Fill each shell with 2 tablespoons shrimp mixture; place in baking dish. Top with the remaining Alfredo sauce.

Cover and bake at 350° for 20-25 minutes or until bubbly. Serve with lemon and parsley. **yield: 3 servings.**

mustard salmon puff

prep: 15 min. • bake: 35 min.

This recipe is a delicious way to use leftover salmon. With its mayonnaise-based topping, this is not your typical salmon casserole.
—Perlene Hoekema, Lynden, Washington

- 2 eggs, lightly beaten
- 2/3 cup 2% milk
- 1/2 cup sour cream
- 3/4 cup dry bread crumbs
- 1 teaspoon seafood seasoning
- 1/2 teaspoon lemon-pepper seasoning
- 1/4 teaspoon dill weed
- 3 cups fully cooked flaked salmon
- 3 tablespoons chopped celery
- 2 tablespoons chopped onion
- 4-1/2 teaspoons lemon juice

TOPPING:
- 1-1/3 cups mayonnaise
- 1 tablespoon prepared mustard
- 1 egg white
- 2 tablespoons minced parsley

In a large bowl, combine the eggs, milk and sour cream until smooth. Add the bread crumbs, seafood seasoning, lemon-pepper and dill. Stir in the salmon, celery, onion and lemon juice.

Transfer to greased 11-in. x 7-in. baking dish. Bake at 350° for 25-30 minutes or until a knife inserted near the center comes out clean.

Meanwhile, in a small bowl, combine mayonnaise and mustard. In a small bowl, beat egg white until stiff peaks form; fold into mayonnaise mixture. Spread over salmon mixture.

Bake 10-15 minutes longer or until lightly browned. Sprinkle with parsley. **yield: 8 servings.**

KITCHEN TIP

If you don't have cooked salmon, you can quickly prepare a fillet by poaching it. To poach, bring 3 cups water, 2 onion slices, 2 lemon slices and bay leaf to a boil in a large skillet. Reduce heat; add salmon and poach, uncovered, for 5-10 minutes or until fish flakes easily with a fork.

broccoli tuna squares

prep: 15 min. • bake: 35 min. + standing

Family and friends always ask for this recipe because it's different than traditional tuna casserole. I make it when I need something in minutes, which is often. We're always on the go.

—*Janet Juncker, Geneva, Ohio*

---

1 tube (8 ounces) refrigerated crescent rolls

1 cup (4 ounces) shredded Monterey Jack cheese

3 cups frozen chopped broccoli, cooked and drained

4 eggs, lightly beaten

1 can (10-3/4 ounces) condensed cream of broccoli soup, undiluted

2 tablespoons mayonnaise

3/4 teaspoon onion powder

1/2 teaspoon dill weed

1 can (12 ounces) tuna, drained and flaked

1 tablespoon diced pimientos, drained

Unroll crescent roll dough into one long rectangle; place in an ungreased 13-in. x 9-in. baking dish. Seal seams and perforations; press onto bottom and 1/2 in. up the sides. Sprinkle with cheese and broccoli.

In a large bowl, combine the eggs, soup, mayonnaise, onion powder and dill. Stir in tuna and pimientos; pour over broccoli.

Bake, uncovered, at 350° for 35-40 minutes or until a knife inserted near the center comes out clean. Let stand for 10 minutes before serving. **yield: 8 servings.**

salmon biscuit bake

prep/total time: 25 min.

The combination of mayonnaise and milk makes the filling in this delicious bake extra creamy.

—*Eleanor Mengel*
  Summerfield, Florida

- 1 can (14-3/4 ounces) salmon, drained, bones and skin removed
- 1 cup frozen peas, thawed
- 1/4 cup 2% milk
- 1/4 cup mayonnaise
- 2 tablespoons finely chopped green pepper
- 1/4 teaspoon lemon-pepper seasoning
- 1 cup (4 ounces) shredded cheddar cheese

TOPPING:

- 1 cup biscuit/baking mix
- 1/3 cup 2% milk
- 2 tablespoons mayonnaise

In a large bowl, combine the salmon, peas, milk, mayonnaise, green pepper and lemon-pepper. Transfer to a greased 9-in. pie plate. Sprinkle with the cheese.

Combine the biscuit mix, milk and mayonnaise just until moistened. Drop eight mounds onto salmon mixture.

Bake at 425° for 10-15 minutes or until bubbly and biscuits are golden brown. **yield: 4-6 servings.**

de-lightful tuna casserole

prep: 15 min. • bake: 25 min.

This mild homemade tuna casserole will truly satisfy your family's craving for comfort food without all the fat!

—*Colleen Willey, Hamburg, New York*

- 1 package (7 ounces) elbow macaroni
- 1 can (10-3/4 ounces) reduced-fat reduced-sodium condensed cream of mushroom soup, undiluted
- 1 cup sliced fresh mushrooms
- 1 cup (4 ounces) shredded reduced-fat cheddar cheese
- 1 cup fat-free milk
- 1 can (5 ounces) light water-packed tuna, drained and flaked
- 2 tablespoons diced pimientos
- 3 teaspoons dried minced onion
- 1 teaspoon ground mustard
- 1/4 teaspoon salt
- 1/3 cup crushed cornflakes

Cook macaroni according to package directions. Meanwhile, in a large bowl, combine the soup, mushrooms, cheese, milk, tuna, pimientos, onion, mustard and salt. Drain macaroni; add to tuna mixture and mix well.

Transfer to a 2-qt. baking dish coated with cooking spray. Sprinkle with cornflakes. Bake, uncovered, at 350° for 25-30 minutes or until bubbly. **yield: 5 servings.**

makeover shrimp rice casserole

prep: 40 min. • bake: 30 min.

I am fond of this lighter version of my shrimp casserole. It has only half the calories and sodium and less fat than my original recipe but still tastes great.
—*Marie Roberts, Lake Charles, Louisiana*

  1 pound uncooked medium shrimp, peeled and deveined
  2 tablespoons butter, *divided*
 12 ounces fresh mushrooms, sliced
  1 large green pepper, chopped
  1 medium onion, chopped
  3 tablespoons all-purpose flour
  3/4 teaspoon salt
  1/8 teaspoon cayenne pepper
1-1/3 cups fat-free milk
  3 cups cooked brown rice
  1 cup (4 ounces) shredded reduced-fat cheddar cheese, *divided*

In a large nonstick skillet, saute shrimp in 1 tablespoon butter for 2-3 minutes or until shrimp turn pink. Remove and set aside. In the same skillet, saute the mushrooms, green pepper and onion in remaining butter until tender.

Stir in the flour, salt and cayenne. Gradually add milk until blended. Bring to a boil; cook and stir for 2 minutes or until thickened. Add the rice, 1/2 cup cheese and shrimp; stir until combined.

Pour into a 1-1/2-qt. baking dish coated with cooking spray. Cover and bake at 325° for 30-35 minutes or until heated through. Sprinkle with remaining cheese; cover and let stand for 5 minutes or until cheese is melted. **yield: 6 servings.**

sea shell crab casserole

prep: 20 min. • bake: 30 min.

This crab casserole gets color and flavor from green pepper, celery and ripe olives.
—*Brandi Jergenson, Vaughn, Montana*

1-1/2 cups uncooked medium shell pasta
  1 large onion, chopped
  1 medium green pepper, chopped
  3 celery ribs, chopped
  3 tablespoons butter
  1 can (12 ounces) evaporated milk
1/2 cup mayonnaise
  1 teaspoon salt
  1 teaspoon ground mustard
  1 teaspoon paprika
  1 teaspoon Worcestershire sauce
  1 can (2-1/2 ounces) sliced ripe olives, drained
  2 packages (8 ounces *each*) imitation crabmeat, flaked

Cook pasta according to package directions. Meanwhile, in a large skillet, saute the onion, green pepper and celery in butter until tender.

In a large bowl, combine milk and mayonnaise until blended. Stir in the salt, mustard, paprika and Worcestershire sauce. Drain pasta; add the pasta, olives, crab and vegetables to milk mixture.

Transfer to a greased shallow 2-qt. baking dish. Cover and bake at 350° for 25 minutes. Uncover; bake 5-10 minutes longer or until heated through. **yield: 6 servings.**

salmon supper

prep/total time: 30 min.

With a husband and four children to cook for, I'm always on the lookout for quick recipes. This recipe was given to me many years ago by my mother-in-law. It's one my family asks me to make time and again.
—*Debra Knippel, Medford, Wisconsin*

- 1/3 cup chopped green pepper
- 3 tablespoons chopped onion
- 2 tablespoons canola oil
- 1/4 cup all-purpose flour
- 1/2 teaspoon salt
- 1-1/2 cups 2% milk
- 1 can (10-3/4 ounces) condensed cream of celery soup, undiluted
- 2 pouches (3 ounces *each*) boneless skinless pink salmon
- 1 cup frozen peas
- 2 teaspoons lemon juice
- 1 tube (8 ounces) refrigerated crescent rolls

In a large skillet, saute green pepper and onion in oil for 3-4 minutes or until crisp-tender.

In a small bowl, combine the flour, salt, milk and soup until blended. Add to the skillet. Bring to a boil. Reduce heat; cook and stir for 2 minutes or until smooth. Stir in the salmon, peas and lemon juice.

Pour into an ungreased 11-in. x 7-in. baking dish. Do not unroll crescent dough; cut into eight equal slices. Arrange over salmon mixture.

Bake, uncovered, at 375° for 10-12 minutes or until golden brown. **yield: 4 servings.**

cheesy clam manicotti

prep: 30 min. • bake: 25 min.

I created this recipe when I was having company and couldn't decide whether to serve seafood or Italian. It was a big hit! I usually add a little extra hot sauce to give it a special kick.
—*Kathy Kysar, Homer, Alaska*

- 1 jar (26 ounces) meatless spaghetti sauce
- 1/4 teaspoon hot pepper sauce
- 2 cans (6-1/2 ounces *each*) minced clams
- 1 carton (8 ounces) ricotta cheese
- 4 ounces cream cheese, softened
- 1/4 cup spreadable chive and onion cream cheese
- 2 cups (8 ounces) shredded part-skim mozzarella cheese
- 1/3 cup grated Parmesan cheese
- 1 teaspoon minced garlic
- 1/2 teaspoon pepper
- 1/4 teaspoon dried oregano
- 8 manicotti shells, cooked and drained

In a large saucepan, combine spaghetti sauce and hot pepper sauce. Drain one can of clams; add clams to sauce. Stir in clams and juice from second can. Bring to a boil. Reduce heat; simmer, uncovered, for 20 minutes.

Meanwhile, in a large bowl, beat ricotta and cream cheeses until smooth. Stir in the cheeses, garlic, pepper and oregano. Stuff into manicotti shells.

Spread 3/4 cup clam sauce into a greased 11-in. x 7-in. baking dish. Arrange manicotti over sauce; top with remaining sauce.

Bake, uncovered, at 350° for 25-30 minutes or until bubbly. Let stand for 5 minutes before serving. **yield: 4 servings.**

blend of the bayou

prep: 20 min. • bake: 25 min.

My sister-in-law shared this recipe when I first moved to Louisiana. It's been handed down in my husband's family for generations, and I've passed it on to my children, too.
—Ruby Williams, Bogalusa, Louisiana

- 1 package (8 ounces) cream cheese, cubed
- 4 tablespoons butter, *divided*
- 1 large onion, chopped
- 2 celery ribs, chopped
- 1 large green pepper, chopped
- 1 pound cooked medium shrimp, peeled and deveined
- 2 cans (6 ounces *each*) crabmeat, drained, flaked and cartilage removed
- 1 can (10-3/4 ounces) condensed cream of mushroom soup, undiluted
- 3/4 cup cooked rice
- 1 jar (4-1/2 ounces) sliced mushrooms, drained
- 1 teaspoon garlic salt
- 3/4 teaspoon hot pepper sauce
- 1/2 teaspoon cayenne pepper
- 3/4 cup shredded cheddar cheese
- 1/2 cup crushed butter-flavored crackers (about 12 crackers)

In a small saucepan, cook and stir cream cheese and 2 tablespoons butter over low heat until melted and smooth; set aside.

In a large skillet, saute the onion, celery and green pepper in remaining butter until tender. Stir in the shrimp, crab, soup, rice, mushrooms, garlic salt, pepper sauce, cayenne and reserved cream cheese mixture.

Transfer to a greased 2-qt. baking dish. Combine cheddar cheese and cracker crumbs; sprinkle over the top. Bake, uncovered, at 350° for 25-30 minutes or until bubbly. **yield: 6-8 servings.**

creamy seafood casserole

prep: 15 min. • bake: 25 min.

I love this recipe from my mother. It's easy and delicious and can be made the night before, then popped in the oven the next day. Crushed potato chips or french-fried onions make other crunchy topping options.
—Mary Brown
Whitman, Massachusetts

- 1 pound flounder fillets, cut into 1-1/2-inch pieces
- 1 pound uncooked medium shrimp, peeled and deveined
- 1 can (10-3/4 ounces) condensed cream of shrimp soup, undiluted
- 1/4 cup 2% milk
- 1 cup crushed butter-flavored crackers (about 25 crackers)
- 1/4 cup grated Parmesan cheese
- 1 teaspoon paprika
- 2 tablespoons butter, melted

Arrange fish and shrimp in a greased 11-in. x 7-in. baking dish. Combine soup and milk; pour over seafood. Combine the cracker crumbs, cheese, paprika and butter; sprinkle over top.

Bake, uncovered, at 350° for 25-30 minutes or until fish flakes easily with a fork and shrimp turn pink. **yield: 6-8 servings.**

spanish corn with fish sticks

prep: 20 min. • bake: 40 min.

With fish sticks, corn and a tomato-based sauce, this meal in one appeals to most kids, and you can tend to other things while it bakes. This is my old standby for social functions.
—Roberta Nelson, Portland, Oregon

- 1/4 cup chopped onion
- 1/4 cup chopped green pepper
- 1/4 cup butter, cubed
- 1/4 cup all-purpose flour
- 1-1/2 teaspoons salt
- 1/4 teaspoon pepper
- 2 teaspoons sugar
- 2 cans (14-1/2 ounces *each*) stewed tomatoes
- 2 packages (10 ounces *each*) frozen corn, partially thawed
- 2 packages (12 ounces *each*) frozen fish sticks

In a large skillet, saute onion and green pepper in butter until tender. Stir in the flour, salt, pepper and sugar until blended. Add tomatoes; bring to a boil. Cook and stir for 2 minutes or until thickened. Reduce heat; simmer, uncovered, for 3-5 minutes or heated through, stirring occasionally. Stir in the corn.

Transfer to two greased 11-in. x 7-in. baking dishes. Cover and bake at 350° for 25 minutes. Uncover; arrange fish sticks over the top. Bake 15 minutes longer or until fish sticks are heated through. **yield: 8-10 servings.**

baked sole and spinach

prep: 25 min. • bake: 30 min.

This crunched-for-time casserole can be fixed from start to finish in less than an hour. A cheesy pasta layer is topped with sole fillets, spinach and slivered almonds to make a meal that's a delicious change of pace.
—Anna Fuery, Taftville, Connecticut

- 1 package (8 ounces) egg noodles
- 3 tablespoons butter
- 3 tablespoons all-purpose flour
- 3 cups 2% milk
- 1-1/2 cups (6 ounces) shredded cheddar cheese, *divided*
- 1 tablespoon lemon juice
- 1 teaspoon salt
- 1 teaspoon ground mustard
- 1 teaspoon Worcestershire sauce
- 1/8 teaspoon ground nutmeg
- 1/8 teaspoon pepper
- 2 packages (10 ounces *each*) frozen chopped spinach, thawed and squeezed dry
- 1-1/2 pounds sole fillets
- 1/4 cup slivered almonds, toasted

Cook noodles according to package directions. Meanwhile, in a large saucepan, melt butter. Stir in flour until smooth; gradually add milk. Bring to a boil; cook and stir for 2 minutes or until thickened.

Stir in 1 cup cheese, lemon juice, salt, mustard, Worcestershire sauce, nutmeg and pepper until cheese is melted. Set aside half of the cheese sauce. Drain noodles; add to the remaining sauce.

Transfer to a greased 13-in. x 9-in. baking dish. Layer with spinach, sole, reserved cheese sauce and remaining cheese; sprinkle with almonds.

Bake, uncovered, at 375° for 30-35 minutes or until fish flakes easily with a fork. **yield: 6 servings.**

KITCHEN TIP

To keep lumps from forming in a sauce, it is important to stir the flour into the melted butter until completely smooth. Once the milk is added, stir or whisk constantly to prevent any scorching on the bottom of the pan and to keep the sauce smooth.

tasty tuna casserole

prep: 20 min. • bake: 25 min.

Looking for a different tuna casserole? The macaroni and tuna in this recipe are coated in a creamy sauce made from reduced-fat cream cheese, tomato sauce and a dash of oregano.
—Elsie Epp, Newton, Kansas

- 2 cups uncooked elbow macaroni
- 1 can (12 ounces) white water-packed solid tuna
- 1 can (8 ounces) tomato sauce
- 4 ounces reduced-fat cream cheese, cubed
- 1 small onion, finely chopped
- 1/4 teaspoon salt
- 1/2 teaspoon dried oregano

Cook macaroni according to package directions. Meanwhile, in a large bowl, combine the remaining ingredients. Drain macaroni; stir into tuna mixture.

Transfer to a 2-qt. baking dish coated with cooking spray. Cover and bake at 350° for 20-25 minutes or until heated through. **yield: 4 servings.**

individual seafood casseroles

prep: 25 min. • bake: 20 min.

My husband can't get enough of these mini casseroles and is disappointed when there aren't leftovers. This dish is a mainstay on my holiday menus.
—Jaelynne Smigel
  Vancouver, British Columbia

- 1/3 cup chopped onion
- 1/3 cup butter, cubed
- 1/3 cup all-purpose flour
- 1/2 teaspoon salt
- 1/2 teaspoon white pepper
- 1 cup 2% milk
- 1 cup heavy whipping cream
- 3 tablespoons *each* finely chopped sweet red and green pepper
- 2 teaspoons curry powder
- 1 teaspoon ground mustard
- 1/4 teaspoon *each* ground ginger, ground turmeric and dried thyme
- 1/2 teaspoon lemon juice
- 3 to 5 drops hot pepper sauce
- 3 cans (6 ounces *each*) crabmeat, drained, flaked and cartilage removed
- 1 can (6 ounces) tuna, drained and flaked
- 1/4 pound cooked medium shrimp, peeled and deveined
- 2 hard-cooked eggs, chopped

TOPPING:

- 1/2 cup shredded cheddar cheese
- 1/4 cup dry bread crumbs
- 1/4 teaspoon garlic powder
- 1 tablespoon *each* chopped sweet red and green pepper

In a large saucepan, saute onion in butter until tender. Stir in flour, salt and pepper until blended. Gradually whisk in milk and cream. Bring to a boil; cook and stir for 2 minutes or until thickened and bubbly. Stir in the peppers, seasonings, lemon juice and pepper sauce until blended.

Remove from the heat; add the crab, tuna, shrimp and eggs. Transfer to six greased ovenproof 10-oz. dishes.

In a small bowl, combine the cheese, bread crumbs and garlic powder. Sprinkle over seafood mixture.

Bake, uncovered, at 350° for 15 minutes. Sprinkle with peppers. Bake 5-8 minutes longer or until heated through and edges are bubbly. **yield: 6 servings.**

creamy seafood-stuffed shells

prep: 40 min. • bake: 30 min.

Inspired by my love of lasagna, pasta shells and seafood, I created this recipe that's easy to make but special enough to serve company. I serve it with garlic bread and a salad for a complete meal.
—Katie Sloan, Charlotte, North Carolina

- 24 uncooked jumbo pasta shells
- 1 tablespoon finely chopped green pepper
- 1 tablespoon chopped red onion
- 1 teaspoon plus 1/4 cup butter, *divided*
- 2 cans (6 ounces *each*) lump crabmeat, drained
- 1 package (5 ounces) frozen cooked salad shrimp, thawed
- 1 egg, lightly beaten
- 1/2 cup shredded part-skim mozzarella cheese
- 1/4 cup mayonnaise
- 2 tablespoons plus 4 cups milk, *divided*
- 1-1/2 teaspoons seafood seasoning, *divided*
- 1/4 teaspoon pepper
- 1/4 cup all-purpose flour
- 1/4 teaspoon coarsely ground pepper
- 1-1/2 cups grated Parmesan cheese

Cook pasta according to package directions. Meanwhile, in a small skillet, saute green pepper and onion in 1 teaspoon butter until tender; set aside.

In a large bowl, combine the crab, shrimp, egg, mozzarella cheese, mayonnaise, 2 tablespoons milk, 1 teaspoon seafood seasoning, pepper and green pepper mixture.

Drain and rinse pasta; stuff each shell with 1 rounded tablespoon of seafood mixture. Place in a greased 13-in. x 9-in. baking dish.

In a small saucepan, melt remaining butter over medium heat. Whisk in flour and coarsely ground pepper; gradually whisk in remaining milk. Bring to a boil; cook and stir for 2 minutes or until thickened. Stir in Parmesan cheese.

Pour over stuffed shells. Sprinkle with remaining seafood seasoning. Bake, uncovered, at 350° for 30-35 minutes or until bubbly. **yield: 8 servings.**

spinach tuna casserole

prep: 25 min. • bake: 50 min.

This thick, gooey tuna-spinach bake has been a family favorite for years.
—Karla Hamrick, Wapakoneta, Ohio

- 5 cups uncooked egg noodles
- 2 cups (16 ounces) sour cream
- 1-1/2 cups mayonnaise
- 2 to 3 teaspoons lemon juice
- 2 to 3 teaspoons 2% milk
- 1/4 teaspoon salt
- 1 package (10 ounces) frozen chopped spinach, thawed and squeezed dry
- 1 package (6 ounces) chicken stuffing mix
- 1/3 cup seasoned bread crumbs
- 1 can (6 ounces) tuna, drained and flaked
- 3 tablespoons grated Parmesan cheese

Cook noodles according to package directions. In a bowl, combine sour cream, mayonnaise, lemon juice, milk and salt. Stir in spinach, stuffing mix, bread crumbs and tuna until combined.

Drain noodles and place in a greased 13-in. x 9-in. baking dish. Top with tuna mixture; sprinkle with cheese. Cover and bake at 350° for 45 minutes. Uncover; bake 5-10 minutes longer or until lightly browned and heated through. **yield: 8 servings.**

meatless

When you're not in the mood for beef, chicken or pork, or if you're looking for something a little different, turn to these recipes for some exceptional fare. These dishes are so hearty and satisfying, you won't even miss the meat.

« pictured left

mostaccioli bake

prep: 15 min. • bake: 40 min.

This homey lasagna-style casserole will appeal to the whole family. There's plenty of spaghetti sauce to keep the layers of tender pasta and spinach-cheese mixture moist.
—Dorothy Bateman, Carver, Massachusetts

        8 ounces uncooked mostaccioli
        1 egg
        1 egg white
        2 cups (16 ounces) 1% cottage cheese
        1 package (10 ounces) frozen chopped spinach, thawed and squeezed dry
        1 cup (4 ounces) shredded part-skim mozzarella cheese, *divided*
    2/3 cup shredded Parmesan cheese, *divided*
    1/3 cup minced fresh parsley
    1/4 teaspoon salt
    1/4 teaspoon pepper
 2-1/2 cups meatless spaghetti sauce, *divided*

Cook pasta according to package directions. Meanwhile, in a large bowl, combine the egg, egg white, cottage cheese, spinach, 2/3 cup mozzarella cheese, 1/3 cup Parmesan cheese, parsley, salt and pepper; set aside. Drain pasta; stir in 2 cups spaghetti sauce.

Layer half of the pasta mixture in a greased 11-in. x 7-in. baking dish coated with cooking spray. Layer with spinach mixture, remaining pasta mixture and remaining spaghetti sauce.

Cover and bake at 350° for 35-40 minutes or until bubbly. Uncover; sprinkle with the remaining mozzarella and Parmesan cheeses. Bake 5 minutes longer or until cheese is melted. **yield: 8 servings.**

KITCHEN TIP

Artichokes are used in meatless entrees for the meaty quality of their dense, thick heart. They also add a slight nutty flavor to dishes. For best flavor, rinse canned artichoke hearts before using.

four-vegetable bake

prep: 20 min. • bake: 20 min.

Several members of my family enjoy meatless dishes, and I'm partial to casseroles, so this tasty dish pleases everyone. It lets the goodness of the veggies come through.
—Ruby Williams, Bogalusa, Louisiana

        3 medium zucchini, cut into 1/4-inch slices
        1 pound sliced fresh mushrooms
        1 medium onion, chopped
    1/2 cup chopped green onions
        8 tablespoons butter, *divided*
    1/4 cup all-purpose flour
        1 cup 2% milk
        1 can (14 ounces) water-packed artichoke hearts, rinsed, drained and quartered
    3/4 cup shredded Swiss cheese
    1/2 teaspoon salt
    1/4 teaspoon pepper
    3/4 cup seasoned bread crumbs

In a skillet, saute zucchini, mushrooms and onions in 3 tablespoons butter until zucchini is crisp-tender; remove and set aside.

In the same skillet, melt 3 tablespoons butter. Stir in flour until smooth. Gradually stir in milk until blended. Bring to a boil; cook and stir for 2 minutes or until thickened. Stir in the zucchini mixture, artichokes, cheese, salt and pepper.

Transfer to a greased 11-in. x 7-in. baking dish. Melt remaining butter; toss with bread crumbs. Sprinkle over the top. Bake, uncovered, at 350° for 20-25 minutes or until bubbly and the topping is lightly browned. **yield: 8 servings.**

brown rice casserole

prep: 30 min. • bake: 35 min.

This hearty dish even passes the test for teenage boys. It is packed with vegetables, nicely seasoned and has a sprinkling of cheddar on top. The brown rice really fills them up.
—*Glenda Schwarz, Morden, Manitoba*

- 8 cups water
- 1-1/2 cups uncooked brown rice
- 1 cup dry split peas
- 1 cup chopped fresh mushrooms
- 2 celery ribs, chopped
- 2 medium carrots, grated
- 1 medium onion, chopped
- 1 tablespoon canola oil
- 2 garlic cloves, minced
- 1 can (14-1/2 ounces) diced tomatoes, undrained
- 1/2 to 1 teaspoon salt
- 1/2 to 1 teaspoon dried thyme
- 1/2 to 1 teaspoon dried oregano
- 1/2 to 1 teaspoon pepper
- 1 cup (4 ounces) shredded cheddar cheese

In a large saucepan, bring water, rice and peas to a boil. Reduce heat; cover and simmer for 20-25 minutes or until tender. Drain and set aside.

In a large skillet, saute mushrooms, celery, carrots and onion in oil until vegetables are tender. Add garlic; cook 1 minute longer. Combine the vegetables, rice mixture, tomatoes and seasonings.

Transfer to a greased 2-1/2-qt. baking dish. Cover and bake at 350° for 30 minutes or until bubbly. Uncover; sprinkle with cheese. Bake 5-10 minutes longer or until the cheese is melted. **yield: 9 servings.**

broccoli rice hot dish

prep: 15 min. • bake: 25 min.

With green broccoli, golden cheese and sweet red peppers, this bountiful rice bake has plenty of eye appeal, and it makes a tasty and satisfying meatless supper.
—*Gretchen Widner, Sun City West, Arizona*

- 2 cups hot cooked rice
- 3/4 cup shredded reduced-fat cheddar cheese
- 1/2 cup egg substitute
- 3/4 teaspoon garlic salt

FILLING:

- 3 cups frozen chopped broccoli, thawed
- 4 ounces chopped fresh mushrooms
- 1/2 cup chopped sweet red pepper
- 1/2 medium onion, chopped
- 1 cup egg substitute
- 1/2 cup fat-free milk
- 1/2 teaspoon onion salt
- 1/2 teaspoon pepper
- 1 cup (4 ounces) shredded reduced-fat cheddar cheese

In a large bowl, combine the rice, cheese, egg substitute and garlic salt. Press firmly into a 2-qt. baking dish coated with cooking spray. Bake at 375° for 10 minutes.

Meanwhile, place the broccoli, mushrooms, red pepper and onion in a steamer basket over 1 in. boiling water in a saucepan. Bring to a boil; cover and steam for 5 minutes or until crisp-tender.

In a large bowl, combine the egg substitute, milk, onion salt and pepper; stir in vegetables. Pour over crust. Sprinkle with cheese. Bake, uncovered, at 375° for 25-30 minutes or until a knife inserted near the center comes out clean. **yield: 6 servings.**

italian cheese-stuffed shells

prep: 1 hour • bake: 50 min.

I found this recipe in a church cookbook and thought it was a great twist on traditional lasagna. I omitted the meat, and it's just as yummy. Italian stewed tomatoes add robust flavor.
—Patty Tappendorf, Galesville, Wisconsin

- 1 medium onion, chopped
- 1/2 cup chopped green pepper
- 1/2 cup chopped sweet red pepper
- 1/2 pound sliced fresh mushrooms
- 2 garlic cloves, minced
- 1-1/2 cups water
- 1 can (14-1/2 ounces) Italian stewed tomatoes
- 1 can (6 ounces) tomato paste
- 1-1/2 teaspoons Italian seasoning
- 2 eggs, lightly beaten
- 1 carton (15 ounces) reduced-fat ricotta cheese
- 2 cups (8 ounces) shredded part-skim mozzarella cheese, *divided*
- 1/2 cup grated Parmesan cheese
- 21 jumbo pasta shells, cooked and drained

In a large nonstick skillet coated with cooking spray, cook onion and peppers over medium heat for 2 minutes. Add mushrooms; cook 4-5 minutes until tender. Add garlic; cook 1 minute longer Stir in the water, tomatoes, tomato paste and Italian seasoning. Bring to a boil. Reduce heat; cover and simmer for 30 minutes.

Meanwhile, in a small bowl, combine the eggs, ricotta, 1/2 cup mozzarella and Parmesan cheeses. Stuff into shells. Spread 1 cup vegetable sauce in a 13-in. x 9-in. baking dish coated with cooking spray. Arrange shells over sauce; top with remaining sauce.

Cover and bake at 350° for 45 minutes. Uncover; sprinkle with remaining mozzarella. Bake 5-10 minutes longer or until bubbly and cheese is melted. Let stand for 5 minutes before serving. **yield: 7 servings.**

five-cheese stuffed shells

prep: 15 min. • bake: 40 min.

These yummy stuffed pasta shells will make any luncheon special. I experimented with various cheeses, herbs and spices until I found that just-right blend. Try adding chopped walnuts for a little crunch.
—Wendy Lee Guerin
   Fridley, Minnesota

- 20 uncooked jumbo pasta shells
- 2 cups cooked chopped spinach
- 1 cup (8 ounces) fat-free cottage cheese
- 1 cup part-skim ricotta cheese
- 4 slices reduced-fat provolone cheese, finely chopped
- 1/2 cup shredded Parmesan cheese
- 1/2 cup shredded Romano cheese
- 1 egg, lightly beaten
- 2 garlic cloves, minced
- 1 teaspoon Italian seasoning
- 1/2 teaspoon salt
- Dash pepper
- 1 jar (26 ounces) meatless spaghetti sauce

Cook pasta according to package directions; drain. In a large bowl, combine the next 11 ingredients; spoon into shells.

Arrange in a 13-in. x 9-in. baking dish coated with cooking spray. Pour spaghetti sauce over all. Cover and bake at 350° for 40-45 minutes or until heated through. **yield: 10 servings.**

cheesy broccoli rigatoni

prep: 15 min. • bake: 25 min.

This cheese-and-veggie-packed pasta dish always brings compliments. I've also added chicken and shrimp to the mixture. The tasty white sauce can be used on many foods. My husband even likes it spooned over eggs!
—Lisa Csiki, North Windham, Connecticut

- 12 ounces uncooked rigatoni *or* large tube pasta
- 3 garlic cloves, minced
- 1/4 cup butter, cubed
- 1/4 cup all-purpose flour
- 1 teaspoon salt
- 1 tablespoon olive oil
- 2-1/2 cups fat-free milk
- 5 cups fresh broccoli florets
- 2 cups (8 ounces) shredded part-skim mozzarella cheese, *divided*

Cook pasta according to package directions. Meanwhile, in a large saucepan, saute garlic in butter over medium heat for 1 minute. Stir in flour and salt until blended. Gradually add milk. Bring to a boil; cook and stir for 2 minutes or until thickened. Remove from the heat; set aside. Drain pasta and toss with oil; set aside.

In a large saucepan, bring 1 in. of water and broccoli to a boil. Reduce heat; cover and simmer for 5-8 minutes or until crisp-tender. Drain and rinse with cold water.

In a 13-in. x 9-in. baking dish coated with cooking spray, layer 1 cup white sauce, half of the pasta and broccoli and 1/2 cup cheese. Repeat layers. Top with remaining sauce and cheese.

Cover and bake at 350° for 25-30 minutes or until heated through. **yield: 10 servings.**

southwest corn bread bake

prep/total time: 30 min.

Warm up chilly nights with this hearty meatless dish. It's loaded with beans and corn, then topped with a from-scratch corn bread. We usually double the ingredients, place it in a 9x13 baking dish and bake it for a bit longer.
—Duane and Christine Geyer, Coralville, Iowa

- 1 can (16 ounces) chili beans, undrained
- 1 can (8-3/4 ounces) whole kernel corn, drained
- 2 tablespoons chopped onion
- 1/2 teaspoon ground cumin
- 1/2 cup all-purpose flour
- 1/2 cup cornmeal
- 2 tablespoons sugar
- 1-1/4 teaspoons baking powder
- 1/4 teaspoon salt
- 1/2 cup plus 1 tablespoon milk
- 1-1/2 teaspoons canola oil

In a large bowl, combine the chili beans, corn, onion and cumin. Transfer to an 8-in. square baking dish coated with cooking spray.

In another bowl, combine the dry ingredients. Combine milk and oil; stir into dry ingredients just until moistened.

Drop by tablespoons over chili mixture; carefully spread over the top. Bake, uncovered, at 350° for 20-25 minutes or until golden brown. **yield: 4 servings.**

asparagus breakfast strata

prep: 15 min. + chilling • bake: 1 hour

Filled with tasty ingredients like mushrooms, cheddar cheese and asparagus, this dish makes for hearty fare. You can prepare it the night before for a no-fuss breakfast, brunch or dish to pass.
—Maryellen Hays
  Fort Wayne, Indiana

- 3 cups fat-free milk
- 2 cups egg substitute
- 1 tablespoon Dijon mustard
- 2 teaspoons dried basil
- 1 teaspoon salt
- 2 tablespoons butter, melted
- 2 tablespoons all-purpose flour
- 2 cups (8 ounces) shredded reduced-fat cheddar cheese
- 1 package (10 ounces) frozen cut asparagus, thawed *or* 2 cups cut fresh asparagus, cooked
- 2 cups sliced fresh mushrooms
- 10 cups cubed reduced-calorie bread

In a large bowl, beat the milk, egg substitute, mustard and basil. Gently stir in remaining ingredients.

Pour into a 13-in. x 9-in. baking dish coated with cooking spray. Cover and refrigerate 8 hours or overnight.

Remove from the refrigerator 30 minutes before baking. Bake, uncovered, at 350° for 1 hour or until a knife inserted near the center comes out clean. Let stand 5 minutes before cutting. **yield: 12 servings.**

baked lentils with cheese

prep: 10 min. • bake: 65 min.

Onions, garlic, tomatoes, green pepper and several herbs and spices give a hearty punch to this cheesy bean dish. These are the only beans my family will eat anymore.
—Pamela Ulrich
    Charlottesville, Virginia

2-1/4 cups water
1-3/4 cups dried lentils, rinsed
  1 cup chopped onion
  2 medium carrots, thinly sliced
1/2 cup thinly sliced celery
  2 garlic cloves, minced
  1 teaspoon salt
1/4 teaspoon pepper
1/8 teaspoon dried marjoram
1/8 teaspoon rubbed sage
1/8 teaspoon dried thyme
  1 bay leaf
  2 cups chopped fresh tomatoes
1/2 cup finely chopped green pepper
  2 tablespoons minced fresh parsley
2-1/2 cups (10 ounces) shredded reduced-fat cheddar cheese

In a 13-in. x 9-in. baking dish, combine the first 12 ingredients. Cover and bake at 350° for 45 minutes.

Stir in the tomatoes and green pepper. Cover and bake 15 minutes longer. Sprinkle with parsley and cheese. Bake, uncovered, for 5-10 minutes or until cheese is melted. Discard bay leaf. **yield: 8 servings.**

vegetarian enchilada bake

prep: 20 min. • bake: 20 min. + standing

I've had this budget-friendly vegetarian recipe for years. You'll enjoy the delicious Tex-Mex flavors, and you won't even miss the meat.
—Barbara Stelluto, Devon, Pennsylvania

  1 cup shredded zucchini
  1 tablespoon finely chopped sweet red pepper
  1 teaspoon olive oil
  1 garlic clove, minced
3/4 cup frozen corn
3/4 cup black beans, rinsed and drained
1/8 teaspoon salt
1/8 teaspoon ground cumin
3/4 cup salsa
  2 tablespoons minced fresh cilantro
  3 corn tortillas (6 inches)
3/4 cup shredded cheddar cheese
Sour cream, optional

In a large skillet, saute zucchini and pepper in oil until pepper is crisp-tender. Add garlic; cook 1 minute longer. Add the corn, beans, salt and cumin; saute 2-3 minutes longer. Stir in salsa and cilantro.

Place a tortilla in the bottom of a 1-1/2-qt. round baking dish coated with cooking spray. Spread with 2/3 cup vegetable mixture; sprinkle with 1/4 cup cheese. Repeat layers twice.

Bake, uncovered, at 350° for 20-25 minutes or until heated through and cheese is melted. Let stand for 10 minutes before serving. Serve with sour cream if desired. **yield: 3 servings.**

upside-down meatless pizza

prep: 25 min. • bake: 20 min.

I experimented with a recipe for upside-down pizza and made it into a meatless dish. It turned out very tasty.

—Marie Figueroa, Wauwatosa, Wisconsin

- 1 small onion, chopped
- 1/4 cup chopped green pepper
- 3 tablespoons canola oil, *divided*
- 2 tablespoons plus 1 cup all-purpose flour, *divided*
- 1/2 teaspoon dried basil
- 1/2 teaspoon fennel seed
- 1 package (10 ounces) frozen chopped spinach, thawed and squeezed dry
- 1 cup sliced fresh mushrooms
- 1 can (15 ounces) tomato sauce
- 2 cups (8 ounces) shredded cheddar cheese
- 2 eggs
- 3/4 cup 2% milk
- 1/2 teaspoon salt
- 2 tablespoons grated Parmesan cheese

In a large skillet, saute onion and green pepper in 2 tablespoons oil until tender. Stir in 2 tablespoons flour, basil and fennel until blended. Add the spinach, mushrooms and tomato sauce. Bring to a boil; cook and stir for 2 minutes or until thickened.

Pour into a greased 11-in. x 7-in. baking dish. Sprinkle with cheddar cheese. Place the remaining flour in a large bowl. Whisk the eggs, milk, salt and remaining oil until smooth. Stir in Parmesan cheese. Pour over vegetable mixture.

Bake, uncovered, at 425° for 20-25 minutes or until a thermometer reads 160°. **yield: 8 servings.**

artichoke spinach shells

prep: 15 min. • bake: 30 min.

I found this recipe in a magazine years ago. If you're looking for a vegetarian meal, it's wonderful as the main course. We like to serve it with hot dinner rolls and a salad.

—Rachel Balsamo, Lewiston, Maine

- 4 cups uncooked medium pasta shells
- 10 ounces fresh spinach, chopped
- 3 cups (12 ounces) shredded cheddar cheese
- 1 can (14-1/2 ounces) Italian stewed tomatoes
- 1 can (14 ounces) water-packed artichoke hearts, rinsed, drained and quartered
- 1 cup (8 ounces) sour cream
- 1/2 teaspoon garlic salt

In a Dutch oven, cook pasta according to package directions for 5 minutes. Add spinach; cook, uncovered, for 6-8 minutes or until pasta is tender. Drain. In a large bowl, combine the remaining ingredients. Stir in pasta mixture.

Transfer to a 3-qt. baking dish. Bake, uncovered, at 350° for 30-35 minutes or until heated through. **yield: 6-8 servings.**

zippy strata

prep: 15 min. + chilling
bake: 1-1/4 hours + standing

The taste of this sandwich bake will remind you of pizza. Red tomatoes add color and cayenne delivers the zip.
—Jean Parè, Vermilion, Alberta

- 12 slices white bread, *divided*
- 6 slices process mozzarella cheese
- 15 thin slices tomato
- 1 can (8 ounces) mushroom stems and pieces, drained
- 3 tablespoons dried minced onion
- 1/4 cup all-purpose flour
- 3/4 teaspoon dried oregano
- 1/2 teaspoon salt
- 1/2 teaspoon dried basil
- 1/4 teaspoon garlic powder
- 1/4 teaspoon cayenne pepper
- 1/8 teaspoon pepper
- 3 cups 2% milk
- 5 eggs, lightly beaten
- 1/2 cup grated Parmesan cheese

Line a greased 13-in. x 9-in. baking dish with 6 bread slices. Layer with mozzarella cheese, tomato, mushrooms, minced onion and remaining bread.

In a large bowl, combine the flour, seasonings, milk and eggs until smooth. Pour over bread; sprinkle with Parmesan cheese. Cover and refrigerate overnight.

Remove from the refrigerator 30 minutes before baking. Uncover; bake at 325° for 1-1/4 hours or until a knife inserted near the center comes out clean. Let stand for 10 minutes before cutting. **yield: 6-12 servings.**

three-bean cassoulet

prep: 5 min. • bake: 1 hour

Brimming with a trio of bean varieties, this is as easy as one, two, three. It makes a satisfying meatless main dish. The veggies add an interesting mix of tastes, colors and textures.
—Carol Berigan, Golden, Colorado

- 2 cans (14-1/2 ounces *each*) stewed tomatoes
- 1 can (16 ounces) butter beans, rinsed and drained
- 1 can (15-1/2 ounces) great northern beans, rinsed and drained
- 1 can (15 ounces) garbanzo beans *or* chickpeas, rinsed and drained
- 1 cup finely chopped carrots
- 1 cup finely chopped onion
- 2 garlic cloves, minced
- 1 bay leaf
- 2 teaspoons dried parsley flakes
- 1 teaspoon dried basil
- 1/2 teaspoon salt
- 1/2 teaspoon dried thyme
- 1/8 teaspoon pepper

In an ungreased 3-qt. baking dish, combine all ingredients. Cover and bake at 350° for 60-70 minutes or until vegetables are tender, stirring occasionally. Discard bay leaf. **yield: 5 servings.**

over-the-top mac 'n' cheese

prep: 15 min. • bake: 40 min.

This fantastic bake is the ultimate comfort food. A blend of five cheeses, it makes a beautiful entree or a special side.
—Connie McDowell, Greenwood, Delaware

- 1 package (16 ounces) elbow macaroni
- 2 ounces Muenster cheese, shredded
- 1/2 cup *each* shredded mild cheddar, sharp cheddar and Monterey Jack cheese
- 1/2 cup plus 1 tablespoon butter, *divided*
- 2 cups half-and-half cream
- 2 eggs, lightly beaten
- 1 cup cubed process cheese (Velveeta)
- 1/4 teaspoon seasoned salt
- 1/8 teaspoon pepper

Cook macaroni according to package directions. Meanwhile, in a large bowl, combine the Muenster, cheddar and Monterey Jack cheeses; set aside.

In a large saucepan, melt 1/2 cup butter over medium heat. Stir in the cream, eggs, process cheese, seasoned salt, pepper and 1-1/2 cups of the cheese mixture. Drain pasta; add to the cheese sauce and stir to coat.

Transfer to a greased 2-1/2-qt. baking dish. Sprinkle with remaining cheese mixture and dot with remaining butter. Bake, uncovered, at 350° for 40-45 minutes or until a thermometer reads 160°. **yield: 7 servings.**

zesty rice 'n' bean casserole

prep: 35 min. • bake: 15 min.

A savory mix of seasonings adds zip to this dish that's loaded with beans, rice, vegetables and cheese. We enjoy it as a light entree with garlic bread and fresh spinach salad.
—Daphne Blandford
  Gander, Newfoundland and
  Labrador

- 2 medium green peppers, chopped
- 1-1/2 cups sliced fresh mushrooms
- 1 medium onion, chopped
- 1/2 cup water
- 1 teaspoon canola oil
- 2 garlic cloves, minced
- 1 can (28 ounces) diced tomatoes, undrained
- 1 can (16 ounces) kidney beans, rinsed and drained
- 3/4 cup uncooked long grain rice
- 2 teaspoons ground cumin
- 1 teaspoon chili powder
- 1/4 teaspoon cayenne pepper
- 1 cup (4 ounces) shredded part-skim mozzarella cheese, *divided*

In a large nonstick skillet, saute the green peppers, mushrooms and onion in water and oil until onion is tender. Add garlic; cook 1 minute longer. Add the tomatoes, beans, rice and seasonings. Bring to a boil.

Reduce heat; cover and simmer for 25 minutes or until rice is tender and most of the liquid is absorbed. Remove from the heat; stir in 1/2 cup cheese.

Transfer to a 2-1/2-qt. baking dish coated with cooking spray. Sprinkle with the remaining cheese. Bake, uncovered, at 350° for 15-20 minutes or until the cheese is melted. **yield: 8 servings.**

broccoli pasta bake

prep: 30 min. • bake: 45 min.

I came up with this recipe in the middle of broccoli season, using ingredients I had on hand. My family loves this light and pleasing casserole.
—*Evelyn Peterson, Corvallis, Montana*

- 12 ounces uncooked spaghetti
- 8 cups chopped fresh broccoli
- 2 cans (10-3/4 ounces *each*) reduced-fat reduced-sodium condensed cream of mushroom soup, undiluted
- 1/4 cup fat-free milk
- 2 cups sliced fresh mushrooms
- 1 medium onion, finely chopped
- 1 can (8 ounces) whole water chestnuts, drained, halved and thinly sliced
- 1 can (3.8 ounces) sliced ripe olives, drained
- 1 teaspoon salt
- 1/2 teaspoon pepper
- 2 cups (8 ounces) shredded reduced-fat cheddar cheese, *divided*
- 1/4 cup sunflower kernels

Cook spaghetti according to package directions for 7 minutes. Add broccoli; return to a boil. Cook 2 minutes longer or until spaghetti is tender; drain.

In a large bowl, combine soup and milk. Add the mushrooms, onion, water chestnuts, olives, salt, pepper and 1 cup cheese. Stir in spaghetti and broccoli.

Transfer to a 13-in. x 9-in. baking dish coated with cooking spray (dish will be full). Cover and bake at 350° for 40 minutes. Uncover; sprinkle with sunflower kernels and remaining cheese. Bake 5-10 minutes longer or until heated through and cheese is melted. **yield: 8 servings.**

italian zucchini bake

prep: 15 min. + standing • bake: 40 min.

Kids of all ages are sure to like this fun vegetarian spin on pizza! You can't even tell there's zucchini in this dish. If you have meat eaters in your family, try adding turkey pepperoni or sausage.
—*Carol Mieske, Red Bluff, California*

- 3-1/2 cups shredded zucchini
- 1/2 teaspoon salt
- 3/4 cup egg substitute
- 1/2 cup dry bread crumbs
- 1/4 cup all-purpose flour
- 2 teaspoons Italian seasoning
- 1/2 pound fresh mushrooms, sliced
- 2 teaspoons olive oil
- 1 can (15 ounces) pizza sauce, *divided*
- 3/4 cup chopped green pepper
- 1/4 cup sliced ripe olives, drained
- 1-1/2 cups (6 ounces) shredded part-skim mozzarella cheese, *divided*

Place zucchini in a colander over a plate; sprinkle with salt and toss. Let stand for 15 minutes. Rinse and drain well.

In a large bowl, combine the zucchini, egg substitute, bread crumbs, flour and Italian seasoning. Spread in an 11-in. x 7-in. baking dish coated with cooking spray. Bake, uncovered, at 350° for 25 minutes.

In a nonstick skillet, saute mushrooms in oil until crisp-tender. Spread half of the pizza sauce over zucchini mixture; sprinkle with the mushrooms, green pepper, olives and half of the cheese. Top with remaining pizza sauce and cheese. Bake 15 minutes longer or until hot and bubbly. **yield: 6 servings.**

KITCHEN TIP

Salting zucchini draws out its natural moisture. Once the liquid is drawn out, the salt is rinsed off to prevent the final dish from being too salty. Then it is drained well. Salting helps prevent the zucchini from watering out and making a recipe too soggy.

black bean cornmeal pie

prep: 30 min. • bake: 20 min.

This hearty, meatless Southwestern entree is delicious. If desired, you can vary the beans used. I like to serve it with salsa and reduced-fat sour cream.
—Tari Ambler, Shorewood, Illinois

    1 large onion, chopped
    1 large green pepper, chopped
    1 teaspoon canola oil
1-1/2 teaspoons chili powder
    1 garlic clove, minced
  3/4 teaspoon ground cumin
  1/4 teaspoon pepper
    1 can (14-1/2 ounces) diced tomatoes, undrained
    2 cans (15 ounces *each*) black beans, rinsed and drained
    1 cup frozen corn

TOPPING:
  3/4 cup whole wheat pastry flour
  3/4 cup yellow cornmeal
    2 teaspoons sugar
    2 teaspoons baking powder
    2 teaspoons chopped seeded jalapeno pepper
  1/4 teaspoon salt
    1 egg
  3/4 cup fat-free milk
    1 tablespoon canola oil
Salsa and reduced-fat sour cream, optional

In a large skillet, saute onion and green pepper in oil until tender. Add the chili powder, garlic, cumin and pepper; saute 1 minute longer. Add tomatoes and bring to a boil. Reduce heat; cover and simmer for 5 minutes.

Stir in beans and corn; heat through. Transfer to an 11-in. x 7-in. baking dish coated with cooking spray.

For topping, in a small bowl, combine the flour, cornmeal, sugar, baking powder, jalapeno and salt. Whisk the egg, milk and oil; stir into dry ingredients just until moistened. Spoon over filling; gently spread to cover the top.

Bake at 375° for 20-25 minutes or until filling is bubbly and a toothpick inserted into topping comes out clean. Serve with salsa and sour cream if desired. **yield: 6 servings.**

editor's note: We recommend wearing disposable gloves when cutting hot peppers. Avoid touching your face.

sides

Casseroles add pizzazz to plain vegetables, noodles and rice, making them fun to eat. Fussy eaters might not care for cauliflower, peas or beans, but watch them ask for seconds when the same veggies are baked in casseroles with rich, velvety sauces and crunchy toppings.

<< pictured left

dijon scalloped potatoes

prep: 25 min. • bake: 50 min. + standing

My family enjoys this creamy and colorful recipe for cheesy potatoes. What's not to love? It has both sweet and white potatoes, lots of rich, buttery flavor and a pretty golden-crumb topping.
—Carolyn Putnam, Norwalk, Ohio

- 2/3 cup chopped onion
- 2 teaspoons canola oil
- 1 can (14-1/2 ounces) chicken broth
- 2 packages (3 ounces *each*) cream cheese, cubed
- 1 tablespoon Dijon mustard
- 3 medium russet potatoes, peeled and thinly sliced
- 2 medium sweet potatoes, peeled and thinly sliced
- 1-1/2 to 2 cups crushed butter-flavored crackers
- 3 tablespoons grated Parmesan cheese
- 2 tablespoons butter, melted
- 2 teaspoons minced fresh parsley

In a Dutch oven, saute onion in oil until tender. Reduce heat to medium; stir in the broth, cream cheese and mustard until blended. Remove from the heat. Stir in the potatoes.

Transfer to a 13-in. x 9-in. baking dish coated with cooking spray. In a small bowl, combine the crushed crackers, cheese and butter; sprinkle over the top.

Bake, uncovered, at 350° for 50-60 minutes or until potatoes are tender. Sprinkle with parsley. Let stand for 10 minutes before serving. **yield: 8 servings.**

baked ratatouille

prep: 15 min. • bake: 50 min.

Ratatouille is usually a seasoned stew made of eggplant, tomatoes, green peppers, squash and sometimes meat. Bacon and cheese make my recipe exceptional. This version is heavenly when made with homegrown vegetables. It's so good, I sometimes make the casserole all for myself, then eat it for lunch a few days in a row.
—Catherine Lee, Chandler, Arizona

- 4 bacon strips, cut into 2-inch pieces
- 1 cup sliced onion
- 1 can (14-1/2 ounces) diced tomatoes, undrained
- 1/3 cup tomato paste
- 1/4 cup olive oil
- 1 large garlic clove, minced
- 1 teaspoon salt
- 1 teaspoon Italian seasoning
- 1 large eggplant (about 1-1/4 pounds), peeled and cubed
- 4 medium zucchini, sliced
- 1 large green pepper, cut into strips
- 8 to 12 ounces sliced Monterey Jack cheese

In a large skillet, cook bacon and onion over medium heat until bacon is crisp; drain. Stir in the tomatoes, tomato paste, oil, garlic, salt and Italian seasoning.

Spread half of the tomato mixture into a greased 13-in. x 9-in. baking dish. Layer with half of the eggplant, zucchini, green pepper and cheese. Repeat layers. Bake, uncovered, at 375° for 50-55 minutes or until hot and bubbly. **yield: 8 servings.**

spiced apple-carrot casserole

prep: 20 min. • bake: 35 min.

Fresh carrots and crisp apples combine for wonderful flavor in this unusual casserole with sugar-and-spice goodness. What a nice addition to a special meal!

—Barbara Waltz
  Cinnaminson, New Jersey

---

  2 cups sliced carrots
  1 tablespoon brown sugar
  1/4 teaspoon ground ginger
  1/8 teaspoon ground nutmeg
  3 medium apples, peeled and thinly sliced
  1 tablespoon butter

Place 1 in. of water in a saucepan; add carrots. Bring to a boil. Reduce heat; cover and simmer for 7-9 minutes or until crisp-tender. Drain. In a small bowl, combine the brown sugar, ginger and nutmeg.

In a greased 1-1/2-qt. baking dish, layer half of the apples and carrots. Sprinkle with half of the brown sugar mixture. Repeat the layers. Dot with the butter.

Cover and bake at 350° for 35-40 minutes or until apples are crisp-tender and carrots are tender. **yield: 6-8 servings.**

noodle pudding

prep: 20 min. • bake: 25 min.

Whenever I bring this creamy dish to gatherings, it always prompts recipe requests. The surprising sweet taste comes from apricot nectar, and everyone enjoys the golden buttery topping.

—Eileen Meyers, Scott Township, Pennsylvania

7-1/2 cups uncooked wide egg noodles
  1 package (8 ounces) cream cheese, softened
  6 tablespoons butter, softened
1/2 cup sugar
  3 eggs
  1 cup 2% milk
  1 cup apricot nectar
TOPPING:
  1 cup cornflake crumbs
1/2 cup sugar
  6 tablespoons butter, melted
1/2 teaspoon ground cinnamon

Cook noodles according to package directions. Meanwhile, in a large bowl, beat the cream cheese, butter and sugar until smooth. Beat in eggs. Gradually stir in milk and apricot nectar.

Drain noodles; place in a large bowl. Add cream cheese mixture and toss to coat. Transfer to a greased 13-in. x 9-in. baking dish.

Combine the topping ingredients; sprinkle over noodles. Bake, uncovered, at 350° for 25-30 minutes or until a thermometer reads 160°. **yield: 9 servings.**

almond cranberry squash bake

prep: 20 min. • bake: 50 min.

When my husband and I visit family in North Dakota, I bring along the ingredients to make this squash dish. It is very popular with my entire gang.
—Ronica Brownson, Madison, Wisconsin

- 4 cups mashed cooked butternut squash
- 4 tablespoons butter, softened, *divided*
- 1/2 teaspoon salt
- 1/2 teaspoon ground cinnamon
- 1/4 teaspoon ground allspice
- 1/4 teaspoon ground nutmeg
- 1 can (14 ounces) whole-berry cranberry sauce
- 1/2 cup sliced almonds
- 1/4 cup packed brown sugar

In a large bowl, combine the squash, 2 tablespoons butter, salt, cinnamon, allspice and nutmeg. Transfer to a greased 2-qt. baking dish. Stir cranberry sauce until softened; spoon over squash.

Combine the almonds, brown sugar and remaining butter; sprinkle over cranberry sauce.

Bake, uncovered, at 350° for 50-60 minutes or until golden brown and bubbly. **yield: 8 servings.**

cauliflower au gratin

prep: 20 min. • bake: 15 min.

I've found that even folks who aren't wild about cauliflower like it when it's dressed up with a delicious cheese sauce. This side dish is simple to fix but it feels like you fussed.

—Kathyrn Herman, Villisca, Iowa

- 1 medium head cauliflower (about 1-1/2 pounds), broken into florets
- 2 garlic cloves, minced
- 6 tablespoons butter, cubed
- 2 tablespoons all-purpose flour
- 1-1/2 cups 2% milk
- 4 bacon strips, cooked and crumbled
- 1/4 teaspoon salt
- 1/8 teaspoon pepper

Dash cayenne pepper

- 1 cup (4 ounces) shredded Swiss cheese

In a large saucepan, bring cauliflower and 1 in. of water to a boil. Reduce heat; cover and cook for 6-7 minutes or until crisp-tender. Drain well; set aside.

In another saucepan, saute garlic in butter for 1 minute. Stir in flour until blended; gradually add milk. Bring to a boil; cook and stir for 2 minutes or until thickened.

Remove from the heat; stir in the cauliflower, bacon, salt, pepper and cayenne. Pour into a greased 1-1/2-qt. baking dish. Sprinkle with cheese.

Bake, uncovered, at 400° for 15-20 minutes or until cheese is melted. **yield: 5-7 servings.**

buttery sweet potato casserole

prep: 15 min. • bake: 20 min.

Whenever we get together as a family for major holidays, my kids, nieces and nephews beg me to make this dish. It goes together in minutes with canned sweet potatoes, which is ideal for the busy holiday season.

—Sue Miller, Mars, Pennsylvania

- 2 cans (15-3/4 ounces *each*) sweet potatoes, drained and mashed
- 1/2 cup sugar
- 1 egg
- 1/4 cup butter, melted
- 1/2 teaspoon ground cinnamon

Dash salt

TOPPING:

- 1 cup coarsely crushed butter-flavored crackers (about 25 crackers)
- 1/2 cup packed brown sugar
- 1/4 cup butter, melted

In a large bowl, combine the first six ingredients. Transfer to a greased 8-in. square baking dish. Combine the topping ingredients; sprinkle over sweet potato mixture.

Bake, uncovered, at 350° for 20-25 minutes or until a thermometer reads 160°. **yield: 6-8 servings.**

cheesy broccoli cauliflower casserole

prep: 35 min. • bake: 25 min.

After I found this recipe in an old church cookbook, I adjusted it to make it lower in calories and fat. The velvety cheese sauce makes it a tasty way to get children to eat their vegetables.
—Nancy Whitford, Edwards, New York

- 1 tablespoon butter
- 4-1/2 teaspoons all-purpose flour
- 1-1/4 cups 1% milk
- 3/4 cup shredded reduced-fat cheddar cheese
- 1/3 cup grated Parmesan cheese
- 5 cups frozen broccoli florets, thawed
- 2-1/4 cups frozen cauliflowerets, thawed
- 1 cup cubed fully cooked lean ham
- 1 cup soft bread crumbs

Butter-flavored cooking spray

In a large saucepan, melt butter. Stir in flour until smooth; gradually add milk. Bring to a boil; cook and stir for 1-2 minutes or until thickened. Remove from the heat. Add cheeses; stir until melted.

Place vegetables in a 2-qt. baking dish coated with cooking spray; sprinkle with ham. Pour sauce over ham. Place bread crumbs in a small bowl; spray with butter-flavored spray. Sprinkle around the edge of casserole.

Bake, uncovered, at 350° for 25-30 minutes or until heated through and bubbly. **yield: 5 servings.**

herbed vegetable squares

prep: 30 min.
bake: 25 min. + standing

Flavorful veggies form the foundation of this colorful casserole. You can serve it as a side dish with beef or chicken or as an appetizer.
—Dorothy Pritchett, Wills Point, Texas

- 1 package (10 ounces) frozen chopped spinach, thawed and squeezed dry
- 2 tablespoons canola oil
- 1-1/2 cups chopped zucchini
- 1 package (9 ounces) frozen cut green beans, thawed
- 1 large onion, chopped
- 1/4 cup water
- 1 garlic clove, minced
- 1-1/2 teaspoons dried basil
- 1-1/2 teaspoons salt
- 1/8 teaspoon pepper
- 1/8 teaspoon ground nutmeg
- 4 eggs, lightly beaten
- 1/4 cup grated Parmesan cheese

Paprika

In a large skillet, saute spinach in oil for 2 minutes. Stir in the zucchini, beans, onion, water, garlic, basil, salt, pepper and nutmeg. Cover and simmer for 10 minutes, stirring occasionally. Remove from the heat.

In a small bowl, add eggs; gradually stir in 1-1/2 cups hot vegetable mixture. Return all to pan and mix well. Transfer to a greased 11-in. x 7-in. baking dish.

Place in a 13-in. x 9-in. baking dish; fill larger dish with hot water to a depth of 1 in. Bake at 350° for 25-30 minutes or until a knife inserted near the center comes out clean. Sprinkle with cheese and paprika. Let stand for 10 minutes before cutting. **yield: 6-8 servings.**

apple-sweet potato bake

prep: 45 min. • bake: 25 min.

*Apples and sweet potatoes are perfect partners in this slightly sweet casserole.
Every bite tastes like fall!*
—Taste of Home Test Kitchen

- 3 **pounds sweet potatoes**
- 4 **medium tart apples, peeled**
- 1/4 **cup lemon juice**
- 1/2 **cup chopped pecans**
- 1/2 **cup butter, cubed**
- 1/2 **cup packed brown sugar**
- 1/2 **cup honey**
- 2 **tablespoons orange juice**
- 1/2 **teaspoon ground cinnamon**
- 1/4 **teaspoon ground ginger**

Scrub and pierce potatoes. Bake at 400° for 30-60 minutes or until tender. Cool slightly; peel potatoes and cut into 1/4-in. slices.

Cut the apples into 1/4-in. slices; toss with lemon juice. In a greased 11-in. x 7-in. baking dish, alternately arrange sweet potato and apple slices. Sprinkle with pecans.

In a small saucepan, combine the butter, brown sugar, honey, orange juice, cinnamon and ginger. Bring to a boil, stirring constantly. Remove from the heat; pour over potatoes and apples.

Bake, uncovered, at 400° for 25-30 minutes or until tender. **yield: 8 servings.**

go for the grains casserole

prep: 25 min. • bake: 55 min.

This savory side is delectable. It has two types of grains and a host of colorful vegetables. A friend of mine gave me the recipe when I was compiling a file of healthier recipes.

—Melanie Blair, Warsaw, Indiana

- 5 medium carrots, thinly sliced
- 2 cups frozen corn, thawed
- 1 medium onion, diced
- 1 cup quick-cooking barley
- 1/2 cup bulgur
- 1/3 cup minced fresh parsley
- 1 teaspoon salt
- 1/2 teaspoon pepper
- 3 cups vegetable broth
- 1 can (15 ounces) black beans, rinsed and drained
- 1-1/2 cups (6 ounces) shredded reduced-fat cheddar cheese

In a large bowl, combine the carrots, corn, onion, barley, bulgur, parsley, salt and pepper. Stir in broth and beans. Transfer to a 13-in. x 9-in. baking dish coated with cooking spray.

Cover and bake at 350° for 50-55 minutes or until grains are tender, stirring once. Sprinkle with cheese. Bake, uncovered, 3-5 minutes longer or until cheese is melted. **yield: 10 servings.**

cheesy beans and rice

prep: 15 min. • bake: 35 min.

After my dad had heart trouble years ago, my mom adapted an old recipe to come up with this colorful all-in-one dish. It has been a dinnertime hit for a long time. Even my kids like it, and they can be quite picky!

—Linda Rindels, Littleton, Colorado

1	cup uncooked brown rice
1	can (16 ounces) kidney beans, rinsed and drained
1	large onion, chopped
1	tablespoon canola oil
1	can (14-1/2 ounces) diced tomatoes and green chilies, undrained
2	teaspoons chili powder
1/4	teaspoon salt
1-1/4	cups shredded reduced-fat cheddar cheese, *divided*

Cook rice according to package directions. Transfer to a large bowl; add the beans. In a nonstick skillet, saute onion in oil for 4-5 minutes. Stir in the tomatoes, chili powder and salt. Bring to a boil; remove from the heat.

In a 2-qt. baking dish coated with cooking spray, layer a third of the rice mixture, cheese and tomato mixture. Repeat layers. Layer with remaining rice mixture and tomato mixture.

Cover and bake at 350° for 30 minutes or until heated through. Uncover; sprinkle with remaining cheese. Bake 5-10 minutes longer or until cheese is melted. **yield: 6 servings.**

monterey corn bake

prep: 15 min. • bake: 25 min.

This vegetable bake came from my mother-in-law, who taught me how to cook. I've served it to my family time and again because they like it so much.

—Irene Redick, Trenton, Ontario

1	medium onion, chopped
5	tablespoons butter, *divided*
2	cups sliced fresh mushrooms
1	medium sweet red pepper, chopped
1/2	teaspoon salt
1/4	teaspoon pepper
1	garlic clove, minced
1	package (16 ounces) frozen corn, thawed
2	cups (8 ounces) shredded Colby-Monterey Jack cheese
2	teaspoons brown sugar
1/2	cup dry bread crumbs
2	tablespoons minced fresh parsley

In a large skillet, saute onion in 2 tablespoons butter until tender. Add the mushrooms, red pepper, salt and pepper; cook and stir for 5 minutes or until vegetables are tender. Add garlic; cook 1 minute longer.

In a greased 2-qt. baking dish, layer half of the corn, mushroom mixture, cheese and brown sugar; repeat layers.

Melt the remaining butter; toss with bread crumbs and parsley. Sprinkle over casserole.

Bake, uncovered, at 375° for 25-30 minutes or until golden brown. **yield: 4-6 servings.**

KITCHEN TIP

Mushrooms will absorb water like a sponge, so you do not want to soak them in water to clean them. The best ways to clean button mushrooms is to wipe them with a damp paper towel or quickly rinse under running water and gently scrub with a mushroom brush.

cranberry cornmeal dressing

prep: 30 min. • bake: 40 min.

This moist dressing is perfect when paired with poultry or even pork. The sweet-tart flavor of the dried cranberries really complements the dish's turkey sausage.

—Corinne Portteus, Albuquerque, New Mexico

- 3 cups reduced-sodium chicken broth, *divided*
- 1/2 cup yellow cornmeal
- 1/2 teaspoon salt
- 1/2 teaspoon white pepper
- 1/2 pound Italian turkey sausage links, casings removed
- 1 large onion, diced
- 1 large fennel bulb, diced (about 1 cup)
- 1 garlic clove, minced
- 1 egg yolk
- 4 cups soft French *or* Italian bread crumbs
- 3/4 cup dried cranberries
- 2 tablespoons minced fresh parsley
- 1 tablespoon balsamic vinegar
- 1 teaspoon minced fresh sage
- 1 teaspoon minced fresh savory
- 1/4 teaspoon ground nutmeg

In a small bowl, whisk 1 cup broth, cornmeal, salt and pepper until smooth. In a large saucepan, bring remaining broth to a boil. Add cornmeal mixture, stirring constantly. Return to a boil; cook and stir for 3 minutes or until thickened. Remove from the heat; set aside.

Crumble the sausage into a large nonstick skillet, add onion and fennel. Cook over medium heat until sausage is no longer pink. Add garlic; cook 1 minute longer; drain. Stir in egg yolk and cornmeal mixture. Add the bread crumbs, cranberries, parsley, vinegar, sage, savory and nutmeg.

Transfer the mixture to a 1-1/2-qt. baking dish coated with cooking spray. Cover and bake at 350° for 40-45 minutes or until a thermometer reads 160°. **yield: 8 servings.**

pineapple casserole

prep: 15 min. • bake: 35 min.

I think this is perfect for Easter Sunday. It is a wonderful side dish with ham.

—Sandy Moyer
  Gilbertsville, Pennsylvania

- 1 cup butter, softened
- 1 cup sugar
- 4 eggs
- 1 can (20 ounces) unsweetened crushed pineapple, drained
- 5 slices white bread, cubed

In a large bowl, cream butter and sugar until light and fluffy. Add eggs, one at a time, beating well after each addition. Stir in pineapple. Gently fold in bread cubes.

Spoon into a greased 2-qt. baking dish. Bake, uncovered, at 350° for 35-40 minutes or until a thermometer reads 160°. Serve warm. **yield: 10 servings.**

scalloped potatoes with ham

prep: 15 min. • bake: 1-1/4 hours

This dish is a crowd-pleaser with its smooth sauce, chunks of ham and potato slices. I always enjoyed it when Mother made it. I added the parsley and the thyme, and now my husband and five children request it often.

—Wendy Rhoades, Yacolt, Washington

- 6 tablespoons butter, *divided*
- 1/4 cup all-purpose flour
- 1 teaspoon dried parsley flakes
- 1 teaspoon salt
- 1/2 teaspoon dried thyme
- 1/4 teaspoon pepper
- 3 cups 2% milk
- 6 cups thinly sliced peeled potatoes
- 1-1/2 cups chopped fully cooked ham
- 1 small onion, grated

In a large saucepan, melt 4 tablespoons butter. Stir in flour, parsley, salt, thyme and pepper until smooth. Gradually add milk; bring to a boil. Cook and stir for 2 minutes.

Combine potatoes, ham and onion; place half in a greased 2-1/2-qt. baking dish. Top with half of the sauce; repeat layers.

Cover and bake at 375° for 65-75 minutes or until potatoes are almost tender. Dot with remaining butter. Bake, uncovered, 15-20 minutes longer or until potatoes are tender. **yield: 4 servings.**

cheesy green chili rice

prep: 25 min. • bake: 20 min.

Looking for a hearty addition to a spicy meal? Give this dish a try. When I first tasted it at a potluck, I knew I had to have the recipe.

—Laurie Fisher, Greeley, Colorado

- 1 large onion, chopped
- 2 tablespoons butter
- 4 cups hot cooked long grain rice
- 2 cups (16 ounces) sour cream
- 1 cup (8 ounces) 4% cottage cheese
- 1/2 teaspoon salt
- 1/8 teaspoon pepper
- 2 cans (4 ounces *each*) chopped green chilies, drained
- 2 cups (8 ounces) shredded cheddar cheese

In a large skillet, cook onion in butter until tender. Remove from the heat. Stir in the rice, sour cream, cottage cheese, salt and pepper. Spoon half of the mixture into a greased 11-in. x 7-in. baking dish. Layer with half of the chilies and cheese. Repeat layers.

Bake, uncovered, at 375° for 20-25 minutes or until heated through and bubbly. **yield: 6-8 servings.**

Place potatoes in a large saucepan; cover with water. Bring to a boil. Reduce heat; cover and cook for 10-15 minutes or until tender. Drain.

In a large bowl, mash the potatoes. Add the cream cheese, butter and cream; beat until blended. Stir in the green pepper, onions, pimientos, salt and pepper. Stir in 1/3 cup cheddar cheese and 1/3 cup Parmesan cheese.

Transfer to a greased 11-in. x 7-in. baking dish. Sprinkle with remaining cheeses. Bake, uncovered, at 350° for 20-25 minutes or until heated through. **yield: 8 servings.**

pea and broccoli bake

prep/total time: 30 min.

When I'm pressed for time, I find this take-along casserole is easy to fix. The crouton-topped combination is not only attractive but tasty, too.
—Pat Waymire, Yellow Springs, Ohio

- 1 package (16 ounces) frozen peas, thawed
- 1 package (16 ounces) frozen chopped broccoli, thawed and drained
- 1 can (10-3/4 ounces) condensed cream of mushroom soup, undiluted
- 1 jar (8 ounces) process cheese sauce
- 1 cup seasoned salad croutons

In a large bowl, combine the peas, broccoli, soup and cheese sauce. Transfer to a greased 2-qt. baking dish. Sprinkle with croutons.

Bake, uncovered, at 350° for 12-17 minutes or until bubbly. **yield: 4-6 servings.**

mashed potatoes supreme

prep: 40 min. • bake: 20 min.

My relatives and friends think these potatoes are just exceptional. They are rich, creamy and taste like twice-baked. The dish offers make-ahead convenience, so it's great for potlucks.
—Julia Daubresse, Sun City Center, Florida

- 3 pounds medium red potatoes, quartered
- 2 packages (3 ounces *each*) cream cheese, cubed
- 1/2 cup butter, cubed
- 1/2 cup half-and-half cream *or* milk
- 1 medium green pepper, chopped
- 4 green onions, thinly sliced
- 1 jar (2 ounces) sliced pimientos, drained
- 1/2 teaspoon salt
- 1/4 teaspoon pepper
- 1/2 cup shredded cheddar cheese, *divided*
- 1/2 cup grated Parmesan cheese, *divided*

zucchini tomato bake

prep: 30 min. • bake: 25 min.

This flavorful side makes the most of the summer bounty of tomatoes and zucchini. Melted Swiss cheese and sour cream lend a touch of decadence to this healthy, appealing dish.

—Tina Repak, Johnstown, Pennsylvania

- 1 **medium onion, chopped**
- 1 **tablespoon butter**
- 3 **medium zucchini (about 1 pound), shredded and patted dry**
- 3 **medium tomatoes, seeded and chopped**
- 1 **cup (4 ounces) shredded reduced-fat Swiss cheese,** *divided*
- 1/3 **cup reduced-fat sour cream**
- 1 **teaspoon paprika**
- 1/2 **teaspoon salt**
- 1/2 **teaspoon garlic powder**
- 1/4 **teaspoon pepper**
- 2 **tablespoons shredded Parmesan cheese**

In a large nonstick skillet, saute onion in butter until tender. Transfer to a large bowl. Add the zucchini, tomatoes, 1/2 cup Swiss cheese, sour cream and seasonings; mix well.

Transfer to an 11-in. x 7-in. baking dish coated with cooking spray. Sprinkle with Parmesan cheese and remaining Swiss cheese. Bake, uncovered, at 350° for 25-30 minutes or until vegetables are tender. **yield: 6 servings.**

crumb-topped asparagus casserole

prep: 20 min. • bake: 20 min.

When we lived on a farm, we had an abundance of fresh vegetables, so I also made this family favorite with broccoli or green beans instead of asparagus.

—Mrs. E. Allen Orem, Rochester, New York

- 2 pounds fresh asparagus, trimmed and cut into 1-inch pieces
- 2 cans (10-3/4 ounces *each*) condensed cream of celery soup, undiluted
- 1/2 cup heavy whipping cream
- 1/2 cup mayonnaise
- 1 tablespoon Heinz 57 steak sauce
- 1/4 teaspoon ground cloves
- 1/4 teaspoon ground nutmeg
- 1 cup (4 ounces) shredded cheddar cheese
- 2-1/2 cups crushed seasoned stuffing
- 5 tablespoons butter, melted

In a large saucepan, bring 1/2 in. of water to a boil. Add asparagus; cover and boil for 3-5 minutes or until crisp-tender. Drain well. Place in a greased 11-in. x 7-in. baking dish; set aside.

In a small bowl, combine the soup, cream, mayonnaise, steak sauce, cloves and nutmeg. Spread over asparagus; sprinkle with cheese.

In another small bowl, toss stuffing with butter; sprinkle over casserole. Bake, uncovered, at 350° for 20-25 minutes or until bubbly. **yield: 8 servings.**

barley bake

prep: 25 min. • bake: 1-1/4 hours

For a fantastic change of pace from a typical potato casserole, try this dish. Slivered almonds give it a nice crunch.

—Lamar Lyons Parker, Peoria, Illinois

- 1/2 pound fresh mushrooms, sliced
- 1 celery rib, chopped
- 1/2 cup chopped green onions
- 5 tablespoons butter, cubed
- 1 cup uncooked quick-cooking barley
- 2 cups vegetable broth, *divided*
- 1/2 cup minced fresh parsley
- 1/2 cup slivered almonds

In a large skillet, saute mushrooms, celery and onions in butter until tender. Add the barley; cook and stir until the barley is golden brown, about 6-7 minutes.

In a greased 2-qt. baking dish, combine the barley mixture, 1 cup broth and parsley. Cover and bake at 350° for 30 minutes.

Uncover; stir in the almonds and remaining broth. Bake 45-50 minutes longer or until barley is tender. **yield: 8 servings.**

harvest carrots

prep: 15 min. • bake: 30 min.

I make this tasty side dish quite often. Once in a while, I add leftover turkey or chicken breasts and turn it into a main dish.
—Marty Rummel
    Trout Lake, Washington

- 4 **cups sliced carrots**
- 2 **cups water**
- 1 **medium onion, chopped**
- 1/2 **cup butter,** *divided*
- 1 **can (10-3/4 ounces) condensed cream of celery soup, undiluted**
- 1/2 **cup shredded cheddar cheese**
- 1/8 **teaspoon pepper**
- 3 **cups seasoned stuffing croutons**

In a large saucepan, bring carrots and water to a boil. Reduce heat; cover and simmer for 5-8 minutes or until tender. Drain. In a small skillet, saute onion in 3 tablespoons butter until tender.

In a large bowl, combine the carrots, onion, soup, cheese and pepper. Melt remaining butter; toss with stuffing. Fold into carrot mixture.

Transfer to a greased 2-qt. baking dish. Cover and bake at 350° for 20 minutes. Uncover; bake 10 minutes longer or until lightly browned. **yield: 6 servings.**

wild rice medley

prep: 1-1/4 hours • bake: 30 min.

For an autumn feel at any meal, serve this distinctive side dish starring wild rice.
—Antonia Seguin, Westlock, Alberta

- 1-3/4 **cups reduced-sodium chicken broth**
- 1 **teaspoon dill weed**
- 1/2 **teaspoon dried basil**
- 1/8 **teaspoon pepper**
- Pinch **dried thyme**
- 3/4 **cup uncooked wild rice**
- 1 **cup chopped green pepper**
- 1 **small onion, chopped**
- 1 **tablespoon olive oil**
- 1 **garlic clove, minced**
- 6 **fresh mushrooms, sliced**
- 1 **large tomato, diced**
- 1/4 **cup shredded part-skim mozzarella cheese**

In a large saucepan, combine broth and seasonings; bring to a boil. Add rice; cover and simmer for 55-60 minutes or until liquid is absorbed.

In a large skillet, saute green pepper and onion in oil. Add garlic; cook 1 minute longer. Add mushrooms; saute until tender. Stir in rice and tomato.

Transfer to a greased 1-1/2-qt. baking dish. Cover and bake at 350° for 25 minutes. Sprinkle with cheese. Bake, uncovered, 5 minutes longer or until cheese is melted. **yield: 8 servings.**

KITCHEN TIP

Did you know that wild rice isn't really a rice? Wild rice is actually long-grain marsh grass. It has a nutty flavor and a chewy texture. Wild rice should be cleaned before using. Soak it in a bowl of cold water and remove any particles that float to the surface.

creamy pea casserole

prep: 15 min. • bake: 25 min.

My sister-in-law shared this classic treatment for peas with me a few years back. It's a welcome addition to church or family dinners.
—*Mary Pauline Maynor*
  Franklinton, Louisiana

- 1 medium onion, chopped
- 3 celery ribs, finely chopped
- 1/2 medium sweet red pepper, chopped
- 6 tablespoons butter
- 1 can (10-3/4 ounces) condensed cream of mushroom soup, undiluted
- 1 tablespoon 2% milk
- 2 cups frozen peas, thawed
- 1 can (8 ounces) sliced water chestnuts, drained
- 1/2 to 3/4 cup crushed butter-flavored crackers (about 12 crackers)

In a large skillet, saute the onion, celery and red pepper in butter for 8-10 minutes or until tender. Stir in soup and milk; heat through. Stir in peas and water chestnuts.

Transfer the soup mixture to a greased 1-1/2-qt. baking dish. Sprinkle with the cracker crumbs. Bake, uncovered, at 350° for 25-30 minutes or until bubbly. **yield: 6 servings.**

rich 'n' creamy potato casserole

prep: 25 min. • bake: 30 min.

My husband, a pastor, and our three children enjoy these potatoes so much that I don't wait until the holidays to make them. This casserole often comes out when we invite church members over for a family-style meal.
—*Mary White, Pawnee City, Nebraska*

- 6 medium potatoes
- 2 cups (16 ounces) sour cream
- 2 cups (8 ounces) shredded cheddar cheese
- 4 tablespoons butter, melted, *divided*
- 3 green onions, thinly sliced
- 1 teaspoon salt
- 1/4 teaspoon pepper

Place potatoes in a large saucepan and cover with water. Bring to a boil. Reduce heat; cover and cook for 15-20 minutes or until tender. Drain and cool. Peel and grate potatoes; place in a large bowl. Add the sour cream, cheddar cheese, 3 tablespoons butter, green onions, salt and pepper.

Transfer to a greased 2-1/2-qt. baking dish. Drizzle with remaining butter. Bake, uncovered, at 350° for 30-35 minutes or until heated through. Refrigerate any leftovers. **yield: 8-10 servings.**

spinach surprise

prep: 20 min. • bake: 20 min.

If you're looking for a good way to get kids to eat spinach, try this zippy side dish flavored with picante sauce. My teenage daughter likes it so much she makes it herself.

—Sandra Weaver
   Fort Gordon, Georgia

- 1 medium onion, chopped
- 2 tablespoons butter
- 2 tablespoons all-purpose flour
- 1/2 teaspoon salt
- 3/4 to 1 cup 2% milk
- 2 packages (10 ounces *each*) frozen chopped spinach, thawed
- 1/2 cup picante sauce *or* salsa
- 1 cup (4 ounces) shredded cheddar cheese, *divided*

In a large saucepan, saute onion in butter until tender. Stir in flour and salt until blended. Gradually stir in milk. Bring to a boil; cook and stir for 2 minutes or until thickened and bubbly. Stir in spinach and picante sauce. Stir in 3/4 cup cheese.

Transfer to a greased 8-in. square baking dish. Sprinkle with remaining cheese. Bake, uncovered, at 350° for 20-25 minutes or until heated through. **yield: 4-6 servings.**

spicy spanish rice

prep: 10 min. • bake: 55 min.

This is a tasty dish to perk up any ho-hum dinner. We especially like it with chicken enchiladas. I also prepare it for potlucks and family get-togethers. It's a little different to bake rice, but it's handy to not have to watch it on the stove. You can make the rice less spicy with a more mild variety of canned tomatoes with green chilies.

—Marilyn Warner, Shirley, Arkansas

- 1 cup uncooked long grain rice
- 1 small onion, chopped
- 1 can (2-1/4 ounces) sliced ripe olives, drained
- 1 teaspoon ground cumin
- 2 cans (10 ounces *each*) diced tomatoes and green chilies, undrained
- 1 cup water
- 2 tablespoons canola oil
- 1 cup (4 ounces) shredded Monterey Jack cheese
- 2 tablespoons minced fresh cilantro, optional

In a greased 2-qt. baking dish, combine the rice, onion, olives, cumin, tomatoes, water and oil. Cover the dish and bake at 350° for 45 minutes.

Stir in cheese. Bake, uncovered, 10-15 minutes longer or until the rice is tender and liquid is absorbed. Stir in cilantro if desired. **yield: 6-8 servings.**

shredded potato casserole

prep: 10 min. • bake: 45 min.

The classic combination of potatoes, cheese and sour cream make this dish perfect with any entree. Make it ahead and have it ready to pop into the oven. The topping of cornflake crumbs and Parmesan cheese adds a nice crunch.
—Paula Zsiray, Logan, Utah

- 1 can (10-3/4 ounces) condensed cream of mushroom soup, undiluted
- 1 cup (8 ounces) sour cream
- 1/2 cup 2% milk
- 1 cup (4 ounces) shredded cheddar cheese
- 1/2 cup butter, melted, *divided*
- 1 package (30 ounces) frozen shredded hash brown potatoes, thawed
- 1 cup cornflake crumbs
- 1/4 cup grated Parmesan cheese

In a large bowl, combine the soup, sour cream, milk, cheddar cheese and 1/4 cup butter. Stir in the hash browns. Transfer to a greased 13-in. x 9-in. baking dish.

In a small bowl, combine cornflake crumbs, Parmesan cheese and remaining butter; sprinkle over top. Bake, uncovered, at 325° for 45-50 minutes or until heated through. **yield: 6-8 servings.**

vidalia onion bake

prep: 25 min. • bake: 20 min.

The mild taste of Vidalias makes this bake appealing to onion lovers and nonfans alike. It's an excellent accompaniment to beef, pork or chicken.
—Katrina Stitt, Zephyrhills, Florida

- **6 large sweet onions, sliced (about 12 cups)**
- **1/2 cup butter, cubed**
- **2 cups crushed butter-flavored crackers**
- **1 cup shredded Parmesan cheese**
- **1/2 cup shredded cheddar cheese**
- **1/4 cup shredded Romano cheese**

In a large skillet, saute onions in butter until tender and liquid has evaporated. Place half of the onions in a greased 2-qt. baking dish; sprinkle with half of the cracker crumbs and cheeses. Repeat layers.

Bake, uncovered, at 325° for 20-25 minutes or until golden brown. **yield: 8 servings.**

elegant green beans

prep: 20 min. • bake: 50 min.

Mushrooms and water chestnuts give new life to ordinary green bean casserole. Every time I make it for friends, I'm asked to share this delicious recipe.
—Linda Poe, Sandstone, Minnesota

- 1 can (8 ounces) sliced water chestnuts, drained
- 1 small onion, chopped
- 1 jar (4-1/2 ounces) sliced mushrooms, drained
- 6 tablespoons butter, *divided*
- 1/4 cup all-purpose flour
- 1 cup 2% milk
- 1/2 cup chicken broth
- 1 teaspoon reduced-sodium soy sauce
- 1/8 teaspoon hot pepper sauce

Dash salt
- 1 package (16 ounces) frozen French-style green beans, thawed
- 1/2 cup shredded cheddar cheese
- 1 cup crushed french-fried onions

In a small skillet, saute the water chestnuts, onion and mushrooms in 2 tablespoons butter for 4-5 minutes or until crisp-tender; set aside.

In large skillet, melt the remaining butter; stir in flour until smooth. Stir in the milk, broth, soy sauce, pepper sauce and salt. Bring to a boil; cook and stir for 2 minutes or until thickened. Remove from the heat; stir in green beans and cheese.

Spoon half of the bean mixture into a greased 1-1/2-qt. baking dish. Layer with water chestnut mixture and remaining bean mixture.

Bake, uncovered, at 350° for 45 minutes. Top with french-fried onions. Bake 5 minutes longer or until heated through. **yield: 8 servings.**

baked creamy spinach

prep: 10 min. • bake: 30 min.

Even folks not fond of spinach find this creamy casserole irresistible. It's a classic for the holidays.
—Sue Dodd, Friendsville, Tennessee

- 1 large onion, chopped
- 1 tablespoon butter
- 1 package (8 ounces) cream cheese, cubed
- 1/4 cup 2% milk
- 1-1/2 cups (6 ounces) shredded Parmesan cheese, *divided*
- 1/2 teaspoon cayenne pepper
- 1/4 teaspoon salt
- 1/8 teaspoon pepper
- 2 packages (10 ounces *each*) frozen chopped spinach, thawed and squeezed dry

In a large saucepan, saute onion in butter until tender. Add cream cheese and milk; stir until melted. Stir in 1 cup Parmesan cheese, cayenne, salt and pepper. Stir in the spinach.

Transfer to a greased 1-1/2-qt. baking dish. Sprinkle with remaining Parmesan cheese. Bake, uncovered, at 350° for 30-35 minutes or until hot and bubbly. **yield: 6-8 servings.**

cheese 'n' grits casserole

prep: 10 min. • bake: 30 min. + standing

Grits are a staple in Southern cooking. Serve this as a brunch item with bacon or as a side dish for dinner.
—Jennifer Wallis
  Goldsboro, North Carolina

- 4 cups water
- 1 cup uncooked old-fashioned grits
- 1/2 teaspoon salt
- 1/2 cup 2% milk
- 1/4 cup butter, melted
- 2 eggs, lightly beaten
- 1 cup (4 ounces) shredded cheddar cheese
- 1 tablespoon Worcestershire sauce
- 1/8 teaspoon cayenne pepper
- 1/8 teaspoon paprika

In a large saucepan, bring water to a boil. Slowly stir in grits and salt. Reduce heat; cover and simmer for 5-7 minutes or until thickened. Cool slightly. Gradually whisk in the milk, butter and eggs. Stir in the cheese, Worcestershire sauce and cayenne.

Transfer to a greased 2-qt. baking dish. Sprinkle with paprika. Bake, uncovered, at 350° for 30-35 minutes or until bubbly. Let stand 10 minutes before serving. **yield: 8 servings.**

nana's chilies rellenos

prep: 20 min. • bake: 40 min. + standing

This zesty dish is not for the faint of heart. My family has been enjoying it for three generations, and will be doing so for years to come!
—Peta-Marie Lamb, Poulsbo, Washington

- 1 can (27 ounces) whole green chilies, drained
- 4 cups (16 ounces) shredded sharp cheddar cheese
- 4 egg, lightly beaten
- 1 can (12 ounces) evaporated milk
- 1/4 cup all-purpose flour
- 1 can (29 ounces) tomato sauce
- 1 envelope taco seasoning
- 8 ounces sharp cheddar cheese, cut into 1-inch cubes

Slice chilies in half and remove seeds. Arrange half of the chilies in a greased 13-in. x 9-in. baking dish. Sprinkle with shredded cheddar cheese. Cover with remaining chilies. In a small bowl, whisk the eggs, milk and flour until smooth; pour over cheese. Bake, uncovered, at 350° for 30 minutes.

In a small bowl, combine tomato sauce and taco seasoning; pour over casserole. Carefully place cheese cubes on top in a checkerboard pattern; bake 10-15 minutes longer or until top is set. Let stand for 10 minutes before serving. **yield: 8-10 servings.**

editor's note: Wear disposable gloves when cutting hot peppers. Avoid touching your face.

KITCHEN TIP

Grits are dried corn that has been coarsely ground. You can purchase old-fashioned grits, quick-cooking grits, instant grits and flavored instant grits. Old-fashioned grits take the longest to cook; instant the quickest. Use before the use-by date on the package.

butternut squash casserole

prep/total time: 30 min.

Here's a recipe that has really stood the test of time in my kitchen. It pairs perfectly with pork or chicken.

—*Cathy Dwyer, Freedom, New Hampshire*

- 2 cups sliced tart apples
- 1 tablespoon sugar
- 2 tablespoons butter, *divided*
- 1 cup mashed cooked butternut squash
- 1 teaspoon brown sugar
- 1/8 teaspoon salt

Dash white pepper

TOPPING:

- 1/2 cup frosted cornflakes, coarsely crushed
- 2 tablespoons chopped pecans
- 2 tablespoons brown sugar
- 2 teaspoons butter, melted

In a large skillet, saute apples and sugar in 1 tablespoon butter for 4-5 minutes or until crisp-tender. Place in a 1-qt. baking dish coated with cooking spray; set aside.

In a small bowl, combine the squash, brown sugar, salt, pepper and remaining butter; spoon over apples. Combine topping ingredients; sprinkle over casserole.

Bake, uncovered, at 350° for 15-20 minutes or until heated through and topping is browned. **yield: 3 servings.**

pesto potatoes

prep: 15 min. • bake: 45 min.

This hearty potato dish keeps us warm during our long Alaskan winters. Each summer, I make lots of homemade pesto and freeze it to enjoy throughout the year.

—*Jennifer Reese, Wasilla, Alaska*

- 1 cup firmly packed fresh basil leaves
- 1/2 cup packed fresh parsley
- 1/2 cup grated Parmesan *or* grated Romano cheese
- 1/4 cup chopped walnuts
- 1 garlic clove
- 1-1/4 teaspoons salt
- 1/2 teaspoon pepper
- 1/2 cup olive oil, *divided*
- 4 large potatoes, peeled and cubed
- 5 plum tomatoes, cut into 1/4-inch slices
- 2 cups (8 ounces) shredded mozzarella cheese

In a food processor or blender, combine the first seven ingredients. Cover and process until smooth. While processing, gradually add 1/4 cup oil in a steady stream.

In a large roasting pan, combine potatoes and tomatoes; drizzle with remaining oil. Top with basil mixture; toss to coat.

Bake, uncovered, at 400° for 40-45 minutes or until potatoes are tender. Sprinkle with mozzarella cheese. Bake 5 minutes longer or until cheese is melted. **yield: 8 servings.**

kentucky spoon bread

prep: 20 min. • bake: 40 min.

This is a traditional Kentucky recipe. It's a popular side dish served all year long. If you've never tried spoon bread before, I think you'll enjoy it.

—Caroline Brown
  Lexington, Kentucky

 4 cups 2% milk, *divided*
 1 cup cornmeal
 3 teaspoons sugar
 1 teaspoon salt
 1/2 teaspoon baking powder
 2 tablespoons butter
 3 eggs, *separated*

In a large saucepan, heat 3 cups milk over medium heat until bubbles form around sides of pan.

Meanwhile, in a small bowl, combine the cornmeal, sugar, salt and remaining milk until smooth. Slowly whisk cornmeal mixture into hot milk.

Cook and stir until mixture comes to a boil. Reduce heat; simmer for 5 minutes, stirring constantly.

Remove from the heat. Sprinkle baking powder over the cornmeal mixture, then stir it in with the butter. In a small bowl, beat egg yolks; stir in a small amount of hot cornmeal mixture. Return all to the pan and mix well.

In another small bowl, beat egg whites until stiff peaks form. Fold a fourth of the egg whites into the cornmeal mixture. Fold in remaining egg whites until blended.

Transfer to a greased 2-1/2-qt. baking dish. Bake, uncovered, at 350° for 40-45 minutes or until puffed and golden brown. Serve immediately. **yield: 8 servings.**

mixed vegetable casserole

prep: 15 min. • bake: 55 min.

I found a recipe for a layered veggie casserole then modified it to use produce I had on hand. I sometimes sprinkle bread crumbs or grated cheese on top for a tasty variation.

—Marilou Robinson, Portland, Oregon

 2 medium tomatoes, cut into wedges
 1 cup sliced celery
 1 cup sliced fresh carrots
 1 cup cut fresh green beans
 1 medium onion, sliced
 1 small sweet red pepper, julienned
 1/2 cup canned sliced water chestnuts, drained
 1-1/2 teaspoons sugar
 1-1/2 teaspoons all-purpose flour
 1 teaspoon dried oregano
 1/4 teaspoon salt
 1/4 teaspoon pepper
 2 tablespoons butter

In a large bowl, combine the first seven ingredients. Place half in a greased 1-1/2-qt. baking dish.

In a small bowl, combine the sugar, flour, oregano, salt and pepper. Sprinkle half over vegetables in the baking dish. Layer with remaining vegetables and seasoning mixture. Dot with butter.

Cover and bake at 350° for 55-60 minutes or until vegetables are tender. **yield: 4 servings.**

macaroon sweet potato bake

prep: 15 min. • bake: 30 min.

This is a special sweet potato bake. The almond flavor gives it a rich taste, and the crumbled macaroon topping adds a festive touch. To save some time the day of your dinner, you can make this the night before and refrigerate it.

—William Waller, Lady Lake, Florida

- 6 cups mashed sweet potatoes (about 3-1/2 pounds)
- 6 tablespoons plus 4-1/2 teaspoons butter, melted, *divided*
- 1/2 cup packed brown sugar
- 1/4 cup amaretto liqueur *or* 1/4 teaspoon almond extract
- 1/2 teaspoon salt
- 1/2 teaspoon ground ginger
- 1/2 cup chopped pecans
- 1/4 cup orange marmalade
- 6 macaroons, crumbled

In a large bowl, combine the sweet potatoes, 6 tablespoons butter, brown sugar, amaretto or extract, salt and ginger; beat until smooth. Stir in the pecans and marmalade.

Transfer to a greased 11-in. x 7-in. baking dish. Toss macaroons with remaining butter; sprinkle over casserole. Bake, uncovered, at 325° for 30-35 minutes or until heated through. **yield: 8 servings.**

winter squash souffle

prep: 20 min. • bake: 45 min.

My large family gets together quite often. To make it easy on the host, everyone brings a dish to pass. We often swap recipes, and I've shared this one many times.

—Colleen Birchill
  Spokane, Washington

- 3 cups mashed cooked winter squash
- 1/4 cup shredded Swiss cheese
- 2 tablespoons butter, melted
- 2 tablespoons heavy whipping cream
- 3/4 teaspoon salt
- 1/4 teaspoon pepper
- 1/4 teaspoon dried thyme
- 3 eggs, *separated*

In a large bowl, combine the squash, cheese, butter, cream, salt, pepper and thyme. Beat egg yolks; add to squash mixture.

In a small bowl, beat egg whites until stiff peaks form. Fold into squash mixture. Transfer to a greased 2-qt. baking dish.

Bake, uncovered, at 375° for 45-50 minutes or until the top is puffed and center appears set. Serve immediately. **yield: 6-8 servings.**

acorn squash puree

prep: 1 hour • bake: 20 min.

I originally created this recipe to have a healthy alternative to go along with our Thanksgiving meal. It's now become one of our traditional sides, and everyone looks forward to sampling it.
—Ann Hennessy
　　Burnsville, Minnesota

- 4 medium acorn squash
- 8 ounces fat-free cream cheese, cubed
- 1/2 cup fat-free milk
- 2 tablespoons reduced-fat butter, melted
- 2 tablespoons dried minced onion
- 2 tablespoons minced chives
- 2 teaspoons dried basil
- 3 tablespoons chopped pecans

Cut squash in half; discard seeds. Place squash cut side down in a 15-in. x 10-in. x 1-in. baking pan; add 1/2 in. of hot water. Bake, uncovered, at 350° for 35 minutes. Drain water from pan; turn squash cut side up. Bake 5-10 minutes longer or until tender. Cool slightly.

Carefully scoop out squash; add to food processor. Add the cream cheese, milk, butter, onion, chives and basil; cover and process until blended.

Transfer to a 2-qt. baking dish coated with cooking spray; sprinkle with pecans. Cover and bake at 350° for 20-25 minutes or until heated through. **yield: 8 servings.**

editor's note: This recipe was tested with Land O'Lakes light stick butter.

family-favorite baked beans

prep: 20 min. • bake: 1 hour

Here's a quick and easy recipe familiar to most at reunions and other large gatherings. The sweet and hearty dish includes three kinds of beans and plenty of beef and bacon.
—Lea Ann Anderson, Tulsa, Oklahoma

- 1/2 pound ground beef
- 1/2 pound sliced bacon, diced
- 1 small onion, chopped
- 1/2 cup ketchup
- 1/2 cup barbecue sauce
- 1/3 cup packed brown sugar
- 2 tablespoons molasses
- 1 can (16 ounces) kidney beans, rinsed and drained
- 1 can (16 ounces) butter beans, rinsed and drained
- 1 can (15-3/4 ounces) pork and beans

In a large skillet, cook the beef over medium heat until no longer pink; drain and set aside. In the same skillet, cook the bacon over medium heat until crisp. Remove with a slotted spoon to paper towels to drain.

In a large bowl, combine the onion, ketchup, barbecue sauce, brown sugar and molasses. Stir in the beans, beef and bacon.

Transfer to a greased 3-qt. baking dish. Cover and bake at 350° for 1 hour or until beans reach desired thickness. **yield: 8 servings.**

scalloped corn

prep: 10 min. • bake: 1 hour

Sunny corn kernels are tucked into a creamy custard for a super-yummy side. My mom got this recipe, and many other excellent ones, from her mother. This was popular when we were growing up. By the time it got around the table, my father, sister, brothers and I would have almost scraped the dish clean.
—Sandy Jenkins, Elkhorn, Wisconsin

- 4 cups fresh *or* frozen corn
- 3 eggs, lightly beaten
- 1 cup 2% milk
- 1 cup crushed saltines (about 30 crackers), *divided*
- 3 tablespoons butter, melted
- 1 tablespoon sugar
- 1 tablespoon finely chopped onion

Salt and pepper to taste

In a large bowl, combine the corn, eggs, milk, 3/4 cup cracker crumbs, butter, sugar, onion, salt and pepper. Transfer to a greased 1-1/2-qt. baking dish. Sprinkle with remaining cracker crumbs.

Bake, uncovered, at 325° for 1 hour or until a thermometer reads 160°. **yield: 6 servings.**

cauliflower casserole

prep: 15 min. • bake: 30 min.

To dress up cauliflower, Mom used a delightful mixture of a cheesy sauce, bright red and green pepper pieces, and crushed cornflakes. We enjoyed this so much that leftovers were rare.
—Linda McGinty, Parma, Ohio

- 1 medium head cauliflower, broken into florets
- 1 cup (8 ounces) sour cream
- 1 cup (4 ounces) shredded cheddar cheese
- 1/2 cup crushed cornflakes
- 1/4 cup chopped green pepper
- 1/4 cup chopped sweet red pepper
- 1 teaspoon salt
- 1/4 cup grated Parmesan cheese

Paprika

Place 1 in. of water in a saucepan; add the cauliflower. Bring to a boil. Reduce heat; cover and simmer for 5-10 minutes or until cauliflower is crisp-tender. Drain.

In a large bowl, combine the cauliflower, sour cream, cheddar cheese, cornflakes, peppers and salt; transfer to a greased 2-qt. baking dish. Sprinkle with Parmesan cheese and paprika.

Bake, uncovered, at 325° for 30-35 minutes or until heated through. **yield: 6-8 servings.**

coconut carrot casserole

prep: 15 min. • bake: 35 min.

I can about 30 pounds of carrots every fall, so I'm always looking for new ways to prepare them. This recipe is one that my family really likes.
—Mary Beth Keim
  Crawfordsville, Indiana

- 1/4 cup butter, softened
- 1/2 cup sugar
- 2 eggs
- 1/3 cup 2% milk
- 1 teaspoon vanilla extract
- 3 cans (15 ounces *each*) sliced carrots, drained and mashed
- 1/2 cup flaked coconut

TOPPING:
- 1/2 cup packed brown sugar
- 1/2 cup chopped pecans
- 1/4 cup all-purpose flour
- 2 tablespoons butter, melted

In a large bowl, cream butter and sugar until light and fluffy. Beat in eggs, milk, vanilla and carrots. Stir in coconut.

Pour into a greased 2-qt. baking dish. Combine topping ingredients; sprinkle over the top. Bake, uncovered, at 350° for 35-40 minutes or until a thermometer reads 160°. **yield: 6-8 servings.**

broccoli souffle

prep: 25 min. • bake: 35 min.

A great way to sneak broccoli into a brunch, lunch or supper, this curry-flavored side dish is light, airy and beginner-easy.
—Jane Shapton, Irvine, California

- 4 egg whites
- 2 teaspoons plus 3 tablespoons all-purpose flour, *divided*
- 1 cup chopped fresh broccoli
- 1/4 cup water
- 1 tablespoon lemon juice
- 2 tablespoons butter
- 1/4 teaspoon salt
- 1 cup soy milk
- 1/2 cup minced fresh cilantro
- 1 teaspoon curry powder

Place egg whites in a small bowl; let stand at room temperature for 30 minutes. Coat a 1-qt. baking dish with cooking spray and lightly sprinkle with 2 teaspoons flour; set aside.

Place broccoli and water in a microwave-safe bowl; cover and microwave on high for 2-3 minutes or until tender. Let stand for 5 minutes; drain. Place broccoli and lemon juice in a small food processor; cover and process until blended.

In a small saucepan over medium heat, melt butter. Stir in salt and remaining flour until blended. Gradually whisk in soy milk. Bring to a boil; cook and stir for 1-2 minutes or until thickened. Transfer to a small bowl; stir in the broccoli mixture, cilantro and curry.

Beat egg whites until stiff peaks form. With a spatula, fold a fourth of the egg whites into broccoli mixture until no white streaks remain. Fold in remaining egg whites until combined.

Transfer to prepared dish. Bake at 350° for 35-40 minutes or until top is puffed and center appears set. Serve immediately. **yield: 4 servings.**

---

editor's note: This recipe was tested in a 1,100-watt microwave.

hearty maple beans

prep: 15 min. • bake: 25 min.

I modified this recipe to suit my family's taste. It's great for any get-together because it can be made in advance and kept warm in a slow cooker for hours without losing any flavor.
—*Margaret Glassic, Easton, Pennsylvania*

- 6 **bacon strips, diced**
- 1/2 **pound smoked kielbasa** *or* **Polish sausage, sliced**
- 1 **small onion, chopped**
- 1 **can (16 ounces) kidney beans, rinsed and drained**
- 1 **can (16 ounces) butter beans, rinsed and drained**
- 1 **can (15-3/4 ounces) pork and beans**
- 1/2 **cup maple syrup**
- 3 **tablespoons white vinegar**
- 3 **tablespoons ketchup**
- 3 **tablespoons prepared mustard**

In a large skillet, cook bacon over medium heat until crisp. Using a slotted spoon, remove to paper towels. Drain, reserving 1 tablespoon drippings. In drippings, cook sausage and onion over medium-high heat until sausage is lightly browned. Stir in bacon and remaining ingredients.

Transfer to an ungreased 2-qt. baking dish. Bake, uncovered, at 350° for 25-30 minutes or until bubbly. **yield: 8 servings.**

mushroom casserole

prep: 30 min. • bake: 25 min.

When I make this buttery-tasting casserole, my family fights over every last bite. The Swiss cheese provides a mild flavor when it melts.
—*Susan Vetter, Cape Coral, Florida*

- 1 **package (16 ounces) wide egg noodles**
- 2 **pounds fresh mushrooms, sliced**
- 1/2 **cup butter,** *divided*
- 1-1/2 **teaspoons salt**
- 3/4 **teaspoon pepper**
- 4 **cups (16 ounces) shredded Swiss cheese**

Cook noodles according to package directions; drain. In a large skillet, saute mushrooms in 1/4 cup butter for 10-15 minutes or until tender.

Place a third of the noodles in a greased 13-in. x 9-in. baking dish; sprinkle with 1/2 teaspoon salt and 1/4 teaspoon pepper. Layer with 1-1/3 cups cheese and a third of the mushrooms. Repeat layers twice. Dot with remaining butter.

Bake, uncovered, at 350° for 25-30 minutes or until bubbly and cheese is melted. **yield: 8-10 servings.**

potato puff

prep: 25 min. • bake: 40 min.

This sensational, rich potato casserole complements a variety of main courses. I've shared the recipe with so many people, I can almost recite it by heart!
—Donna Cline, Pensacola, Florida

　2　**pounds potatoes, peeled and quartered**
　3　**eggs,** *separated*
　1　**cup 2% milk**
3/4　**teaspoon salt**
1/2　**teaspoon dried basil**
1/4　**teaspoon white pepper**
1-1/2　**cups (6 ounces) shredded Monterey Jack cheese,** *divided*

Place potatoes in a large saucepan and cover with water. Bring to a boil. Reduce heat; cover and cook for 15-20 minutes or until tender. Drain and mash.

In a small bowl, whisk the egg yolks, milk, salt, basil and pepper. Gradually stir into mashed potatoes. Fold in 1 cup cheese. In a small bowl, beat egg whites on high speed until stiff peaks form; fold into potato mixture.

Spoon into a greased 1-1/2-qt. baking dish. Sprinkle with remaining cheese. Bake, uncovered, at 350° for 40-45 minutes or until a thermometer reads 160°. **yield: 8 servings.**

asparagus onion casserole

prep: 20 min. • bake: 35 min.

This vegetable dish goes great with just about any meal. I've prepared it ahead of time, then popped it in the oven so it's ready with the rest of the supper.
—Judy Fleetwood, Beulah, Michigan

- 1 pound fresh asparagus, cut into 1-inch pieces *or* 2 packages (10 ounces *each*) asparagus cuts, thawed
- 2 medium onions, sliced
- 5 tablespoons butter, *divided*
- 2 tablespoons all-purpose flour
- 1 cup 2% milk
- 1 package (3 ounces) cream cheese, cubed
- 1 teaspoon salt
- 1/8 teaspoon pepper
- 1/2 cup shredded cheddar cheese
- 1 cup soft bread crumbs

In a large skillet, saute asparagus and onions in 1 tablespoon of butter until crisp-tender, about 8 minutes. Transfer to an ungreased 1-1/2-qt. baking dish.

In a large saucepan, melt 2 tablespoons butter. Stir in flour until smooth; gradually add milk. Bring to a boil; cook and stir for 2 minutes or until thickened.

Reduce heat. Add the cream cheese, salt and pepper; stir until cheese is melted. Pour over vegetables. Sprinkle with cheddar cheese. Melt remaining butter; toss with bread crumbs. Sprinkle over the casserole.

Bake, uncovered, at 350° for 35-40 minutes or until heated through. **yield: 4-6 servings.**

basil pasta shells

prep/total time: 30 min.

Basil and cherry tomatoes add pizazz to this cheesy pasta dish. It goes with many entrees.
—Marcia Hostetter, Canton, New York

- 2-1/2 cups uncooked medium pasta shells
- 8 green onions, thinly sliced
- 2 teaspoons olive oil
- 1 pint cherry tomatoes, halved
- 1/4 pound Canadian bacon, diced
- 1/4 cup minced fresh basil *or* 1-1/2 teaspoons dried basil
- 1/2 teaspoon coarsely ground pepper
- 3/4 cup shredded part-skim mozzarella cheese, *divided*

Cook pasta according to package directions. Meanwhile, in a large skillet, saute onions in oil until tender. Stir in the tomatoes, bacon, basil and pepper; cook and stir until tomatoes are softened. Rinse and drain pasta; stir into tomato mixture. Add half of the cheese.

Transfer the pasta mixture to a 1-1/2-qt. baking dish coated with cooking spray. Sprinkle with the remaining cheese. Bake, uncovered, at 375° for 8-10 minutes or until cheese is melted. **yield: 4 servings.**

quick & easy

When you don't want to spend a lot of time in the kitchen, turn to these recipes. They just take a few minutes to prep before you pop them in the oven. Nothing could be easier!

<< pictured left

lattice chicken potpie

prep: 10 min. • bake: 35 min.

My sister shared this great potpie with me. Because it features all four food groups, it's the only item you need to prepare for dinner.
—Angie Cottrell, Sun Prairie, Wisconsin

- 1 package (16 ounces) frozen California-blend vegetables
- 2 cups cubed cooked chicken
- 1 can (10-3/4 ounces) condensed cream of potato soup, undiluted
- 1 cup 2% milk
- 1 cup (4 ounces) shredded cheddar cheese
- 1 can (2.8 ounces) french-fried onions
- 1/2 teaspoon seasoned salt
- 1 tube (8 ounces) refrigerated crescent rolls

In a large saucepan, combine the vegetables, chicken, soup and milk; bring to a boil. Remove from the heat. Stir in the cheese, onions and seasoned salt. Transfer to a greased shallow 2-qt. baking dish.

Unroll the crescent roll dough and separate into two rectangles. Seal the perforations; cut each rectangle lengthwise into 1/2-in. strips. Form a lattice crust over the chicken mixture. Bake, uncovered, at 375° for 35-40 minutes or until golden brown. **yield: 4-6 servings.**

apricot sweet potato bake

prep/total time: 25 min.

I dress up convenient canned sweet potatoes and apricots with brown sugar, cinnamon and raisins. This speedy side dish is delicious for holiday dinners.
—Jessie Sarrazin, Livingston, Montana

- 2 cans (15 ounces *each*) cut sweet potatoes
- 1 can (15-1/4 ounces) apricot halves
- 3 tablespoons brown sugar
- 1 tablespoon cornstarch
- 1/4 teaspoon salt
- 1/8 teaspoon ground cinnamon
- 3 tablespoons dry sherry *or* chicken broth
- 1/3 cup raisins
- 1/8 teaspoon grated orange peel

Drain sweet potatoes and apricots, reserving 1/2 cup juice from each; set aside. Cut apricots in half. Place sweet potatoes and apricots in a greased shallow 1-qt. baking dish; set aside.

In a small saucepan, combine the brown sugar, cornstarch, salt and cinnamon; stir in reserved juices until smooth. Bring to a boil, stirring constantly. Cook and stir for 2 minutes or until thickened. Remove from the heat; stir in the sherry, raisins and orange peel.

Pour over sweet potato mixture. Bake, uncovered, at 375° for 12-15 minutes or until bubbly. **yield: 6 servings.**

vegetable bake

prep: 10 min. • bake: 30 min.

Even finicky eaters may change their minds about vegetables when they taste this cheesy casserole. It couldn't be easier to whip up, and it's so creamy and yummy that no one suspects how nutritious it is.
—Violet Klause, Onoway, Alberta

- 1 package (16 ounces) frozen cauliflower, thawed
- 1 can (15-1/4 ounces) whole kernel corn, drained
- 4 cups frozen broccoli florets, thawed
- 1 can (14-3/4 ounces) cream-style corn
- 1 can (10-3/4 ounces) condensed cream of celery soup, undiluted
- 2 cups (8 ounces) shredded Swiss cheese
- 1 jar (4-1/2 ounces) sliced mushrooms, drained
- 1-1/2 cups soft rye bread crumbs (about 3 slices)
- 2 tablespoons butter, melted

In a large bowl, combine the first seven ingredients. Pour into a greased 13-in. x 9-in. baking dish. Combine bread crumbs and butter; sprinkle over top.

Bake, uncovered, at 375° for 30-35 minutes or until bubbly. Let stand for 5 minutes before serving. **yield: 8-10 servings.**

onion-topped hot dish

prep: 10 min. • bake: 50 min.

With ground beef, vegetables, potatoes and onion rings, one hearty serving of this dish satisfies hunger in a hurry.
—Marilisa Fagerlind, Glidden, Iowa

- 1-1/2 pounds ground beef
- 1 package (16 ounces) frozen California-blend vegetables, thawed
- 1 can (10-3/4 ounces) condensed cheddar cheese soup, undiluted
- 1 cup (4 ounces) shredded part-skim mozzarella cheese
- 1/2 cup 2% milk
- 1/2 teaspoon salt
- 1/4 teaspoon pepper
- 1 package (32 ounces) frozen shredded hash brown potatoes, thawed
- 1/4 cup butter, melted
- 1/2 teaspoon seasoned salt
- 20 frozen large onion rings
- 1 cup (4 ounces) shredded cheddar cheese

In a large skillet, cook beef over medium heat until no longer pink; drain. Stir in the vegetables, soup, mozzarella cheese, milk, salt and pepper. Transfer to a greased 13-in. x 9-in. baking dish. Sprinkle with potatoes; drizzle with the butter. Top with seasoned salt and onion rings.

Cover and bake at 350° for 45-50 minutes or until heated through. Uncover; sprinkle with cheddar cheese. Bake 3-5 minutes longer or until cheese is melted. **yield: 6-8 servings.**

KITCHEN TIP

Many cheeses will work well as a topping for casseroles or mixed in with the other ingredients. If you don't have the cheese called for in the recipe, try cheddar, Swiss, Monterey Jack, pepper Jack, Colby or mozzarella.

crumb-topped haddock

prep: 5 min. • bake: 35 min.

With only five simple ingredients, this creamy dish with a crispy topping is a breeze to make.

—Debbie Solt, Lewistown, Pennsylvania

- 2 pounds haddock *or* cod fillets
- 1 can (10-3/4 ounces) condensed cream of shrimp soup, undiluted
- 1 teaspoon grated onion
- 1 teaspoon Worcestershire sauce
- 1 cup crushed butter-flavored crackers (about 25 crackers)

Arrange fillets in a greased 13-in. x 9-in. baking dish. Combine the soup, onion and Worcestershire sauce; pour over fish.

Bake, uncovered, at 375° for 20 minutes. Sprinkle with cracker crumbs. Bake 15 minutes longer or until fish flakes easily with a fork. **yield: 6 servings.**

greek spinach feta bake

prep: 10 min. • bake: 1 hour

"Spanakopita" is the Greek name for this traditional dish featuring spinach and feta cheese. You can serve it as a side dish or meatless main dish. My dad and I used to fight over the last piece!
—Sharon Olney, Galt, California

2 cups (16 ounces) 4% cottage cheese
1 package (10 ounces) frozen chopped spinach, thawed and squeezed dry
8 ounces crumbled feta cheese
6 tablespoons all-purpose flour
1/2 teaspoon pepper
1/4 teaspoon salt
4 eggs, lightly beaten

In a large bowl, combine the cottage cheese, spinach and feta cheese. Stir in the flour, pepper and salt. Add eggs and mix well.

Spoon into a greased 9-in. square baking dish. Bake, uncovered, at 350° for 1 hour or until a thermometer reads 160°. **yield: 6 servings.**

potato ham bake

prep: 10 min. • bake: 1-1/2 hours

Turn leftover baked ham into a sensational, hearty meal with this wonderful recipe.
—Arthur Heidorn, Hillside, Illinois

---

3 medium potatoes, peeled and thinly sliced
2 cups cubed fully cooked ham
1 medium onion, sliced and separated into rings
8 slices process American cheese
1 can (10-3/4 ounces) condensed cream of mushroom soup, undiluted
1/2 cup frozen peas, thawed

In a greased 3-qt. baking dish, layer half of the potatoes, ham, onion, cheese and soup. Repeat layers. Cover and bake at 350° for 1-1/4 hours or until potatoes are almost tender.

Sprinkle with peas. Bake, uncovered, for 10 minutes or until heated through. **yield: 6 servings.**

four-cheese rice casserole

prep: 10 min. • bake: 40 min.

My husband and I developed this recipe as an alternative to a broccoli and rice casserole that we had relied on for years. Now his folks won't let us visit during the holidays without this dish in hand.
—Gretchen Kavanaugh, Oklahoma City, Oklahoma

---

1 medium sweet onion, chopped
1/4 cup butter, cubed
4 cups cooked long grain rice
2 packages (10 ounces *each*) frozen chopped spinach, thawed and squeezed dry
3 cups (12 ounces) shredded part-skim mozzarella cheese, *divided*
1-1/2 cups shredded Parmesan cheese, *divided*
2 packages (8 ounces *each*) cream cheese, softened
1 carton (15 ounces) ricotta cheese
3/4 cup 2% milk
1/2 teaspoon garlic powder
1/2 teaspoon beau monde seasoning

In a small skillet, saute onion in butter until tender. In a large bowl, combine the rice, spinach, 1-1/2 cups mozzarella cheese, 1 cup Parmesan cheese and onion mixture.

In a large bowl, beat cream cheese, ricotta, milk, garlic powder and beau monde seasoning until smooth. Add to rice mixture and mix well.

Spoon into a greased 13-in. x 9-in. baking dish. Sprinkle with remaining mozzarella and Parmesan cheeses. Bake, uncovered, at 325° for 40-45 minutes or until heated through and the cheese is melted. **yield: 12 servings.**

---

editor's note: This recipe was tested with Spice Islands beau monde seasoning. It is a blend of salt, onion powder and celery seed.

creamy beef with biscuits

prep: 10 min. • bake: 35 min.

With 11 children, my mom had lots of cooking experience. She generously passed down to me her knowledge and recipes. This home-style dinner was one that Mom usually served to company.
—Mary Miller, Shreve, Ohio

- 2 pounds ground beef
- 1 medium onion, chopped
- 1 package (8 ounces) cream cheese, cubed
- 1 can (10-3/4 ounces) condensed cream of mushroom soup, undiluted
- 3/4 cup 2% milk
- 1/2 cup ketchup
- 1/2 teaspoon salt
- 1/4 teaspoon pepper
- 1 tube (12 ounces) refrigerated buttermilk biscuits

In a large skillet, cook beef and onion over medium heat until meat is no longer pink; drain. Add cream cheese, stirring until melted. Stir in the soup, milk, ketchup, salt and pepper.

Transfer to a greased 13-in. x 9-in. baking dish. Cover and bake at 375° for 15 minutes. Uncover; arrange biscuits over top. Bake 20-25 minutes longer or until biscuits are golden brown. **yield: 8-10 servings.**

baked shredded carrots

prep: 10 min. • bake: 45 min.

Everyone who samples this crisp and tender carrot dish loves it. I make it often when we have fresh produce from our garden. Its bright orange color looks so pretty on our Thanksgiving table.
—Carole Hartwig, Horicon, Wisconsin

- 6 cups shredded carrots (about 2 pounds)
- 3/4 cup chopped green onions
- 2 tablespoons sugar
- 1/2 teaspoon salt
- 1/2 teaspoon celery salt
- 1/4 cup butter, cubed

In a large bowl, combine the carrots, onions, sugar, salt and celery salt. Transfer to an ungreased 1-1/2-qt. baking dish. Dot with butter.

Cover and bake at 325° for 45-50 minutes or until carrots are crisp-tender. **yield: 6 servings.**

cajun-style brunch bake

prep: 10 min. + chilling • bake: 45 min. + standing

It's so handy to fix this hearty breakfast casserole the night before and refrigerate it until morning. It was given to me by a coworker and has turned out to be a family hit! I adapted it by adding onion, potato and Cajun seasoning.
—Kathie Deusser, Church Point, Louisiana

6 eggs, lightly beaten

2 cups 2% milk

1 pound sliced bacon, cooked and crumbled

6 slices bread, cubed

1 medium potato, peeled and diced

1 cup (4 ounces) shredded cheddar cheese

1/2 cup finely chopped onion

1 to 1-1/2 teaspoons Cajun seasoning

1 teaspoon salt

In a large bowl, combine all ingredients. Transfer to a greased 11-in. x 7-in. baking dish. Cover and refrigerate overnight.

Remove from the refrigerator 30 minutes before baking. Bake, uncovered, at 350° for 45-50 minutes or until a knife inserted near the center comes out clean. Let stand for 10 minutes before cutting. **yield: 6 servings.**

hearty calico bean bake

prep: 10 min. • bake: 1 hour

For years, my mother made this savory-sweet bean dish. I was always thrilled when it was on the menu, and now I serve it often to my own family. You can vary the types of beans used if you wish.
—Heather Biedler
  Martinsburg, West Virginia

- 1 can (16 ounces) pork and beans, undrained
- 1 can (16 ounces) kidney beans, rinsed and drained
- 1 can (16 ounces) chili beans, undrained
- 1 can (15-1/2 ounces) great northern beans, rinsed and drained
- 1 can (14-1/2 ounces) cut wax beans, drained
- 1-1/2 cups packed brown sugar
- 1-1/2 cups cubed fully cooked ham
- 1-1/2 cups cubed cheddar cheese
- 1/2 cup ketchup
- 1 small onion, chopped
- 2 tablespoons Worcestershire sauce

In a large bowl, combine all ingredients. Transfer to a greased shallow 3-qt. baking dish.

Bake, uncovered, at 350° for 1 hour or until bubbly and heated through. **yield: 10 servings.**

sombrero bake

prep: 10 min. • bake: 45 min.

Green chilies and hot pepper sauce bring a little zip to this Southwestern-style supper that uses up leftover cooked chicken.
—Mary Tallman, Arbor Vitae, Wisconsin

- 2-1/2 cups cubed cooked chicken
- 1 can (4 ounces) chopped green chilies
- 1 cup (4 ounces) shredded cheddar cheese
- 1 medium tomato, chopped
- 1 can (10-3/4 ounces) condensed cream of chicken soup, undiluted
- 1/2 cup 2% milk
- 1/2 teaspoon hot pepper sauce

BISCUIT TOPPING:

- 3/4 cup biscuit/baking mix
- 1/2 cup cornmeal
- 2/3 cup 2% milk
- 1 can (2.8 ounces) french-fried onions, *divided*
- 1/2 cup shredded cheddar cheese

In a greased 13-in. x 9-in. baking dish, layer with chicken, chilies, cheese and tomato. In a small bowl, combine the soup, milk and hot pepper sauce. Pour over chicken mixture. Cover and bake at 375° for 20 minutes.

In a small bowl, combine the biscuit mix, cornmeal, milk and 3/4 cup onions. Drop into eight mounds over casserole.

Bake, uncovered, for 20 minutes (topping will spread). Sprinkle with cheese and remaining onions. Bake 5 minutes longer or until cheese is melted. **yield: 6 servings.**

KITCHEN TIP

Leftover cooked chicken will keep in the refrigerator for up to 4 days. For longer storage, spread out chicken in a flat layer in a freezer bag (it will defrost more quickly this way) and squeeze out the air. Don't forget to label and date the bag before you place it in the freezer.

gaucho casserole

prep/total time: 30 min.

When our daughters graduated from college, my husband and I made recipe books for their closest friends. From the comments we received, this one was a big hit.
—*Dianne Hennis, King George, Virginia*

- 1 pound lean ground beef (90% lean)
- 1 medium onion, chopped
- 1 small green pepper, chopped
- 1 can (16 ounces) kidney beans, rinsed and drained
- 1 can (14-1/2 ounces) diced tomatoes, undrained
- 1 can (8 ounces) tomato sauce
- 1/4 cup water
- 1 envelope reduced-sodium taco seasoning
- 1 teaspoon chili powder
- 1-1/3 cups uncooked instant rice
- 1 cup (4 ounces) shredded reduced-fat Mexican cheese blend

Crumble the beef into an ungreased 2-1/2-qt. microwave-safe dish. Add onion and green pepper. Cover and microwave on high for 4-1/2 minutes or until meat is no longer pink, stirring every 2 minutes; drain.

Stir in the beans, tomatoes, tomato sauce, water, taco seasoning and chili powder. Cover and microwave on high for 3-1/2 to 4-1/2 minutes or until bubbly, stirring every 2 minutes. Stir in rice.

Transfer to a shallow 2-1/2-qt. microwave-safe dish coated with cooking spray. Cover and let stand for 6-8 minutes or until the liquid is absorbed. Sprinkle with the cheese. Cover and microwave on high for another minute or until the cheese is melted. **yield: 8 servings.**

editor's note: This recipe was tested in a 1,100-watt microwave.

spinach rice ham bake

prep: 10 min. • bake: 25 min.

When I was in college, my best friend gave me this casserole recipe. When my children were toddlers, I made it because it was an easy way for them to eat rice. We still enjoy it today.
—*Ramona Parris, Marietta, Georgia*

- 8 ounces process cheese (Velveeta), cubed
- 1/2 cup 2% milk
- 3 cups cooked rice
- 2 cups cubed fully cooked ham
- 1 package (10 ounces) frozen chopped spinach, thawed and squeezed dry

In a microwave-safe bowl, combine the cheese and milk. Microwave, uncovered, on high for 1-1/2 minutes or until cheese is melted; stir until smooth. Stir in rice, ham and spinach.

Transfer to a greased 1-1/2-qt. baking dish. Cover and bake at 350° for 25-30 minutes or until heated through. **yield: 3 servings.**

editor's note: This recipe was tested in a 1,100-watt microwave.

apple turkey potpie

prep: 10 min. • bake: 25 min.

Leftover holiday turkey turns into something special in this delicious potpie. Apples and raisins add sweetness to the savory filling.
—Georgia MacDonald
   Dover, New Hampshire

- 1/4 **cup chopped onion**
- 1 **tablespoon butter**
- 2 **cans (10-3/4 ounces *each*) condensed cream of chicken soup, undiluted**
- 3 **cups cubed cooked turkey**
- 1 **large unpeeled tart apples, cubed**
- 1/3 **cup golden raisins**
- 1 **teaspoon lemon juice**
- 1/4 **teaspoon ground nutmeg**
- **Pastry for a single-crust pie (9 inches)**

In a large saucepan, saute onion in butter until tender. Add the soup, turkey, apple, raisins, lemon juice and nutmeg. Spoon into an ungreased 11-in. x 7-in. baking dish.

On a lightly floured surface, roll out pastry to fit top of dish. Place over filling; flute edges and cut slits in top.

Bake at 425° for 25-30 minutes or until crust is golden brown and filling is bubbly. **yield: 6 servings.**

upside-down meat pie

prep/total time: 30 min.

Thanks to the sloppy joe flavor of this dinner, kids will dig right in and adults will, too. Plus, I can get it on the table in just a half an hour.
—Jennifer Eilts, Lincoln, Nebraska

- 1 **pound ground beef**
- 1/2 **cup chopped celery**
- 1/2 **cup chopped onion**
- 1/4 **cup chopped green pepper**
- 1 **can (10-3/4 ounces) condensed tomato soup, undiluted**
- 1 **teaspoon prepared mustard**
- 1-1/2 **cups biscuit/baking mix**
- 1/3 **cup water**
- 3 **slices process American cheese, halved diagonally**
- **Green pepper rings, optional**

In a large skillet, cook the beef, celery, onion and green pepper over medium heat until the meat is no longer pink; drain. Stir in soup and mustard. Transfer to a greased 9-in. pie plate.

Meanwhile, in a large bowl, combine dry baking mix and water until a soft dough forms. Turn onto a lightly floured surface; roll into a 9-in. circle.

Place over meat mixture. Bake at 425° for 20 minutes or until golden brown. Cool for 5 minutes.

Run a knife around edge to loosen biscuit; invert onto a serving platter. Arrange cheese slices in a pinwheel pattern on top. Garnish with green pepper rings if desired. **yield: 6 servings.**

hot chicken salad

prep: 10 min. • bake: 30 min.

I know you'll enjoy this rich and creamy chicken dish. Topped with crunchy potato chips and almonds, the delicious casserole is a fabulous way to use up leftover chicken.

—Doris Heath, Franklin, North Carolina

- 2 cups diced cooked chicken
- 1 can (10-3/4 ounces) condensed cream of chicken soup, undiluted
- 2 celery ribs, finely chopped
- 1/2 cup mayonnaise
- 1 can (4 ounces) mushroom stems and pieces, drained
- 2 tablespoons finely chopped onion
- 1/2 cup crushed butter-flavored crackers (about 12 crackers)
- 1/2 cup crushed potato chips
- 1/2 cup sliced almonds, toasted

In a large bowl, combine the chicken, soup, celery, mayonnaise, mushrooms and onion. Stir in cracker crumbs. Spoon into a greased 1-1/2-qt. baking dish.

Bake, uncovered, at 375° for 15 minutes. Sprinkle with potato chips and almonds. Bake 15 minutes longer or until bubbly and lightly browned. **yield: 4 servings.**

nacho mac 'n' cheese

prep/total time: 25 min.

Your entire family will find the taste of this Tex-Mex inspired stove-top casserole very appealing. Most of the ingredients are mixed in one pot, making cleanup a breeze!

—Taste of Home Test Kitchen

---

3 cups uncooked gemelli *or* spiral pasta

1 pound ground beef

2 cups chopped sweet red peppers

1/4 cup butter, cubed

1/4 cup all-purpose flour

1 envelope taco seasoning

1/4 teaspoon pepper

2-1/4 cups 2% milk

2 cups (8 ounces) shredded cheddar cheese

1 cup frozen corn, thawed

1 cup coarsely crushed tortilla chips

Cook gemelli according to package directions. Meanwhile, in a Dutch oven, cook beef and red peppers over medium heat until meat is no longer pink; drain.

Stir in the butter, flour, taco seasoning and pepper until blended. Gradually stir in milk. Bring to a boil; cook and stir for 2 minutes or until thickened. Remove from the heat. Stir in cheese and corn until cheese is melted.

Drain gemelli; add to beef mixture and stir to coat. Sprinkle with tortilla chips. **yield: 6 servings.**

salmon casserole

prep: 10 min. • bake: 30 min.

Canned salmon is the key ingredient in this budget-friendly supper. Bread crumbs give it a soft texture, and mayonnaise, mustard and cheese add a lot of flavor to this old-fashioned favorite.

—Agnes Moon, Ionia, Michigan

- 1 can (7-1/2 ounces) salmon, drained, bones and skin removed
- 4 cups soft bread crumbs
- 1/2 cup chopped celery
- 1/2 cup chopped green pepper
- 1/4 cup chopped onion
- 1 tablespoon minced fresh parsley
- 3/4 cup fat-free milk
- 1 tablespoon reduced-fat mayonnaise
- 1 teaspoon ground mustard
- 1/4 teaspoon pepper
- 1 tablespoon grated Parmesan cheese
- 1/4 teaspoon paprika

In a large bowl, combine the salmon, bread crumbs, celery, green pepper, onion and parsley. In a small bowl, combine the milk, mayonnaise, mustard and pepper. Pour over salmon mixture; toss to coat evenly.

Transfer to a 1-qt. baking dish coated with cooking spray. Sprinkle with cheese and paprika. Bake, uncovered, at 350° for 30-35 minutes or until heated through and top is golden brown. **yield: 4 servings.**

chicken veggie casserole

prep: 10 min. • bake: 1 hour

This all-in-one meal is great when you want something filling and nutritious without spending a lot of time in the kitchen. To assemble it even quicker, you can substitute a package of frozen vegetables.

—Bonnie Smith, Goshen, Indiana

- 3 cups cubed cooked chicken
- 4 medium carrots, cut into chunks
- 3 medium red potatoes, cut into chunks
- 3 celery ribs, sliced
- 1 can (10-3/4 ounces) condensed cream of chicken soup, undiluted
- 2/3 cup water
- 1/2 teaspoon salt
- 1/4 teaspoon pepper

Place chicken in a greased shallow 2-qt. baking dish. Top with the carrots, potatoes and celery. Combine the soup, water, salt and pepper; pour over vegetables.

Cover and bake at 350° for 60-75 minutes or until vegetables are tender. **yield: 5 servings.**

cheesy beef casserole

prep: 10 min. • bake: 30 min.

When it comes to family-pleasing supper, this dish can't miss! The taco flavor, ground beef and Mexican cheese ensure satisfied smiles.

—Sharon Crider, Junction City, Kansas

- 1-1/2 **pounds ground beef**
- 1 **envelope taco seasoning**
- 2 **cups water**
- 2 **cups uncooked instant rice**
- 1 **can (10-3/4 ounces) condensed cream of chicken soup, undiluted**
- 1 **can (10-3/4 ounces) condensed cream of mushroom soup, undiluted**
- 1 **can (4 ounces) chopped green chilies, undrained**
- 2 **cups (8 ounces) shredded Mexican cheese blend**

In a large skillet, cook beef over medium heat until no longer pink; drain. Stir in the taco seasoning, water, rice, soups and chilies. Transfer to a greased 13-in. x 9-in. baking dish.

Cover and bake at 350° for 25 minutes. Uncover; sprinkle with cheese. Bake 5 minutes longer or until heated through and cheese is melted. **yield: 6-8 servings.**

meat lover's pizza casserole

prep: 10 min. • bake: 40 min.

My children have busy schedules, so I need suppers that are sure to satisfy. This one has been a popular choice ever since a friend shared it with me.

—Karin Ptak, Elburn, Illinois

- 1 **pound ground beef**
- 1 **medium onion, chopped**
- 1 **can (15 ounces) pizza sauce**
- 8 **ounces elbow macaroni, cooked and drained**
- 2 **cups (8 ounces) shredded part-skim mozzarella cheese**
- 1 **package (3-1/2 ounces) sliced pepperoni, quartered**
- 1/2 **teaspoon salt**

In a large skillet, cook beef and onion over medium heat until meat is no longer pink; drain. Stir in remaining ingredients.

Transfer to a greased 2-qt. baking dish. Bake, uncovered, at 350° for 40-45 minutes or until heated through. **yield: 6 servings.**

tomato crouton casserole

prep: 10 min. • bake: 30 min.

This old-fashioned side uses lots of delicious tomatoes and seasonings that give it an Italian twist. Every time I serve it, someone asks for the recipe.
—Norma Nelson, Punta Gorda, Florida

- 8 medium tomatoes, peeled and cut into wedges
- 8 slices bread, crusts removed, cubed
- 1/2 cup plus 2 tablespoons butter, melted
- 1 teaspoon salt
- 1 teaspoon dried basil
- 1 teaspoon dried thyme
- 3/4 cup grated Parmesan cheese

Arrange tomatoes in a greased 13-in. x 9-in. baking dish. Top with bread cubes. Combine the butter, salt, basil and thyme; drizzle over bread and tomatoes. Sprinkle with cheese.

Bake, uncovered, at 350° for 30-35 minutes or until tomatoes are tender. **yield: 8-10 servings.**

green bean turkey bake

prep/total time: 20 min.

Let the microwave help you out in the kitchen. This speedy meal in one uses leftover turkey and mashed potatoes, and a few pantry staples. In just 20 minutes, dinner is served. If you, don't have leftover potatoes, make some instant mashed potatoes.
—Ann Wood
  Battle Ground, Washington

- 2 cups frozen cut green beans, thawed
- 1-1/2 cups cubed cooked turkey breast
- 1 can (10-3/4 ounces) condensed cream of mushroom soup, undiluted
- 1 cup (4 ounces) shredded cheddar cheese
- 1/3 cup 2% milk
- 3 cups mashed potatoes
- 1/2 cup cheese-flavored snack crackers, crushed

In a 2-qt. microwave-safe dish, combine the green beans, turkey, soup, cheese and milk. Cover and microwave on high for 5-6 minutes or until bubbly, stirring once.

Carefully spread mashed potatoes over turkey mixture; sprinkle with cracker crumbs. Cover and cook on high for 2-4 minutes or until heated through. Let stand for 5 minutes before serving. **yield: 6 servings.**

editor's note: This recipe was tested in a 1,100-watt microwave.

serves two

Do casseroles leave you with lots of leftovers? Well now you can indulge in this comfort food without having to worry about making too much. These recipes are perfectly sized for two servings.

« pictured left

sweet potato shepherd's pie

prep: 25 min. • bake: 25 min.

As a child, shepherd's pie was one of my favorites. But now, having cut white potatoes out of our diet, I experimented with sweet potatoes. The result is different but just as yummy!
—Tanya Marcketti, Golden, Colorado

- 1 large sweet potato
- 1/2 pound lean ground beef (90% lean)
- 1/4 cup chopped onion
- 1 can (8-3/4 ounces) whole kernel corn, drained
- 1/2 cup tomato sauce
- Dash *each* ground cinnamon, allspice and nutmeg
- 1 tablespoon butter
- 1 tablespoon 2% milk
- 1/8 teaspoon salt
- 1/8 teaspoon pepper

Scrub and pierce sweet potato; place on a microwave-safe plate. Microwave, uncovered, on high for 10-12 minutes or until tender, turning once.

Meanwhile, in a large skillet, cook beef and onion until meat is no longer pink; drain. Add the corn, tomato sauce and spices. Place in a 1-qt. baking dish coated with cooking spray; set aside.

When cool enough to handle, cut potato in half; scoop out the pulp and place in a small bowl. Mash with butter, milk, salt and pepper. Spread evenly over meat mixture.

Bake, uncovered, at 350° for 25-30 minutes or until heated through. **yield: 2 servings.**

editor's note: This recipe was tested in a 1,100-watt microwave.

sausage-stuffed shells

prep: 25 min. • bake: 20 min.

I wanted to make manicotti one day but was out of the noodles. So I came up with this recipe using jumbo shells instead. They were much easier to work with.
—Lori Daniels, Beverly, West Virginia

- 1/3 pound bulk Italian sausage
- 1 can (8 ounces) tomato sauce
- 1/4 cup tomato paste
- 2 tablespoons water
- 1 teaspoon brown sugar
- 1/2 teaspoon Italian seasoning
- 1/3 cup 4% cottage cheese
- 3/4 cup shredded part-skim mozzarella cheese, *divided*
- 2 tablespoons beaten egg
- 1/2 teaspoon minced fresh parsley
- 6 jumbo pasta shells, cooked and drained
- Grated Parmesan cheese, optional

In a small saucepan, cook sausage over medium heat until no longer pink; drain. Set half of the sausage aside for filling. Add the tomato sauce, tomato paste, water, brown sugar and Italian seasoning to sausage in pan. Bring to a boil. Reduce heat; simmer, uncovered, for 15 minutes, stirring occasionally.

In a small bowl, combine the cottage cheese, 1/2 cup mozzarella cheese, egg, parsley and reserved sausage. Stuff into shells. Spread 1/4 cup meat sauce in an ungreased 1-qt. shallow baking dish. Place stuffed shells in the dish; drizzle with the remaining meat sauce.

Sprinkle with remaining mozzarella cheese and Parmesan cheese if desired. Bake, uncovered, at 350° for 20-25 minutes or until filling reaches 160°. **yield: 2 servings.**

creamy scalloped potatoes

prep: 25 min. • bake: 40 min.

What's not to like about these tender potatoes with cheese topping? This recipe is a downsized dish full of traditional taste.

—Edie Farm, Farmington, New Mexico

- 2 tablespoons butter
- 2 tablespoons all-purpose flour
- 3/4 teaspoon salt
- Dash pepper
- 1-1/3 cups 2% milk
- 2 medium potatoes, peeled and thinly sliced
- 2 tablespoons finely chopped onion
- 1/4 cup shredded cheddar cheese

In a small saucepan, melt butter. Stir in the flour, salt and pepper until smooth. Gradually stir in milk. Bring to a boil; cook and stir for 2 minutes or until thickened.

In a 1-qt. baking dish coated with cooking spray, layer half of the potatoes, onion and half of the sauce. Top with the remaining potatoes and sauce.

Cover and bake at 375° for 30 minutes. Uncover; sprinkle with cheese. Bake 10-15 minutes longer or until potatoes are tender. **yield: 2 servings.**

biscuit-topped beef casserole

prep: 25 min. • bake: 20 min.

This satisfying recipe has been in our family for years. We just made a few adjustments. It's so flavorful, we try to make this often!

—Debbie Slater, Spokane, Washington

- 1/2 pound lean ground beef (90% lean)
- 1/4 cup chopped onion
- 1/2 cup water
- 1/2 cup tomato sauce
- 1/4 cup tomato paste
- 1/8 teaspoon pepper
- 1 cup frozen mixed vegetables, thawed
- 1/2 cup shredded part-skim mozzarella cheese, *divided*
- 1 tube (6 ounces) refrigerated flaky buttermilk biscuits
- 1 teaspoon butter, melted
- 1/4 teaspoon dried oregano

In a small saucepan, cook beef and onion over medium heat until meat is no longer pink; drain. Stir in the water, tomato sauce, tomato paste and pepper. Bring to a boil. Reduce heat; simmer, uncovered, for 10 minutes.

Remove from the heat; stir in vegetables and 1/4 cup cheese. Transfer to a 1-qt. baking dish coated with cooking spray (dish will be full).

Separate each biscuit horizontally in half; arrange around edge of dish. Brush with butter; sprinkle with oregano. Sprinkle remaining cheese over beef filling.

Bake, uncovered, at 375° for 18-22 minutes or until heated through and biscuits are golden brown. **yield: 2 servings.**

broccoli cheese strata

prep: 15 min. + chilling • bake: 25 min.

For an excellent, easy-to-prepare lunch for two, try this recipe. I enjoy it so much, I frequently fix it for myself and reheat the extra portion in the microwave.
—*Mina Dyck, Boissevain, Manitoba*

- 1 cup coarsely chopped fresh broccoli
- 2 green onions, sliced
- 1 tablespoon water
- 2 slices white bread, cubed
- 1/2 cup shredded cheddar cheese
- 4 eggs
- 1/2 cup 2% milk
- 1/2 teaspoon Dijon mustard
- 1/8 teaspoon dill weed

Dash ground nutmeg

Dash pepper

In a small microwave-safe dish, microwave broccoli and onions in water on high for 1 minute; drain and set aside. Place bread in a shallow 3-cup baking dish coated with cooking spray. Add broccoli mixture and cheese.

In a small bowl, combine the eggs, milk, mustard, dill, nutmeg and pepper; pour over cheese. Cover and refrigerate overnight.

Remove from the refrigerator 30 minutes before baking. Bake, uncovered, at 350° for 25-30 minutes or until a knife inserted near the center comes out clean. **yield: 2 servings.**

carrots au gratin

prep/total time: 30 min.

A luscious cheese sauce coats carrots in this homey side. The cornflake topping adds a nice crunch. I'm an onion lover, so I sometimes double the amount called for in this recipe.

—*Agnes Carone
East Windsor, Connecticut*

- 3 medium carrots, sliced
- 2 tablespoons chopped onion
- 5 teaspoons butter, *divided*
- 1 tablespoon all-purpose flour
- 1/4 teaspoon salt

Dash pepper

- 1/2 cup 2% milk
- 1/3 cup shredded cheddar cheese
- 1 tablespoon minced fresh parsley
- 2 tablespoons crushed cornflakes

Place 1 in. of water in a saucepan; add the carrots. Bring to a boil. Reduce heat. Cover and simmer for 5-8 minutes or until the carrots are almost tender.

Meanwhile, in a small saucepan, saute onion in 3 teaspoons butter until tender. Stir in flour, salt and pepper until blended. Gradually whisk in milk. Bring to a boil; cook and stir 1-2 minutes or until thickened.

Remove from heat; add the cheese and parsley, stirring until cheese is melted. Drain carrots; add to sauce.

Transfer to a greased 2-cup baking dish. Melt remaining butter; stir in cornflakes. Sprinkle over carrots. Bake, uncovered, at 350° for 15-20 minutes or until bubbly and golden brown. **yield: 2 servings.**

puffed pizza casserole

prep: 25 min. • bake: 20 min.

My sister gave me this recipe a while ago. The filling one-dish meal has a fun popover crust, and the pizza flavor makes it a hit with all ages!
—Linda Wilkens
     Maple Grove, Minnesota

- 1/3 **pound lean ground beef (90% lean)**
- 1/4 **cup chopped onion**
- 1/2 **cup tomato sauce**
-   3 **tablespoons water**
-   3 **teaspoons spaghetti sauce mix**
- 1/3 **cup all-purpose flour**
- 1/3 **cup 2% milk**
-   2 **tablespoons beaten egg**
-   1 **teaspoon canola oil**
- 1/2 **cup shredded part-skim mozzarella cheese**
-   2 **tablespoons grated Parmesan cheese**

In a large skillet, cook beef and onion over medium heat until meat is no longer pink; drain. Add the tomato sauce, water and spaghetti sauce mix. Bring to a boil. Reduce heat; simmer, uncovered, for 5 minutes. Meanwhile, place flour in a small bowl. Combine the milk, egg and oil; whisk into flour just until blended.

Pour meat mixture into a 3-cup baking dish coated with cooking spray. Sprinkle with mozzarella cheese. Pour flour mixture over top. Sprinkle with Parmesan cheese.

Bake, uncovered, at 400° for 20-25 minutes or until golden brown and center is set. **yield: 2 servings.**

cheddar bacon penne

prep/total time: 30 min.

In just a half hour you can be sitting down to dinner with this fabulous pasta. I added garlic and crumbled bacon to the original recipe for some pizzazz.
—Sandra Bienz, Calgary, Alberta

-       1 **cup uncooked penne pasta**
-     1/4 **cup chopped onion**
-     1/4 **teaspoon minced garlic**
-       1 **tablespoon butter**
- 4-1/2 **teaspoons all-purpose flour**
-       1 **cup 2% milk**
- 1-1/2 **cups (6 ounces) shredded cheddar cheese, *divided***
-       1 **bacon strip, cooked and crumbled**

Cook pasta according to package directions. Meanwhile, in a small nonstick skillet coated with cooking spray, saute onion until tender. Add garlic; cook 1 minute longer. Set aside.

In a small saucepan, melt butter. Stir in flour until smooth; gradually add milk. Bring to a boil; cook and stir for 1-2 minutes or until thickened. Add 1 cup cheese, stirring until melted.

Drain pasta. Add pasta, bacon and onion mixture to the sauce; stir to coat. Transfer to a 3-cup baking dish coated with cooking spray. Sprinkle with remaining cheese.

Bake, uncovered, at 350° for 15-20 minutes or until cheese is melted. **yield: 2 servings.**

Cook noodles according to package directions. Meanwhile, in a small saucepan, melt 5 teaspoons butter. Stir in the flour, salt and pepper until blended; gradually add milk. Bring to a boil; cook and stir for 1-2 minutes or until thickened. Reduce heat; add the cream cheese, tuna, pimientos and chives. Cook and stir until the cheese is melted.

Drain noodles. Spread 1/4 cup tuna mixture into a 3-cup baking dish coated with cooking spray. Layer with half of the noodles, 1/2 cup tuna mixture and one slice of cheese. Repeat layers.

In a small microwave-safe bowl, melt remaining butter; stir in bread crumbs. Sprinkle over top of casserole. Bake, uncovered, at 350° for 20-25 minutes or until bubbly. **yield: 2 servings.**

sweet onion rice casserole

prep: 15 min. • bake: 45 min.

This creamy onion side dish is warm, delectable and perfect for a cool evening. Everyone who tries it really enjoys it.
—Julie Rea
   Battle Ground, Washington

- 1/3 **cup uncooked instant rice**
- 2-1/2 **cups chopped sweet onions**
- 1 **tablespoon butter**
- 1/4 **cup shredded Swiss cheese**
- 1/4 **cup half-and-half cream**

Cook rice according to package directions. Meanwhile, in a large skillet, saute onions in butter until tender. Stir in the cheese, cream and rice.

Transfer to a 2-cup baking dish coated with cooking spray. Bake, uncovered, at 325° for 45-55 minutes or until golden brown. **yield: 2 servings.**

comforting tuna casserole

prep: 15 min. • bake: 20 min.

My mother gave me the recipe for this classic tuna bake many years ago. Sometimes I use sliced stuffed olives instead of pimientos.
—Dorothy Coleman, Hobe Sound, Florida

- 1-3/4 **cups uncooked wide egg noodles**
- 6 **teaspoons butter,** *divided*
- 4 **teaspoons all-purpose flour**
- 1/4 **teaspoon salt**

Dash pepper

- 3/4 **cup 2% milk**
- 1 **package (3 ounces) cream cheese, softened**
- 1 **pouch (3 ounces) white water-packed tuna**
- 2 **tablespoons diced pimientos**
- 2 **teaspoons minced chives**
- 2 **sliced Muenster cheese (3/4 ounce** *each***)**
- 2 **tablespoons soft bread crumbs**

pork chop-cranberry bake

prep: 20 min. • bake: 45 min.

This recipe was originally for pork chops and apples and it was good. I added cranberry and onion, and it was even more sensational. I like to eat this with mashed potatoes or buttered noodles.

—Shelvy Ritter, Portage, Wisconsin

- 2 boneless pork loin chops (5 ounces *each*)
- 2 teaspoons butter
- 2 medium apples, peeled and sliced
- 3/4 cup whole-berry cranberry sauce
- 1 small sweet onion, halved and thinly sliced
- 2 tablespoons brown sugar
- 1/4 teaspoon ground cinnamon

In a small nonstick skillet, brown pork chops in butter. Meanwhile, in a small bowl, combine the apples, cranberry sauce and onion. Transfer to an 8-in. square baking dish coated with cooking spray. Combine brown sugar and cinnamon; sprinkle over apple mixture. Top with pork chops.

Cover and bake at 325° for 45-50 minutes or until pork reaches 160° and apples are tender. **yield: 2 servings.**

turkey lattice pie

prep: 20 min. • bake: 25 min.

After tasting this savory potpie, you'll find yourself turning to this recipe time and again. Prepared crescent roll dough makes the lattice crust a snap to do.
—Taste of Home Test Kitchen

- 1 **cup water**
- 1/2 **cup frozen mixed vegetables**
- 2 **teaspoons chicken bouillon granules**
- 2 **tablespoons plus 1/2 teaspoon cornstarch**
- 1 **cup 2% milk**
- 1 **cup cubed cooked turkey**
- 1/2 **cup shredded cheddar cheese**
- 2 **teaspoons minced fresh parsley**
- 1/4 **teaspoon salt**
- 1/8 **teaspoon pepper**
- 1 **tube (4 ounces) refrigerated crescent rolls**

In a large saucepan, bring the water, vegetables and bouillon to a boil. Reduce heat; simmer, uncovered, for 3-5 minutes or until vegetables are tender.

In a small bowl, combine cornstarch and milk until smooth; add to the vegetable mixture. Bring to a boil; cook and stir for 1-2 minutes or until thickened. Add the turkey, cheese, parsley, salt and pepper. Pour into a greased 8-in. square baking dish.

Unroll crescent roll dough; separate into two rectangles. Seal seams and perforations. Place long sides together to form a square; pinch edges together to seal. Cut into eight strips; make a lattice crust over hot turkey mixture.

Bake at 375° for 25-30 minutes or until top is golden brown. **yield: 2 servings.**

swiss spinach casserole

prep: 10 min. • bake: 30 min.

I'm a nurse who works 12-hour shifts, so I don't have much time to cook. This goes together quickly and can easily be shared with my husband.
—Mary Ellen Minter
  North Ridgeville, Ohio

- 1 **egg**
- 3 **tablespoons 2% milk**
- 4 **cups chopped fresh spinach**
- 1/2 **cup chopped water chestnuts**
- 1/2 **cup shredded Swiss cheese,** *divided*
- 1 **tablespoon chopped pimientos**
- 1 **tablespoon chopped green onion**
- 1/4 **to 1/2 teaspoon salt**
- 1/8 **teaspoon ground nutmeg, optional**

In a bowl, whisk together egg and milk. Stir in the spinach, water chestnuts, 1/4 cup Swiss cheese, pimientos, green onion, salt and nutmeg if desired.

Transfer to a greased 1-qt. baking dish. Cover and bake at 350° for 25 minutes. Sprinkle with remaining cheese. Bake, uncovered, 5 minutes longer or until cheese is melted. **yield: 2 servings.**

turkey spaghetti pie

prep: 25 min. • bake: 15 min.

This pie is practically a meal in itself. I usually put a green salad and crusty French rolls on the table with it.

—Colleen Sherman
  Bakersfield, California

2 ounces uncooked spaghetti, broken in half

1 egg, lightly beaten

2 tablespoons grated Parmesan cheese

3 tablespoons sour cream

1/2 pound ground turkey

1/4 cup chopped green pepper

2 tablespoons chopped onion

1 teaspoon butter

1/3 cup tomato sauce

1/4 teaspoon garlic salt

1/4 teaspoon dried oregano

Salt and pepper to taste

1/3 cup shredded part-skim mozzarella cheese

Cook spaghetti according to package directions; drain. In a small bowl, combine the egg, Parmesan cheese and spaghetti. Press spaghetti mixture onto the bottom and up sides of a greased shallow 2-cup baking dish or 7-in. pie plate. Spread the top with sour cream.

Crumble turkey into a skillet; add the pepper, onion and butter. Cook over medium heat until meat is no longer pink; drain. Stir in the tomato sauce, garlic salt, oregano, salt and pepper. Spoon into spaghetti crust. Sprinkle with mozzarella cheese. Cover edges loosely with foil.

Bake at 350° for 15-20 minutes or until heated through and cheese is melted. Serve immediately. **yield: 2 servings.**

baked ham tetrazzini

prep: 20 min. • bake: 20 min.

Rich, creamy pasta and cubed ham blend perfectly in this hearty meal for two. It's a great way to use up leftover holiday ham.

—Elvi Kaukinen, Horseheads, New York

4 ounces uncooked spaghetti, broken into 2-inch pieces

1 cup (4 ounces) shredded sharp cheddar cheese

2/3 cup condensed cream of mushroom soup, undiluted

1/2 cup 2% milk

1 tablespoon minced fresh parsley

2 teaspoons diced pimientos, drained

1 teaspoon finely chopped onion

1/2 teaspoon Worcestershire sauce

Dash pepper

3/4 cup cubed fully cooked ham

Cook spaghetti according to package directions. Meanwhile, in a small bowl, combine the cheese, soup, milk, parsley, pimientos, onion, Worcestershire sauce and pepper.

Drain spaghetti; add to soup mixture. Spread half into a 1-1/2-qt. baking dish coated with cooking spray. Layer with the ham and remaining spaghetti mixture.

Bake, uncovered, at 375° for 20-25 minutes or until bubbly. **yield: 2 servings.**

cheesy ham 'n' noodles

prep: 10 min. • bake: 30 min.

I love to prepare this old-fashioned supper with ham. Peas add color and flavor.
—Renee Schwebach, Dumont, Minnesota

- 3/4 cup uncooked egg noodles
- 2 tablespoons butter, *divided*
- 1 tablespoon all-purpose flour
- 2/3 cup 2% milk
- 1/2 cup cubed process cheese (Velveeta)
- 1 cup cubed fully cooked ham
- 1/2 cup frozen peas, thawed
- 2 tablespoons dry bread crumbs
- 1/4 teaspoon dried parsley flakes

Cook noodles according to package directions. Meanwhile, in a saucepan, melt 1 tablespoon butter; stir in flour until smooth. Gradually add milk. Bring to a boil over medium heat; cook and stir for 2 minutes or until thickened. Remove from the heat; stir in the cheese until melted.

Drain noodles. Add the noodles, ham and peas to cheese sauce. Pour into a 3-cup baking dish coated with cooking spray. Melt the remaining butter; toss with bread crumbs and parsley. Sprinkle over the top.

Bake, uncovered, at 350° for 30-35 minutes or until heated through. **yield: 2 servings.**

nacho chicken mushroom casserole

prep: 10 min. • bake: 25 min.

My fiance never tires of this cheesy Southwestern dinner. I like it not only for its flavor, but because it takes only 10 minutes to prepare.
—Caroline Nielsen
  Wausau, Wisconsin

- 1 cup cubed cooked chicken
- 3/4 cup crushed nacho tortilla chips
- 2/3 cup condensed cream of chicken soup, undiluted
- 1/2 cup sliced fresh mushrooms
- 1/4 cup sour cream
- 2 tablespoons 2% milk
- 1 tablespoon chopped green chilies
- 1/2 teaspoon finely chopped jalapeno pepper, optional
- 1/4 cup shredded part-skim mozzarella cheese
- 1/4 cup shredded cheddar cheese

In a large bowl, combine the first eight ingredients. In a small bowl, combine the cheeses; stir half into the chicken mixture.

Transfer to a 1-qt. baking dish coated with cooking spray. Sprinkle with remaining cheeses. Bake, uncovered, at 350° for 25-30 minutes or until cheese is bubbly. **yield: 2 servings.**

editor's note: We recommend wearing disposable gloves when cutting hot peppers. Avoid touching your face.

creamy chicken enchiladas

prep/total time: 30 min.

I love this creamy dish because it's easy, tastes amazing, freezes well and reheats easily in the microwave. If you prefer more zip, substitute pepper Jack cheese for Monterey Jack.
—Rachel Smith, Katy, Texas

- 2/3 cup condensed cream of chicken soup, undiluted
- 2/3 cup sour cream
- 2 cups shredded cooked chicken breast
- 1/2 cup shredded Monterey Jack cheese, *divided*
- 4 flour tortillas (6 inches), warmed

In a small bowl, combine soup and sour cream. Spread half over the bottom of an 8-in. square baking dish coated with cooking spray.

Place 1/2 cup of the chicken and 1 tablespoon cheese down the center of each tortilla; roll up and place in the baking dish. Top with the remaining soup mixture; sprinkle with the remaining cheese.

Bake, uncovered, at 350° for 18-22 minutes or until heated through. **yield: 2 servings.**

macaroni sausage supper

prep: 15 min. • bake: 20 min.

This nourishing and yummy supper been served in my family for decades. Sometimes I add a few fresh mushrooms or substitute cream of celery soup and a stalk of diced celery for extra flavor. I heat up the leftover soup for lunch next day.
—Joyce Clauson, Wisconsin Rapids, Wisconsin

- 3/4 cup uncooked elbow macaroni
- 1/3 pound bulk Italian sausage
- 2 tablespoons chopped onion
- 1 tablespoon chopped green pepper
- 1/4 cup sliced ripe olives, drained
- 2/3 cup condensed cream of mushroom soup, undiluted
- 1/4 cup 2% milk
- 1/8 teaspoon pepper
- 2 ounces process cheese (Velveeta)

Cook macaroni according to package directions. Meanwhile, in a small skillet, cook the sausage, onion and green pepper over medium heat until meat is no longer pink; drain.

Drain macaroni; stir into sausage mixture. Add olives. Transfer to a 1-qt. baking dish coated with cooking spray.

In a small saucepan over low heat, combine the soup, milk and pepper. Gradually add the cheese, stirring until melted. Pour over the sausage mixture.

Bake, uncovered, at 375° for 20-25 minutes or until heated through. **yield: 2 servings.**

KITCHEN TIP

Smaller-portion recipes often call for only part of a sweet pepper (green, red or yellow). To keep the leftover pepper from going bad before you use it, dice or chop the entire pepper. Wrap 1- or 2-tablespoon portions in plastic wrap, then place in freezer bags and freeze for up to 6 months.

corn chip beef bake

prep: 20 min. • bake: 15 min.

After my children left home, I found it difficult to whittle down meals for two, but I eventually succeeded, and this became one of our go-to recipes. You can easily freeze the extra portion if you're cooking for one.

—Barbara Bernard, Holyoke, Massachusetts

- 1/2 pound lean ground beef (90% lean)
- 1/3 cup finely chopped onion
- 1/3 cup thinly sliced celery
- 1/3 cup finely chopped green pepper
- 1/4 teaspoon minced garlic
- 1 cup cooked brown rice
- 1 medium tomato, chopped
- 1 teaspoon lemon juice
- 1/4 teaspoon salt
- 1/4 teaspoon hot pepper sauce
- 1/4 cup mayonnaise
- 1/2 to 1 cup corn chips, crushed

In a large skillet, cook the beef, onion, celery and green pepper over medium heat until meat is no longer pink. Add garlic; cook 1 minute longer; drain. Stir in the rice, tomato, lemon juice, salt and hot pepper sauce; heat through. Stir in mayonnaise.

Spoon into two 15-oz. baking dishes coated with cooking spray. Sprinkle with crushed corn chips. Bake, uncovered, at 350° for 13-15 minutes or until heated through. **yield: 2 servings.**

kielbasa and pepper casserole

prep: 15 min. • bake: 55 min.

This filling supper is packed full of flavor and deliciousness. A few scoops of this will leave you satisfied all night!

—Sara Wilson
  Middlebourne, West Virginia

- 1/2 **pound smoked kielbasa** *or* **Polish sausage, cut into 1/2-inch slices**
- 4 **small red potatoes, halved**
- 1 **medium onion, halved and sliced**
- 1 **medium sweet red pepper, cut into 1-inch pieces**
- 2 **tablespoons olive oil**
- 1/8 **teaspoon salt**
- 1/8 **teaspoon pepper**
- 1/4 **cup heavy whipping cream**

Minced fresh parsley

In a small bowl, combine the sausage, potatoes, onion and red pepper. Drizzle with oil; sprinkle with salt and pepper. Toss to coat. Transfer to a greased 1-qt. baking dish.

Cover and bake at 375° for 45 minutes. Stir in cream; cover and bake 10-15 minutes longer or until vegetables are tender and the cream has thickened. Sprinkle with parsley. **yield: 2 servings.**

creamy chicken casserole

prep: 20 min. • bake: 25 min.

French onion dip lends a tangy accent to this cheesy rice bake. Short prep time means you can eat a scrumptious dinner without spending hours in the kitchen.

—Jaky Broussard, Greensboro, Alabama

- 2/3 **cup uncooked instant rice**
- 1/4 **cup chopped onion**
- 2 **teaspoons butter**
- 1/2 **cup 4% cottage cheese**
- 1/3 **cup French onion dip**
- 3 **tablespoons sour cream**
- 1/4 **teaspoon salt**

Dash white pepper
- 1/2 **cup cubed cooked chicken**
- 1/2 **cup shredded cheddar cheese**
- 2 **tablespoons chopped green chilies**

Cook rice according to package directions. Meanwhile, in a small skillet, saute onion in butter until tender; set aside. In a small bowl, combine the cottage cheese, onion dip, sour cream, salt and pepper. Stir in rice and onion.

Spread half of the rice mixture into a 3-cup baking dish coated with cooking spray. Layer with chicken, 1/4 cup cheddar cheese and green chilies. Top with remaining rice mixture; sprinkle with remaining cheese.

Bake, uncovered, at 350° for 25-30 minutes or until bubbly. **yield: 2 servings.**

southwest turkey casserole

prep: 20 min. • bake: 20 min.

When I was small, my mother and stepfather—who was head cook for an oil company—made this colorful dinner. Whenever I make it, it brings back fond memories.
—*Maria Luisa Reyes, Bastrop, Texas*

- 1/2 cup uncooked elbow macaroni
- 1/4 cup chopped onion
- 1/4 cup chopped sweet red pepper
- 4-1/2 teaspoons butter
- 1 tablespoon canola oil
- 1 tablespoon all-purpose flour
- 1/2 teaspoon salt
- 1/2 teaspoon ground cumin
- Dash pepper
- 1 cup 2% milk
- 1 cup (4 ounces) shredded cheddar cheese
- 1 cup cubed cooked turkey
- 2/3 cup canned diced tomatoes and green chilies
- 1/3 cup frozen corn
- 1/3 cup frozen peas

Cook macaroni according to package directions. Meanwhile, in a large skillet, saute onion and red pepper in butter and oil until tender. Stir in the flour, salt, cumin and pepper until blended; gradually add milk. Bring to a boil; cook and stir for 1-2 minutes or until thickened. Stir in cheese until melted.

Drain macaroni; add to cheese mixture. Stir in the turkey, tomatoes, corn and peas. Transfer to a 1-qt. baking dish coated with cooking spray. Bake, uncovered, at 350° for 20-25 minutes or until bubbly. **yield: 2 servings.**

candied sweet potatoes

prep: 40 min. • bake: 15 min.

This old-fashioned side is perfect for two. It's a dish that can be made often to complement any meal. The touch of pineapple juice adds a nice flavor.
—*Ruby Williams, Bogalusa, Louisiana*

- 1 large sweet potato
- 1/4 cup packed brown sugar
- 2 tablespoons chopped pecans
- 1 tablespoon unsweetened pineapple *or* orange juice
- 1 teaspoon lemon juice
- 1/4 teaspoon ground cinnamon
- 1 tablespoon butter

Place sweet potato in a small saucepan; cover with water. Bring to a boil. Reduce heat; cover and simmer for 30-40 minutes or just until tender. Drain.

When cool enough to handle, peel and cut into 1/4-in. slices. Place in a greased shallow 2-cup baking dish.

In a small bowl, combine the brown sugar, pecans, pineapple juice, lemon juice and cinnamon; sprinkle over sweet potato slices. Dot with butter.

Bake, uncovered, at 350° for 15 minutes or until bubbly and heated through. **yield: 2 servings.**

manicotti for two

prep: 20 min. • bake: 35 min.

Manicotti shells are filled with a three-cheese mixture, then topped with store-bought spaghetti sauce beefed up with flavorful sausage. Enjoy them with sliced canned pears and frozen garlic bread, or accompany the entree with steamed fresh green beans and warm Italian bread.
—Taste of Home Test Kitchen

  4 uncooked manicotti shells
1/2 pound bulk Italian sausage
1-1/2 cups meatless spaghetti sauce
  1 cup ricotta cheese
1/2 cup shredded part-skim mozzarella cheese, *divided*
1/4 cup grated Parmesan cheese
1/2 teaspoon Italian seasoning
1/4 teaspoon garlic powder
1/4 teaspoon pepper

Cook manicotti according to package directions. Meanwhile, in a large skillet, cook the sausage over medium heat until no longer pink; drain. Stir in spaghetti sauce.

Drain manicotti and rinse with cold water. In a small bowl, combine the ricotta cheese, 1/4 cup mozzarella cheese, Parmesan cheese, Italian seasoning, garlic powder and pepper. Carefully stuff manicotti. Place in a greased small baking dish. Top with sausage mixture.

Bake, uncovered, at 350° for 30-35 minutes or until heated through. Sprinkle with remaining mozzarella. Bake 3-5 minutes longer or until cheese is melted. **yield: 2 servings.**

meatball casserole

prep: 40 min. • bake: 20 min.

The mini meatballs in this dish have lots of flavor and give you plenty per serving.
—Anu Riley, Boise, Idaho

3/4 cup uncooked whole wheat penne pasta
  2 tablespoons seasoned bread crumbs
1/4 cup grated Parmesan cheese, *divided*
  2 tablespoons egg substitute
1/2 teaspoon Italian seasoning
1/8 teaspoon onion powder
Dash salt
Dash garlic powder
1/4 pound lean ground turkey
3/4 cup marinara sauce *or* meatless spaghetti sauce
1/4 cup 2% cottage cheese
1/4 cup shredded part-skim mozzarella cheese

Cook pasta according to package directions. Meanwhile, in a small bowl, combine the bread crumbs, 2 tablespoons Parmesan cheese, egg substitute, Italian seasoning, onion powder, salt and garlic powder. Crumble turkey over mixture and mix well.

Shape into 1/2-in. balls; place on a baking sheet coated with cooking spray. Bake at 350° for 9-11 minutes or until no longer pink.

Drain pasta and meatballs. In a small bowl, combine meatballs with marinara sauce. Spoon half of mixture into a 1-qt. baking dish coated with cooking spray. Top with half of the pasta, cottage cheese and mozzarella; sprinkle with 1 tablespoon Parmesan cheese. Repeat layers.

Cover and bake at 350° for 20-25 minutes or until cheese is melted. **yield: 2 servings.**

chicken-ricotta stuffed shells

prep: 25 min. • bake: 30 min.

My husband and I don't care for tomato-based sauces, so I came up with this variation on stuffed shells. It tastes like a chicken Alfredo, and we really enjoy it.
—*Amy Hixon, Ringgold, Georgia*

- 6 uncooked jumbo pasta shells
- 2/3 cup ricotta cheese
- 2 ounces cream cheese, softened
- 1/8 teaspoon chicken bouillon granules
- 2/3 cup shredded cooked chicken breast
- 2 tablespoons shredded Parmesan cheese

SAUCE:
- 1/3 cup heavy whipping cream *or* half-and-half cream
- 1 tablespoon butter
- 5 tablespoons shredded Parmesan cheese, *divided*
- 1/2 teaspoon dried parsley flakes

Cook pasta according to package directions. Meanwhile, in a small bowl, beat the ricotta, cream cheese and bouillon until blended. Stir in chicken and Parmesan cheese. Drain shells; stuff with chicken mixture. Place in a shallow 3-cup baking dish coated with cooking spray.

In a small saucepan, bring the cream and butter to a boil. Whisk in 3 tablespoons cheese and parsley. Stir until the cheese is melted. Pour over shells.

Cover and bake at 350° for 25 minutes. Uncover; sprinkle with remaining cheese. Bake 5-10 minutes longer or until cheese is melted and filling is heated through. **yield: 2 servings.**

crescent brunch bake

prep/total time: 30 min.

Brunch does not always mean a large gathering. This recipe makes a perfect small brunch dish in no time at all and it has a wonderful flavor.
—*Aaron Matthews*
  Montreal, North Carolina

- 1/4 pound bulk pork sausage
- 1 tube (4 ounces) refrigerated crescent rolls
- 2/3 cup shredded cheddar cheese
- 2 eggs, lightly beaten
- 1/4 cup 2% milk

Salt and pepper to taste

Crumble sausage into skillet; cook over medium heat until no longer pink. Drain.

Unroll crescent dough into one long rectangle; seal seams and perforations. Press dough onto the bottom and up the sides of a greased shallow 3-cup baking dish. Trim dough even with edge of dish. Fill with sausage and cheese.

In a small bowl, combine the eggs, milk, salt and pepper. Pour over cheese. Bake, uncovered, at 425°for 16-20 minutes or until a knife comes out clean. **yield: 2 servings.**

ham and spaetzle bake

prep: 20 min. • bake: 15 min.

Tired of the same old ham and scalloped potatoes? Try this yummy change of pace. Creamy and cheesy, the hearty one-dish meal goes together in just minutes using convenient deli or leftover ham.
—Taste of Home Test Kitchen

- 3/4 cup uncooked spaetzle
- 1/3 cup finely chopped onion
- 2 teaspoons butter
- 2 teaspoons all-purpose flour
- 1/2 cup 2% milk
- 3/4 cup fresh broccoli florets
- 1/3 cup shredded Gruyere cheese
- 1/3 cup cubed deli ham
- 1/2 teaspoon ground mustard
- 1/8 teaspoon pepper

Cook spaetzle according to package directions. Meanwhile, in a small saucepan, saute onion in butter until tender. Stir in flour; gradually add milk. Bring to a boil; cook and stir for 2 minutes or until thickened. Remove from the heat.

Drain spaetzle; stir the spaetzle, broccoli, cheese, ham, mustard and pepper into the white sauce. Transfer to a 3-cup baking dish coated with cooking spray.

Bake, uncovered, at 375° for 15-18 minutes or until bubbly. **yield: 2 servings.**

reuben casserole

prep/total time: 30 min.

I've had this recipe in my recipe file for quite some time, and from the stains on it you know it's been well used. Sauerkraut, kielbasa and Swiss cheese combine for a creamy Reuben-style entree.
—Sally Mangel, Bradford, Pennsylvania

- 1-1/2 cups uncooked egg noodles
- 2/3 cup condensed cream of mushroom soup, undiluted
- 1/3 cup 2% milk
- 2 tablespoons chopped onion
- 3/4 teaspoon prepared mustard
- 1 can (8 ounces) sauerkraut, rinsed and well drained
- 1/3 pound smoked kielbasa *or* Polish sausage, cut into 1/2-inch slices
- 1/2 cup shredded Swiss cheese
- 3 tablespoons soft whole wheat bread crumbs
- 1-1/2 teaspoons butter, melted

Cook noodles according to package directions. Meanwhile, in a small bowl, combine the soup, milk, onion and mustard; set aside.

Spread sauerkraut into a 1-qt. baking dish coated with cooking spray. Drain noodles; place over sauerkraut. Layer with soup mixture and kielbasa; sprinkle with cheese.

In a small bowl, combine bread crumbs and butter; sprinkle over casserole. Bake, uncovered, at 350° for 15-20 minutes or until bubbly. **yield: 2 servings.**

In a small bowl, combine the chicken, cheese, sour cream, milk, olives, seasoned salt, pepper and vegetable mixture. Drain macaroni; add to chicken mixture.

Transfer to a 3-cup baking dish coated with cooking spray. Combine bread crumbs and butter; sprinkle over top of casserole. Bake, uncovered, at 350° for 20-25 minutes or until bubbly. **yield: 2 servings.**

chicken macaroni casserole

prep: 20 min. • bake: 20 min.

Start the evening off right with this piping hot, satisfying casserole. Topped with crispy bread crumbs, you'll love the satisfying crunch.
—Quincie Ball, Shelton, Washington

- 2/3 cup uncooked elbow macaroni
- 2/3 cup sliced fresh mushrooms
- 2 tablespoons finely chopped onion
- 1 tablespoon finely chopped green pepper
- 1 tablespoon butter
- 3/4 cup cubed cooked chicken
- 1/2 cup shredded cheddar cheese
- 1/2 cup sour cream
- 2 tablespoons 2% milk
- 1 tablespoon chopped pimiento-stuffed olives
- 1/2 teaspoon seasoned salt
- 1/8 teaspoon pepper
- 1/4 cup soft bread crumbs
- 1 teaspoon butter, melted

Cook macaroni according to package directions. Meanwhile, in a small skillet, saute the mushrooms, onion and green pepper in butter until tender.

tuna noodle casserole

prep: 15 min. • bake: 30 min.

My mom made this tuna casserole, a delicious family dish, through the years. It's good for any occasion, and I often serve it for a luncheon along with garlic bread and a salad.
—Lorraine Rafuse, New Ross, Nova Scotia

- 1 medium onion, chopped
- 2 teaspoons butter
- 1 tablespoon all-purpose flour
- 1/2 teaspoon salt
- 1/4 teaspoon pepper
- 1 cup 2% milk
- 2 cups cooked wide egg noodles
- 1 can (6 ounces) tuna, drained and flaked
- 2/3 cup frozen peas, thawed
- 1/4 cup crushed cornflakes

In a small saucepan, saute onion in butter until tender. Stir in the flour, salt and pepper until blended. Gradually add milk. Bring to a boil; cook and stir for 2 minutes or until thickened. Stir in the noodles, tuna and peas.

Transfer to a greased 1-qt. baking dish. Sprinkle with cornflakes. Bake, uncovered, at 350° for 30-35 minutes or until bubbly around the edges. **yield: 2 servings.**

fiesta bean casserole

prep: 20 min. • bake: 20 min.

I don't recall its origin, but I have had this recipe for many years. A tasty cracker crust makes it a unique meatless option.
—Karen Tjelmeland, Ely, Iowa

 3/4 cup kidney beans, rinsed and drained
 1/4 cup chopped onion
 1/4 cup chopped green chilies, drained
 1/4 teaspoon ground cumin
  16 Triscuits *or* other crackers
 3/4 cup shredded cheddar cheese
 1/2 cup 2% milk
 1/3 cup mayonnaise
   2 tablespoons beaten egg
Sour cream and sliced ripe olives, optional

In a small bowl, combine the beans, onion, green chilies and cumin. Place eight crackers in an 8-in. x 4-in. loaf pan coated with cooking spray. Top with half of the bean mixture; layer with remaining crackers and bean mixture. Sprinkle with cheese.

In a small bowl, combine the milk, mayonnaise and egg; pour over cheese. Bake, uncovered, at 350° for 20-25 minutes or until a thermometer reads 160°. Serve with sour cream and olives if desired. **yield: 2 servings.**

easy chicken biscuit bake

prep: 20 min. • bake: 30 min.

This recipe looks fussy but doesn't take long to assemble, plus it gives me time to put my feet up and read the paper while it bakes. It's great with just a salad and some fruit.
—Gail Betz, Newport, Washington

 1/2 cup plus 1 tablespoon all-purpose flour
 1/2 teaspoon baking powder
Dash salt
   3 tablespoons cold butter
   2 tablespoons beaten egg
 1/4 cup buttermilk
FILLING:
   2 tablespoons butter
   2 tablespoons all-purpose flour
   1 cup 2% milk
   1 tablespoon chicken bouillon granules
Dash poultry seasoning
Dash onion powder
 1/2 cup cubed cooked chicken
 1/2 cup frozen mixed vegetables
 1/2 cup 4% cottage cheese

In a small bowl, combine the flour, baking powder and salt; cut in butter until mixture resembles coarse crumbs. Set aside 1 teaspoon beaten egg; stir remaining egg into buttermilk. Add to crumb mixture; stir until dough forms a ball.

Turn onto a floured surface; knead 10 times or until smooth. Divide dough in half. On a lightly floured surface, roll out one portion to fit the bottom of a greased 1-qt. baking dish. Place in dish.

In a small saucepan, melt butter over medium heat. Stir in flour until smooth. Gradually add the milk, bouillon, poultry seasoning and onion powder. Bring to a boil; cook and stir for 1-2 minutes or until thickened. Remove from the heat. Stir in the chicken, vegetables and cottage cheese. Pour into baking dish.

Roll out remaining dough to fit top of dish; place over filling. Brush with reserved egg. Bake at 350° for 30-35 minutes or until golden brown. **yield: 2 servings.**

creamy pork chop casserole

prep: 15 min. + marinating • bake: 55 min.

Tender pork chops are treated to a sweet-tangy marinade and topped with gooey melted cheese in this delightful meal. The rice and vegetable medley is a great complement.

—Debbie Hankins, Ironton, Ohio

1/4	cup reduced-sodium teriyaki sauce
2	bone-in pork loin chops (8 ounces *each* and 1/2 inch thick)
1	can (10-3/4 ounces) condensed cream of mushroom soup, undiluted
1	cup frozen peas and carrots
3/4	cup water
1/2	small sweet red pepper, chopped
1/3	cup uncooked long grain rice
1	teaspoon dried minced onion
1/8	teaspoon pepper
1/4	cup shredded Mexican cheese blend

Place teriyaki sauce in a large resealable plastic bag; add pork chops. Seal bag and turn to coat; refrigerate for at least 1 hour.

In a large bowl, combine the soup, peas and carrots, water, red pepper, rice, onion and pepper. Transfer to an 11-in. x 7-in. baking dish coated with cooking spray.

Drain and discard marinade. Place pork chops over rice mixture. Cover and bake at 350° for 40 minutes. Uncover; sprinkle with cheese. Bake 15-20 minutes longer or until a meat thermometer reaches 160° and cheese is melted. **yield: 2 servings.**

mini green bean casserole

prep/total time: 20 min.

Warm and soothing, this popular side spells comfort. The pared-down classic features tender green beans, creamy mushroom soup and golden french-fried onions.

—Christy Hinrichs, Parkville, Missouri

1/2	cup condensed cream of mushroom soup, undiluted
3	tablespoons 2% milk
1/2	teaspoon reduced-sodium soy sauce

Dash pepper

1-1/3	cups frozen cut green beans, thawed
1/2	cup french-fried onions, *divided*

In a small bowl, combine the soup, milk, soy sauce and pepper. Stir in green beans and 1/4 cup onions.

Transfer to a 2-cup baking dish coated with cooking spray. Sprinkle with remaining onions. Bake, uncovered, at 400° for 12-15 minutes or until bubbly. **yield: 2 servings.**

serves a crowd

Need a dish to pass? This chapter features entrees and sides that will please a group. You can pass a dish, knowing that you won't bring home leftovers, only compliments for the cook.

≪ pictured left

double-cheese macaroni

prep: 25 min. • bake: 20 min.

A friend passed this recipe on to me, and I made some changes to create this definite crowd-pleaser. I make it for every family get-together and I haven't found anyone—child or adult—who doesn't want some of this ooey, gooey macaroni and cheese.
—Sabrina DeWitt, Cumberland, Maryland

- 1 package (16 ounces) elbow macaroni
- 3 cups (24 ounces) 4% cottage cheese
- 1/2 cup butter, cubed
- 1/2 cup all-purpose flour
- 1 teaspoon salt
- 1/2 teaspoon white pepper
- 1/4 teaspoon garlic salt
- 3 cups half-and-half cream
- 1 cup 2% milk
- 4 cups (16 ounces) shredded cheddar cheese

TOPPING:

- 1 cup dry bread crumbs
- 1/4 cup butter, melted

Cook macaroni according to package directions. Meanwhile, place cottage cheese in a food processor; cover and process until smooth. Set aside.

In a large saucepan, melt butter. Stir in the flour, salt, pepper and garlic salt until smooth. Gradually add cream and milk. Bring to a boil; cook and stir for 2 minutes or until thickened.

Drain macaroni; transfer to a large bowl. Add the cheddar cheese, cottage cheese and white sauce; toss to coat. Transfer to a greased 13-in. x 9-in. baking dish. (Dish will be full.) Combine bread crumbs and butter; sprinkle over the top.

Bake, uncovered, at 400° for 20-25 minutes or until bubbly. **yield: 12 servings (1 cup each).**

KITCHEN TIP

Cheddar cheese can be hard to cube. It is best to use a large sharp knife, such as a French chef's knife, for this task. To cube, cut a 1/2- to 1-inch slice from the cheese. Cut the slice into lengthwise rows the same thickness as the slice, then cut widthwise into the same size.

baked potato casserole

prep: 15 min. • bake: 50 min.

I created this baked potato casserole with input from friends and neighbors. It makes a great all-around side dish for special meals.
—Karen Berlekamp, Maineville, Ohio

- 5 pounds red potatoes, cooked and cubed
- 1 pound sliced bacon, cooked and crumbled
- 1 pound cheddar cheese, cubed
- 4 cups 16 ounces shredded cheddar cheese
- 1 large onion, finely chopped
- 1 cup mayonnaise
- 1 cup (8 ounces) sour cream
- 1 tablespoon minced chives
- 1 teaspoon salt
- 1/2 teaspoon pepper

In a very large bowl, combine the potatoes and bacon. In another large bowl, combine the remaining ingredients; add to potato mixture and gently toss to coat.

Transfer to a greased 4-1/2-qt. baking dish. Bake, uncovered, at 325° for 50-60 minutes or until bubbly and lightly browned. **yield: 20-24 servings.**

tuna noodle cups

prep: 30 min. • bake: 30 min.

Older kids can get a jump on preparing dinner by stirring up these miniature tuna casseroles. Or serve them for brunch with fresh fruit, a tossed salad and rolls.

—Marlene Pugh
  Fort McMurray, Alberta

- 8 ounces medium egg noodles
- 2 cups frozen peas and carrots
- 1 small onion, finely chopped
- 1 can (6-1/2 ounces) tuna, drained
- 2 cups (8 ounces) shredded cheddar cheese
- 3 eggs
- 1 can (12 ounces) evaporated milk
- 1/2 cup water

Cook noodles according to package direction's drain and place in a large bowl. Add the peas and carrots, onion, tuna and cheese. In a small bowl, whisk the eggs, milk and water; stir into noodle mixture. Spoon into greased muffin cups.

Bake at 350° for 30-35 minutes or until a knife inserted near the center comes out clean. Cool for 5 minutes; loosen edges with a knife to remove from cups. Serve warm. **yield: about 1-1/2 dozen.**

ground beef baked beans

prep: 15 min. • bake: 45 min.

I serve this hearty ground beef and bean bake with a tossed salad and some crusty bread for a balanced one-pot meal. It's nice to have this casserole in the freezer for those nights when there's no time to cook.

—Louann Sherbach, Wantagh, New York

- 3 pounds ground beef
- 4 cans (15-3/4 ounces each) pork and beans
- 2 cups ketchup
- 1 cup water
- 2 envelopes onion soup mix
- 1/4 cup packed brown sugar
- 1/4 cup ground mustard
- 1/4 cup molasses
- 1 tablespoon white vinegar
- 1 teaspoon garlic powder
- 1/2 teaspoon ground cloves

In a Dutch oven, cook beef over medium heat until no longer pink; drain. Stir in the remaining ingredients; heat through. Transfer to two greased 2-qt. baking dishes. Cover and freeze one dish for up to 3 months.

Cover and bake the second dish at 400° for 30 minutes. Uncover; bake 10-15 minutes longer or until bubbly.

to use frozen casserole: Thaw in the refrigerator. Cover and bake at 400° for 40 minutes. Uncover; bake 15-20 minutes longer or until bubbly. **yield: 2 casseroles (10-12 servings each).**

breakfast supreme

prep: 20 min. + chilling • bake: 35 min. + standing

Friends shared this recipe with me many years ago, when we spent the night at their home. After one taste, you'll understand why I call this breakfast supreme. It's really that good!
—Laurie Harms, Grinnell, Iowa

---

    1 pound bulk pork sausage
    1 pound ground beef
    1 small onion, chopped
  3/4 cup sliced fresh mushrooms
  1/2 cup chopped green pepper
    1 to 1-1/2 teaspoons salt
  1/4 to 1/2 teaspoon pepper
    2 tablespoons butter, melted
    2 cups (8 ounces) shredded cheddar cheese, *divided*
   12 eggs, lightly beaten
  2/3 cup heavy whipping cream

In a large skillet, cook the sausage, beef, onion, mushrooms and green pepper over medium heat until meat is no longer pink; drain. Stir in salt and pepper; set aside.

Pour butter into an ungreased 13-in. x 9-in. baking dish. Sprinkle with 1 cup cheese. Pour eggs over cheese. Top with sausage mixture.

Pour the cream over sausage mixture. Sprinkle with remaining cheese. Cover and refrigerate for 8 hours or overnight.

Remove from the refrigerator 30 minutes before baking. Bake, uncovered, at 325° for 35-40 minutes or until a knife inserted near the center comes out clean. Let stand for 10 minutes before cutting. **yield: 12 servings.**

mushroom green bean casserole

prep: 15 min. • bake: 25 min.

Most green bean casseroles center around mushroom soup and french-fried onions. This from-scratch version features fresh mushrooms, sliced water chestnuts and slivered almonds.
—Pat Richter, Lake Placid, Florida

- 1 pound fresh mushrooms, sliced
- 1 large onion, chopped
- 1/2 cup butter
- 1/4 cup all-purpose flour
- 1 cup half-and-half cream
- 1 jar (16 ounces) process cheese spread
- 2 teaspoons soy sauce
- 1/2 teaspoon pepper
- 1/8 teaspoon hot pepper sauce
- 1 can (8 ounces) sliced water chestnuts, drained
- 2 packages (16 ounces *each*) frozen French-style green beans, thawed and well drained
- 2 to 3 tablespoons slivered almonds

In a large skillet, saute mushrooms and onion in butter. Stir in flour until blended. Gradually stir in cream. Bring to a boil; cook and stir for 2 minutes or until thickened. Reduce heat; add the cheese sauce, soy sauce, pepper and hot pepper sauce, stirring until cheese is melted. Remove from the heat; stir in water chestnuts.

Place beans in an ungreased 3-qt. baking dish. Pour the cheese mixture over top. Sprinkle with almonds. Bake, uncovered, at 375° for 25-30 minutes or until bubbly. **yield: 14 servings.**

chili tots

prep: 15 min. • bake: 35 min.

Cook once and eat twice with this hearty Southwestern casserole. With help from a few convenience products, it quickly goes together before you freeze it or pop it into the oven to bake.
—Linda Baldwin, Long Beach, California

- 1 pound ground beef
- 2 cans (15 ounces *each*) chili without beans
- 1 can (8 ounces) tomato sauce
- 1 can (2-1/4 ounces) sliced ripe olives, drained
- 1 can (4 ounces) chopped green chilies
- 2 cups (8 ounces) shredded cheddar cheese
- 1 package (32 ounces) frozen Tater Tots

In a large skillet, cook the beef over medium heat until no longer pink; drain. Stir in the chili, tomato sauce, olives and chilies. Transfer to two greased 8-in. square baking dishes. Sprinkle with cheese; top with Tater Tots. Cover and freeze one casserole for up to 3 months.

Cover and bake the remaining casserole at 350° for 35-40 minutes or until heated through.

to use frozen casserole: Remove from the freezer 30 minutes before baking (do not thaw). Cover and bake at 350° for 1-1/4 to 1-1/2 hours or until heated through. **yield: 2 casseroles (6 servings each).**

duo tater bake

prep: 40 min. • bake: 20 min.

Cut down on holiday prep time with this creamy potato dish that combines sweet potatoes with regular spuds. I served this for Thanksgiving, and it was a winner with my family.

—Joan McCulloch, Abbotsford, British Columbia

---

4 pounds russet *or* Yukon Gold potatoes, peeled and cubed

3 pounds sweet potatoes, peeled and cubed

2 cartons (8 ounces *each*) spreadable chive and onion cream cheese

1 cup (8 ounces) sour cream

1/4 cup shredded Colby-Monterey Jack cheese

1/3 cup milk

1/4 cup shredded Parmesan cheese

1/2 teaspoon salt

1/2 teaspoon pepper

TOPPING:

1 cup (4 ounces) shredded Colby-Monterey Jack cheese

1/2 cup chopped green onions

1/4 cup shredded Parmesan cheese

Place russet potatoes in a Dutch oven and cover with water. Bring to a boil. Reduce heat; cover and cook for 10-15 minutes or until tender.

Meanwhile, place sweet potatoes in a large saucepan; cover with water. Bring to a boil. Reduce heat; cover and cook for 10-15 minutes or until tender. Drain; mash with half of the cream cheese and sour cream and all of Colby cheese.

Drain russet potatoes; mash with the remaining cream cheese and sour cream. Stir in the milk, Parmesan cheese, salt and pepper.

Spread 2-2/3 cups russet potato mixture into each of two greased 11-in. x 7-in. baking dishes. Layer with 4 cups sweet potato mixture. Repeat layers. Spread with remaining russet potato mixture.

Bake, uncovered, at 350° for 15 minutes or until heated through. Combine topping ingredients; sprinkle over casseroles. Bake 2-3 minutes longer or until cheese is melted. **yield: 2 casseroles (10 servings each).**

cinnamon-sugar french toast bake

prep: 15 min. + chilling • bake: 45 min. + standing

Cinnamon and sugar top this fuss-free fare that tastes like French toast. Since you assemble it the previous night, you save time in the morning.
—Sharyn Adams, Crawfordsville, Indiana

  1 loaf (1 pound) French bread, cut into 1-inch cubes
  8 eggs, lightly beaten
  3 cups 2% milk
  4 teaspoons sugar
  1 teaspoon vanilla extract
3/4 teaspoon salt

TOPPING:

  2 tablespoons butter
  3 tablespoons sugar
  2 teaspoons ground cinnamon

Maple syrup, optional

Place bread cubes in a greased 13-in. x 9-in. baking dish. In a large bowl, whisk the eggs, milk, sugar, vanilla and salt. Pour over bread. Cover and refrigerate for 8 hours or overnight.

Remove from refrigerator 30 minutes before baking. Dot with butter. Combine sugar and cinnamon; sprinkle over the top.

Cover and bake at 350° for 45-50 minutes or until a knife inserted near the center comes out clean. Let stand for 5 minutes. Serve with maple syrup if desired. **yield: 12 servings.**

chicken noodle casserole

prep: 20 min. • bake: 30 min.

Cayenne pepper gives a little zip to this creamy chicken bake. I sometimes use spinach noodles in place of the egg noodles.
—Cheryl Davidson, Fulshear, Texas

- 5 cups uncooked egg noodles
- 1/4 cup butter, cubed
- 1/2 cup all-purpose flour
- 1-1/2 cups 2% milk
- 1 cup chicken broth
- 2 cups (16 ounces) sour cream
- 1 can (4 ounces) mushroom stems and pieces, drained
- 1 jar (4 ounces) diced pimientos, drained
- 3 teaspoons dried parsley flakes
- 2 teaspoons seasoned salt
- 1/2 teaspoon salt
- 1 teaspoon paprika
- 1/4 to 1/2 teaspoon pepper
- 1/8 to 1/4 teaspoon cayenne pepper
- 4 cups diced cooked chicken
- 1/4 cup dry bread crumbs
- 2 tablespoons shredded Parmesan cheese

Cook noodles according to package directions. Meanwhile, in a large saucepan, melt butter; stir in flour until smooth. Gradually add milk and broth. Bring to a boil. Cook and stir for 2 minutes or until thickened. Remove from the heat. Stir in the sour cream, mushrooms, pimientos and seasonings. Drain pasta.

In a greased 3-qt. baking dish, layer half of the noodles, chicken and sauce. Repeat layers. Combine bread crumbs and Parmesan cheese. Sprinkle over top.

Bake, uncovered, at 350° for 30-35 minutes or until bubbly. **yield: 12 servings.**

jambalaya casserole

prep: 10 min. • bake: 45 min.

Whenever family and friends get together, they request that I bring this jambalaya to the event. It's sensational and easy to fix.
—Evelyn Anderson Lugo, Kenner, Louisiana

- 3 large onions, chopped
- 3 large green peppers, chopped
- 3 celery ribs, chopped
- 1-1/2 cups butter
- 12 garlic cloves, minced
- 3 pounds smoked sausage, cut into 1/2-inch slices
- 9 cups chicken broth
- 6 cups uncooked long grain rice
- 3 cups chopped fresh tomatoes
- 1-1/2 cups chopped green onions
- 1/2 cup minced fresh parsley
- 3 tablespoons Worcestershire sauce
- 3 tablespoons hot pepper sauce
- 3 tablespoons browning sauce, optional
- 1 tablespoon salt
- 1 tablespoon pepper

In several large skillets, saute the onions, green peppers and celery in butter until crisp-tender. Add garlic; cook 1 minute longer. Place in several large bowls; stir in the remaining ingredients.

Transfer to three greased shallow 3-qt. baking dishes. Cover and bake at 375° for 45-50 minutes or until rice is tender, stirring twice. **yield: 3 casseroles (8 servings each).**

makeover favorite corn bake

prep: 20 min.
bake: 30 min. + standing

My family loves this dish—even my picky 5-year-old. The Taste of Home Test Kitchen helped me slash the fat in my recipe for a sweet corn bake with fewer calories but all the flavor of the tasty original.

—RuthAnn Clore, West Peoria, Illinois

  1 cup all-purpose flour
  1 cup cornmeal
  3 tablespoons sugar
  1/2 teaspoon salt
  1/2 teaspoon baking soda
  1 egg
  1 cup (8 ounces) reduced-fat sour cream
  1/4 cup unsweetened applesauce
  1/4 cup butter, melted
  1 can (15-1/4 ounces) whole kernel corn, undrained
  1 can (14-3/4 ounces) cream-style corn

In a large bowl, combine the first five ingredients. In a small bowl, whisk the egg, sour cream, applesauce and butter. Stir in corn. Stir into dry ingredients just until moistened.

Transfer to a 13-in. x 9-in. baking dish coated with cooking spray. Bake at 350° for 30-35 minutes or until a thermometer reads 160°. Serve warm. Refrigerate leftovers. **yield: 12 servings.**

southwest sausage bake

prep: 15 min. + chilling • bake: 1 hour + standing

This layered tortilla dish is not only delicious, but it's a real time-saver because it's put together the night before. The tomato slices provide a nice touch of color. I like to serve this crowd-pleasing casserole with muffins and fresh fruit.

—Barbara Waddel, Lincoln, Nebraska

  6 flour tortillas (10 inches), cut into 1/2-inch strips
  4 cans (4 ounces *each*) chopped green chilies, drained
  1 pound bulk pork sausage, cooked and drained
  2 cups (8 ounces) shredded Monterey Jack cheese
  10 eggs, lightly beaten
  1/2 cup 2% milk
  1/2 teaspoon *each* salt, garlic salt, onion salt, pepper and ground cumin
Paprika
  2 medium tomatoes, sliced
Sour cream and salsa

In a greased 13-in. x 9-in. baking dish, layer half of the tortilla strips, chilies, sausage and cheese. Repeat layers.

In a large bowl, whisk the eggs, milk and seasonings; pour over cheese. Sprinkle with paprika. Cover and refrigerate overnight.

Remove from the refrigerator 30 minutes before baking. Bake, uncovered, at 350° for 50 minutes. Arrange tomato slices over the top. Bake 10-15 minutes longer or until a knife inserted near the center comes out clean. Let stand for 10 minutes before cutting. Serve with sour cream and salsa. **yield: 12 servings.**

KITCHEN TIP

When you bring a dish to a gathering, you should also include a label or name card. Write the recipe name on it and list any items in the dish that people might be allergic to or intolerant of, such as peanuts, nuts, cheese or eggs.

spaghetti beef casserole

prep: 25 min. • bake: 20 min.

We love spaghetti, and as the mother of three boys, I've found this casserole to be a life-saver! It's fast and has mass appeal, which makes it a hit at pregame meals and sports banquets.

—Jane Radtke, Griffith, Indiana

- 1-1/2 **pounds uncooked spaghetti**
- 3 **pounds ground beef**
- 1 **cup chopped onion**
- 2/3 **cup chopped green pepper**
- 1 **teaspoon minced garlic**
- 2 **cans (10-3/4 ounces *each*) condensed cream of mushroom soup, undiluted**
- 2 **cans (10-3/4 ounces *each*) condensed tomato soup, undiluted**
- 1-1/3 **cups water**
- 1 **can (8 ounces) mushroom stems and pieces, drained**
- 3 **cups (12 ounces) shredded cheddar cheese, *divided***

Cook spaghetti according to package directions. Meanwhile, in several large skillets, cook the beef, onion and green pepper over medium heat until meat is no longer pink. Add garlic; cook 1 minute longer. Drain. Stir in the soups, water and mushrooms.

Drain spaghetti. Add spaghetti and 1 cup cheese to beef mixture. Transfer to two greased 13-in. x 9-in. baking dishes. Sprinkle with remaining cheese. Cover and freeze one casserole for up to 3 months. Bake remaining casserole, uncovered, at 350° for 20-25 minutes or until cheese is melted.

to use frozen casserole: Thaw in the refrigerator overnight. Remove from the refrigerator 30 minutes before baking. Cover and bake at 350° for 1 to 1-1/4 hours or until heated through and cheese is melted. **yield: 2 casseroles (8 servings each).**

spinach feta strata

prep: 10 min. + chilling
bake: 40 min.

This breakfast entree is easy to put together and is loaded with yummy ingredients, such as Monterey Jack and feta cheese. The first time my family tasted it, they told me it was a keeper.

—Pat Lane, Pullman, Washington

- 10 slices French bread (1 inch thick) *or* 6 croissants, split
- 6 eggs, lightly beaten
- 1-1/2 cups 2% milk
- 1 package (10 ounces) frozen chopped spinach, thawed and squeezed dry
- 1/2 teaspoon salt
- 1/4 teaspoon ground nutmeg
- 1/4 teaspoon pepper
- 1-1/2 cups (6 ounces) shredded Monterey Jack cheese
- 1 cup (4 ounces) crumbled feta cheese

In a greased 13-in. x 9-in. baking dish, arrange French bread or croissant halves with sides overlapping.

In a large bowl, combine the eggs, milk, spinach, salt, nutmeg and pepper; pour over bread. Sprinkle with cheeses. Cover and refrigerate for 8 hours or overnight.

Remove from the refrigerator 30 minutes before baking. Bake, uncovered, at 350° for 40-45 minutes or until a knife inserted near the center comes out clean. Let stand for 5 minutes before cutting. Serve warm. **yield: 12 servings.**

onions neptune

prep: 20 min. • bake: 35 min.

You can serve this as an entree or appetizer. I often add whatever ingredients I have handy, such as mushrooms or sun-dried tomatoes. Whether I serve it as is or jazz it up, it's always delicious.

—Todd Noon, Galloway, New Jersey

- 5 to 6 medium sweet onions, sliced and separated into rings
- 1/2 cup butter, softened, *divided*
- 2 cans (6 ounces *each)* lump crabmeat, drained, *divided*
- 3 cups (12 ounces) shredded Swiss cheese
- 1 can (10-3/4 ounces) condensed cream of mushroom soup, undiluted
- 1/2 cup evaporated milk
- 1/2 teaspoon salt
- 1/4 teaspoon pepper
- 12 to 16 slices French bread (1/4 inch thick)

In a large skillet, saute onions in 1/4 cup butter until tender. Remove from the heat; gently stir in half of the crab. Spread into a greased 13-in. x 9-in. baking dish. Top with remaining crab. Combine the cheese, soup, milk, salt and pepper; spoon over crab.

Spread remaining butter over one side of each slice of bread; place buttered side up over casserole. Bake, uncovered, at 350° for 35-45 minutes or until golden brown. **yield: 12 servings.**

holiday green beans

prep: 40 min. • bake: 15 min.

Try this perked-up green bean casserole this year and you'll never go back to the old stuff. No one will ever know it's light!
—Laura Fall-Sutton, Buhl, Idaho

8 cups cut fresh green beans (about 2 pounds)
1/2 pound sliced fresh mushrooms
2 tablespoons butter
2 tablespoons all-purpose flour
1 teaspoon dried minced onion
1/2 teaspoon pepper
1/2 cup fat-free milk
1 cup reduced-fat sour cream
1 teaspoon Worcestershire sauce
1-1/2 cups (6 ounces) shredded reduced-fat
Swiss cheese

TOPPING:
1/3 cup slivered almonds
1/3 cup crushed cornflakes
1 tablespoon butter, melted

Place beans in a Dutch oven and cover with water; bring to a boil. Cover and cook for 3-5 minutes or until crisp-tender; drain and set aside.

In a large skillet, saute mushrooms in butter until tender. Stir in the flour, onion and pepper until blended. Gradually stir in milk. Bring to a boil; cook and stir for 1-2 minutes or until thickened. Remove from the heat; stir in sour cream and Worcestershire sauce. Stir in beans and cheese until blended.

Transfer to an 11-in. x 7-in. baking dish coated with cooking spray (dish will be full). Combine topping ingredients; sprinkle over the top.

Bake, uncovered, at 400° for 12-16 minutes or until bubbly and heated through.
yield: 12 servings.

 **KITCHEN TIP**

Fresh green beans are available year-round. When buying green beans, select those that are brightly colored, firm and smooth with unblemished pods. Avoid ones with large seeds. Store unwashed beans in the refrigerator for up to 3 days.

potluck lasagna

prep: 30 min.
bake: 55 min. + standing

This is a variation on a lasagna dish a coworker made for a company potluck. When I was expecting our third son, I often prepared meals and froze them. It was so nice to have a substantial entree like this one to bake.

—Colleen Wolfisberg
   Everson, Washington

    1 pound ground beef
    1 can (14-1/2 ounces) Italian stewed tomatoes, cut up
    1 can (6 ounces) tomato paste
    1 tablespoon minced fresh parsley
  1/2 teaspoon minced garlic
    2 eggs
1-1/2 cups (12 ounces) 4% cottage cheese
1-1/2 cups ricotta cheese
    1 cup grated Parmesan cheese
    1 teaspoon salt
    1 teaspoon pepper
    6 lasagna noodles, cooked and drained
    2 cups (8 ounces) shredded part-skim mozzarella cheese

In a large skillet, cook beef over medium heat until no longer pink; drain. Stir in the tomatoes, tomato paste, parsley and garlic; remove from the heat.

In a large bowl, combine the eggs, cottage cheese, ricotta cheese, Parmesan cheese, salt and pepper. In a greased 13-in. x 9-in. baking dish, layer with three noodles, half of the cottage cheese mixture, 1 cup mozzarella cheese and half of the meat sauce. Repeat layers.

Cover and freeze for up to 3 months. Or, cover and bake 375° for 30 minutes. Uncover; bake 25-30 minutes longer or until a meat thermometer reads 160°. Let stand for 10 minutes before cutting.

to use frozen lasagna: Thaw in refrigerator overnight. Bake as directed. **yield: 12-15 servings.**

curry chicken casserole

prep: 1 hour • bake: 45 min.

When I've invited a crowd over for the holidays, this is the recipe I reach for. It's rich and meaty and makes plenty. I find it satisfies one and all.

—Julia Garnett, Virginia Beach, Virginia

    13 large onions, diced
     4 medium bunches celery, sliced
     6 cans (8 ounces *each*) mushroom stems and pieces, drained
     2 cups butter, cubed
     9 packages (4 ounces *each*) long grain and wild rice mix
13-1/2 cups water
    12 cans (10-3/4 ounces *each*) condensed golden mushroom soup, undiluted
    13 cups sour cream
   1/4 cup curry powder
    72 cups cubed cooked chicken (36 pounds boneless skinless chicken breasts)
     1 can (8 ounces) grated Parmesan cheese

In several large saucepans over medium heat, saute the onions, celery and mushrooms in butter until tender. Stir in rice with contents of seasoning packets and water; bring to a boil. Reduce heat; cover and simmer until rice is tender, about 25 minutes.

Stir in the soup, sour cream and curry powder. Fold in chicken. Spoon into nine greased 13-in. x 9-in. baking dishes. Sprinkle with cheese.

Bake, uncovered, at 350° for 45-60 minutes or until bubbly. **yield: 100 servings.**

2 teaspoons garlic powder

1 teaspoon salt

1/2 teaspoon pepper

1 egg, lightly beaten

2 tablespoons half-and-half cream

Place potatoes in a Dutch oven and cover with water. Bring to a boil; reduce heat. Cover and cook for 10-15 minutes or until tender; drain. In a small skillet, saute onion in 1 tablespoon butter until tender; set aside.

Melt remaining butter. Brush a 13-in. x 9-in. baking dish with some of the butter. Unroll phyllo sheets; trim to fit into dish. (Keep dough covered with plastic wrap and a damp cloth while assembling.) Place one phyllo sheet in prepared dish; brush with butter. Repeat twice.

Top with half of the sour cream, potatoes, onion, ham and cheese. Combine 6 teaspoons dill, garlic powder, salt and pepper; sprinkle half over cheese. Layer with three phyllo sheets, brushing each with butter. Top with remaining sour cream, potatoes, onion, ham, cheese and seasoning mixture.

Layer with remaining phyllo dough, brushing each sheet with butter. Combine egg and cream; brush over top. Sprinkle with remaining dill.

Bake, uncovered, at 350° for 20-25 minutes or until heated through. Let stand for 5 minutes. Cut into squares. **yield: 12-15 servings.**

ham-potato phyllo bake

prep: 30 min. • bake: 20 min.

I'm often asked to bring this entree to potlucks. The phyllo is crisp and golden brown, and the dill tastes so good with the rich filling.
—Tracy Hartsuff, Charlotte, Michigan

3 pounds red potatoes, peeled and thinly sliced

1 medium onion, chopped

8 tablespoons butter, *divided*

20 sheets phyllo dough (14 inches x 9 inches)

2 cups (16 ounces) sour cream

2 cups cubed fully cooked ham

2 cups (8 ounces) shredded cheddar cheese

7 teaspoons dill weed, *divided*

lazy pierogi bake

prep: 25 min. • bake: 35 min.

A favorite dish in our family is pierogi—tasty pockets of dough filled with cottage cheese and onions. Making pierogi is time-consuming, so my mom created this recipe, which has all the flavor but is simple to make.
—Sandy Starks, Amherst, New York

- 1 package (16 ounces) spiral pasta
- 1 pound sliced bacon, diced
- 2 medium onions, chopped
- 2 garlic cloves, minced
- 1/2 pound fresh mushrooms, sliced
- 2 cans (14 ounces *each*) sauerkraut, rinsed and well drained
- 3 cans (10-3/4 ounces *each*) condensed cream of mushroom soup, undiluted
- 1/2 cup milk
- 1/2 teaspoon celery seed
- 1/8 teaspoon pepper

Cook pasta according to package directions. Meanwhile, in a large skillet, cook bacon over medium heat until crisp. Remove to paper towels; drain, reserving 2 tablespoons drippings.

In the drippings, saute onions until tender. Add garlic; cook 1 minute longer. Add mushrooms; cook until tender. Stir in sauerkraut and half of the bacon. In a large bowl, combine the soup, milk, celery seed and pepper. Drain pasta.

Place a fourth of the pasta in two greased 13-in. x 9-in. baking dishes. Layer each with a fourth of the sauerkraut and soup mixture. Repeat layers.

Cover and bake at 350° for 25 minutes. Uncover; sprinkle with remaining bacon. Bake 10-15 minutes longer or until heated through. Let stand for 5-10 minutes before serving. **yield: 16 servings.**

chicken tater bake

prep: 20 min. • bake: 40 min.

Please everyone in the family with this warm and comforting dish that tastes like a chicken potpie with a Tater Tot crust.
—Fran Allen, St. Louis, Missouri

- 2 cans (10-3/4 ounces *each*) condensed cream of chicken soup, undiluted
- 1/2 cup 2% milk
- 1/4 cup butter, cubed
- 3 cups cubed cooked chicken
- 1 package (16 ounces) frozen peas and carrots, thawed
- 1-1/2 cups (6 ounces) shredded cheddar cheese, *divided*
- 1 package (32 ounces) frozen Tater Tots

In a large saucepan, combine the soup, milk and butter. Cook and stir over medium heat until heated through. Remove from the heat; stir in the chicken, peas and carrots and 1 cup cheese.

Transfer to two greased 8-in. square baking dishes. Top with Tater Tots; sprinkle with remaining cheese.

Cover and freeze one casserole for up to 3 months. Cover and bake the remaining casserole at 350° for 35 minutes. Uncover; bake 5-10 minutes longer or until heated through.

to use frozen casserole: Remove from the freezer 30 minutes before baking (do not thaw). Cover and bake at 350° for 1-1/2 to 1-3/4 hours or until heated through. **yield: 2 casseroles (6 servings each).**

spaghetti goulash

prep: 25 min. • bake: 35 min.

My mother always made this inviting supper when we had lots of company or we were going to a church dinner. She'd make two casseroles and save one in the freezer for another time.
—Jinger Newsome, Gainesville, Florida

- 1 package (16 ounces) thin spaghetti, broken in half
- 3/4 pound ground beef
- 3/4 pound bulk pork sausage
- 1 medium green pepper, chopped
- 1 medium onion, chopped
- 2 cans (14-1/2 ounces *each*) diced tomatoes
- 1 bottle (12 ounces) chili sauce
- 1 can (8 ounces) mushroom stems and pieces, drained
- 1 tablespoon Worcestershire sauce
- 1 teaspoon salt
- 1/4 teaspoon pepper
- 1 cup (4 ounces) shredded cheddar cheese, *divided*

Cook spaghetti according to package directions; drain. In a large skillet, cook the beef, sausage, green pepper and onion over medium heat until meat is no longer pink; drain. Add the tomatoes; cover and simmer for 45 minutes.

Remove from heat; stir in the chili sauce, mushrooms, Worcestershire sauce, salt, pepper and spaghetti.

Transfer to a greased 4-qt. baking dish or two greased 2-qt. baking dishes. Sprinkle with cheese. Cover and bake at 350° for 35-40 minutes or until heated through. **yield: 12-16 servings.**

potluck ham and pasta

prep: 40 min. • bake: 25 min.

This easy meal-in-one dish is a real crowd-pleaser on chilly nights. It's creamy and filling and has a wonderful ham and cheese flavor.
—Nancy Foust
   Stoneboro, Pennsylvania

- 1 package (16 ounces) elbow macaroni
- 4 cups fresh broccoli florets
- 1/2 cup finely chopped onion
- 1/2 cup butter, cubed
- 1/2 cup all-purpose flour
- 1 teaspoon ground mustard
- 1 teaspoon salt
- 1/4 teaspoon pepper
- 6 cups 2% milk
- 1 jar (15 ounces) process cheese sauce
- 2 cups (8 ounces) shredded cheddar cheese, *divided*
- 4 cups cubed fully cooked ham

Cook macaroni according to package directions, adding broccoli during the last 3-4 minutes; drain.

In a large Dutch oven, saute onion in butter for 2 minutes. Stir in the flour, mustard, salt and pepper until blended. Gradually stir in milk. Bring to a boil; cook and stir for 2 minutes or until thickened. Stir in cheese sauce and 1 cup cheddar cheese until blended.

Remove from the heat; stir in the ham, macaroni and broccoli. Divide between a greased 13-in. x 9-in. baking dish and a greased 8-in. square baking dish. Sprinkle with remaining cheese.

Bake, uncovered, at 350° for 25-35 minutes or until bubbly and heated through. **yield: 12 servings.**

au gratin party potatoes

prep: 45 min. • bake: 45 min.

When putting on a party for their American Legion Post, my father and uncle prepared this yummy potato dish. I've used the recipe for smaller groups by making a half or quarter of the recipe. It's simple to divide.
—Crystal Kolady, Henrietta, New York

---

20 pounds potatoes, peeled, cubed and cooked

4 cans (12 ounces *each*) evaporated milk

3 packages (16 ounces *each*) process cheese (Velveeta), cubed

1 cup butter, cubed

2 tablespoons salt

2 teaspoons pepper

Paprika, optional

In several large bowls, combine potatoes, milk, cheese, butter, salt and pepper. Transfer to four greased 13-in. x 9-in. baking dishes.

Bake, uncovered, at 350° for 45-50 minutes or until bubbly. Sprinkle with paprika if desired. **yield: about 60 (3/4-cup) servings.**

baked ziti

prep: 20 min. + simmering • bake: 1 hour

This satisfying Italian pasta has a from-scratch spaghetti sauce and a generous combination of cheeses. You can easily double the recipe to serve a larger crowd.
—Kim Neer, Kalamazoo, Michigan

---

1 pound lean ground beef (90% lean)

2 medium onions, chopped

3 garlic cloves, minced

1 jar (28 ounces) reduced-sodium meatless spaghetti sauce

1 can (28 ounces) diced tomatoes, undrained

1 can (12 ounces) tomato paste

3/4 cup water

2 tablespoons minced fresh parsley

1 tablespoon Worcestershire sauce

2 teaspoons dried basil

1-1/2 teaspoons dried oregano, *divided*

1 package (16 ounces) ziti *or* 16 ounces small tube pasta

1 carton (15 ounces) reduced-fat ricotta cheese

2 cups (8 ounces) shredded part-skim mozzarella cheese

1/2 cup grated Parmesan cheese, *divided*

1/2 cup egg substitute

1/2 teaspoon salt

1/2 teaspoon pepper

In a large saucepan, cook beef and onions over medium heat until meat is no longer pink. Add garlic; cook 1 minute longer. Drain. Stir in the spaghetti sauce, tomatoes, tomato paste, water, parsley, Worcestershire sauce, basil and 1 teaspoon oregano. Cover and simmer for 3 hours, stirring occasionally.

Cook pasta according to package directions; drain. In a large bowl, combine the ricotta, mozzarella, 1/4 cup Parmesan cheese, egg substitute, salt and pepper.

In two greased 13-in. x 9-in. baking dishes coated with cooking spray, spread 1 cup of meat sauce. In each dish, layer a fourth of the pasta, 1 cup meat sauce and a fourth of the cheese mixture. Repeat layers of pasta, sauce and cheese mixture.

Top with remaining sauce. Sprinkle with remaining Parmesan cheese and oregano. Cover and bake at 350° for 1 hour or until heated through. **yield: 2 casseroles (12 servings each).**

1 celery rib, chopped

3 garlic cloves, minced

1 tablespoon minced fresh basil *or* 1 teaspoon dried basil

1 teaspoon salt

1 teaspoon chili powder

12 lasagna noodles, cooked and drained

2 cups (8 ounces) shredded part-skim mozzarella cheese

1/2 cup grated Parmesan cheese

In a large skillet, cook beef over medium heat until no longer pink; drain. Add the salsa, beans, vegetables, garlic and seasonings. Bring to a boil. Reduce heat; cover and simmer for 15 minutes.

Spread a fourth of the meat sauce in a greased 13-in. x 9-in. baking dish; top with four noodles. Repeat the layers once. Layer with half of the remaining sauce; sprinkle with half of the cheeses. Layer with the remaining noodles, sauce and cheeses.

Cover and bake at 350° for 30 minutes. Uncover; bake 15-20 minutes longer or until heated through. Let stand for 15 minutes before cutting. **yield: 12 servings.**

lasagna corn carne

prep: 30 min. • bake: 45 min. + standing

My grandkids always want this lasagna when they come to visit. It is sort of like chili in a pan. I came up with the recipe one day using just ingredients I had on hand. It was an instant hit.
—Mary Lou Wills, La Plata, Maryland

1 pound ground beef

1 jar (16 ounces) salsa

1 can (16 ounces) kidney beans, rinsed and drained

1 can (14-3/4 ounces) cream-style corn

1 large onion, chopped

1 medium green pepper, chopped

spinach beef macaroni bake

prep: 55 min. • bake: 25 min.

This filling dish is great to serve at a family reunion or church supper. I've also made half the recipe for family gatherings. My grandson-in-law and great-grandson often ask me to serve it when they stop by to see me.

—Lois Lauppe, Lahoma, Oklahoma

5-1/4 cups uncooked elbow macaroni

2-1/2 pounds ground beef

2 large onions, chopped

3 large carrots, shredded

3 celery ribs, chopped

2 cans (28 ounces *each*) Italian diced tomatoes, undrained

4 teaspoons salt

1 teaspoon garlic powder

1 teaspoon pepper

1/2 teaspoon dried oregano

2 packages (10 ounces *each*) frozen chopped spinach, thawed and squeezed dry

1 cup grated Parmesan cheese

Cook macaroni according to package directions. Meanwhile, in a large Dutch oven, cook the beef, onions, carrots and celery over medium heat until meat is no longer pink; drain. Add the tomatoes, salt, garlic powder, pepper and oregano. Bring to a boil. Reduce heat; cover and simmer for 30 minutes or until vegetables are tender.

Drain macaroni; add macaroni and spinach to beef mixture. Pour into two greased 3-qt. baking dishes. Sprinkle with cheese. Bake, uncovered, at 350° for 25-30 minutes or until heated through. **yield: 2 casseroles (12 servings each).**

roasted veggie pasta

prep: 40 min. • bake: 25 min.

My sister gave me this recipe years ago, and it has become one of my go-to make-ahead and company meals. For a heartier dish, pair it with ham and dinner rolls.

—Robyn Baney, Lexington Park, Maryland

4 small zucchini, halved lengthwise and cut into 1-inch slices

2 large onions, cut into wedges

2 medium yellow summer squash, halved lengthwise and cut into 1-inch slices

2 large sweet yellow peppers, cut into 1-inch pieces

1 cup fresh baby carrots, halved lengthwise

2 tablespoons olive oil

3-1/2 cups uncooked fusilli pasta

2 cups (8 ounces) shredded fontina cheese

1-1/2 cups heavy whipping cream

1/2 cup canned diced tomatoes in sauce

1/2 cup grated Parmesan cheese, *divided*

2 garlic cloves, minced

1/2 teaspoon salt

1/4 teaspoon pepper

In a large bowl, combine the first six ingredients. Transfer to two greased 15-in. x 10-in. x 1-in. baking pans. Bake at 450° for 20-25 minutes or until crisp-tender; set aside. Reduce heat to 350°.

Cook pasta according to package directions; drain. Add the fontina cheese, cream, tomatoes, 1/4 cup Parmesan cheese, garlic, salt and pepper to the pasta. Stir in vegetable mixture.

Transfer to a greased 13-in. x 9-in. baking dish (dish will be full). Sprinkle with remaining Parmesan cheese. Bake, uncovered, for 25-30 minutes or until bubbly. **yield: 16 servings (3/4 cup each).**

tamale casserole

prep: 35 min. • bake: 55 min.

At a large Mexican-themed party I hosted, I served this tamale dish. Its zippy tomato and ground beef sauce was well liked by all.
—Elaine Daniels, Santa Ana, California

- 7 **pounds ground beef**
- 6 **medium onions, chopped**
- 2 **celery ribs, chopped**
- 3 **garlic cloves, minced**
- 2 **cans (14-1/2 ounces *each*) diced tomatoes, undrained**
- 2 **cans (12 ounces *each*) tomato paste**
- 2 **cans (15-1/4 ounces *each*) whole kernel corn, drained**
- 2 **cans (4-1/2 ounces *each*) mushroom stems and pieces, drained**
- 3 **cans (2-1/4 ounces *each*) sliced ripe olives, drained**
- 2-1/4 **to 2-3/4 cups water**
- 2 **to 3 tablespoons chili powder**
- 1 **tablespoon seasoned salt**
- 1/2 **to 1 teaspoon crushed red pepper flakes**
- 1 **teaspoon pepper**
- 3 **jars (13-1/2 ounces *each*) tamales, papers removed and halved**
- 2 **cups (8 ounces) shredded cheddar cheese**

In several Dutch ovens, cook the beef, onions and celery until meat is no longer pink. Add garlic; cook 1 minute longer. Drain. Stir in tomatoes and tomato paste. Add the corn, mushrooms and olives. Stir in water and seasonings. Bring to a boil; remove from the heat.

Spoon into three greased 13-in. x 9-in. baking dishes. Top with tamales. Cover and bake at 350° for 50-60 minutes. Sprinkle with cheese. Bake 5-10 minutes longer or until the cheese is melted. **yield: 3 casseroles (8-10 servings each).**

spinach cheese phyllo squares

prep: 20 min. + chilling • bake: 40 min. + standing

A higher-fat version of this casserole was a big hit when my aunt and I ran a gourmet carryout business. This is my lightened-up version, which is quite good.
—Julie Remer, Gahanna, Ohio

- 6 **sheets phyllo dough (14 inches x 9 inches)**
- 1 **package (10 ounces) frozen chopped spinach, thawed and squeezed dry**
- 2-1/2 **cups (10 ounces) shredded part-skim mozzarella cheese**
- 1-1/2 **cups (6 ounces) shredded reduced-fat cheddar cheese**
- 1-1/2 **cups (12 ounces) fat-free cottage cheese**
- 4 **eggs**
- 1-1/2 **teaspoons dried parsley flakes**
- 3/4 **teaspoon salt**
- 6 **egg whites**
- 1-1/2 **cups fat-free milk**

Layer three phyllo sheets in a 13-in. x 9-in. baking dish coated with cooking spray, lightly spraying the top of each sheet with cooking spray.

In a large bowl, combine the spinach, cheeses, 2 eggs, parsley flakes and salt; spread over phyllo dough. Top with remaining phyllo sheets, lightly spraying the top of each sheet with cooking spray. Using a sharp knife, cut into 12 squares; cover and chill for 1 hour.

In a large bowl, beat the egg whites, milk and remaining eggs until blended; pour over casserole. Cover and refrigerate overnight.

Remove from the refrigerator 1 hour before baking. Bake, uncovered, at 375° for 40-50 minutes or until a knife inserted near the center comes out clean. Let stand for 10 minutes before cutting. **yield: 12 servings.**

black-eyed pea casserole

prep: 20 min. • bake: 25 min.

This group-size dish is quick, simple and tasty. People always ask for "just a little more." I guess you could call it one of my Southern favorites.
—Kathy Rogers, Natchez, Mississippi

2 packages (6 ounces *each*) long grain and wild rice mix

2 pounds ground beef

2 medium onions, chopped

2 small green peppers, chopped

4 cans (15-1/2 ounces *each*) black-eyed peas with jalapenos, rinsed and drained

2 cans (10-3/4 ounces *each*) condensed cream of mushroom soup, undiluted

1-1/3 cups shredded cheddar cheese

In a large saucepan, cook the rice mixes according to package directions. Meanwhile, in a large skillet, cook the beef, onions and green peppers over medium heat until the meat is no longer pink; drain.

In a large bowl, combine the peas, soup, rice and beef mixture. Transfer to two greased 2-1/2-qt. baking dishes.

Cover and bake at 350° for 20-25 minutes or until heated through. Uncover; sprinkle with cheese. Bake 5 minutes longer or until cheese is melted. **yield: 2 casseroles (10-12 servings each).**

harvest vegetable casserole

prep: 35 min. • bake: 1-1/2 hours

This is a great way to use fresh garden vegetables on a large scale with only minimal preparation. It's colorful, flavorful and nutritious.
—JoLynn Hill, Roosevelt, Utah

4 large onions, thinly sliced

1/4 cup canola oil

2 large green peppers, cut into chunks

1 large sweet red pepper, cut into chunks

4 large carrots, cut into chunks

4 large tomatoes, cut into chunks

3 medium zucchini, cut into 1-inch pieces

1-1/2 pounds green beans, trimmed and cut into 1-inch pieces

1 medium head cauliflower, cut into florets

1 package (10 ounces) frozen peas

1 to 2 tablespoons salt

1 tablespoon chicken bouillon granules

3 cups boiling water

1 cup medium pearl barley

3 garlic cloves, minced

1/4 cup lemon juice

2 teaspoons paprika

Minced fresh parsley

In several large skillets, saute onions in oil until tender. Add peppers; cook and stir for 1 minute. Stir in the carrots, tomatoes, zucchini, beans, cauliflower, peas and salt.

In a large bowl, dissolve bullion in water; stir in the barley and garlic. Transfer to three greased 13-in. x 9-in. baking dishes. Top with vegetable mixture. Drizzle with lemon juice; sprinkle with paprika.

Cover and bake at 350° for 1-1/2 hours or until barley and vegetables are tender. Sprinkle with parsley. **yield: about 28 servings.**

KITCHEN TIP

To seed and slice a bell pepper, hold the pepper by the stem. Using a chef's knife, slice from the top of the pepper down. Use this technique to slice around the seeds when a recipe calls for julienned or chopped bell peppers.

Place apples in a large bowl; sprinkle with lemon juice. Add the sweet potatoes, syrup, butter, salt and pepper; toss to coat.

Transfer to a 3-qt. baking dish coated with cooking spray. Bake, uncovered, at 400° for 35-40 minutes or until apples are tender, stirring once.

In a small bowl, combine the bread crumbs, oil, cinnamon, nutmeg and vinegar; sprinkle over potato mixture. Bake 10-15 minutes longer or until topping is golden brown. **yield: 12 servings.**

broccoli supreme
prep: 10 min. • bake: 50 min.

I really don't know how long I've had this recipe, but it is a great vegetable side dish. I've shared it with many friends, too.
—Lucy Parks, Birmingham, Alabama

- 2 tablespoons all-purpose flour
- 2 cans (10-3/4 ounces *each*) condensed cream of chicken soup, undiluted
- 1 cup (8 ounces) sour cream
- 1/2 cup grated carrot
- 2 tablespoons grated onion
- 1/2 teaspoon pepper
- 3 packages (10 ounces *each*) frozen broccoli cuts, thawed
- 1-1/2 cups crushed seasoned stuffing
- 1/4 cup butter, melted

In a large bowl, combine the flour, soup and sour cream. Stir in the carrot, onion and pepper. Fold in the broccoli.

Transfer to a greased 2-1/2-qt. baking dish. Combine the stuffing and butter; sprinkle over top. Bake, uncovered, at 350° for 50-60 minutes or until the casserole is bubbly and heated through. **yield: 12 servings.**

sweet potatoes and apples au gratin
prep: 25 min. • bake: 45 min.

This is a favorite of ours that we make every year. People from both sides of the family rave about it! The spices go beautifully with the apples and sweet potatoes, and the maple syrup adds a lovely sweetness.
—Erika Vickerman, Hopkins, Minnesota

- 3 cups thinly sliced tart apples (about 3 large)
- 1 teaspoon lemon juice
- 3 pounds sweet potatoes (about 5 medium), peeled and thinly sliced
- 1/4 cup maple syrup
- 1 tablespoon butter, melted
- 1/2 teaspoon salt
- 1/4 teaspoon pepper
- 1 cup soft bread crumbs
- 2 teaspoons olive oil
- 1/4 teaspoon ground cinnamon
- 1/4 teaspoon ground nutmeg
- 1/4 teaspoon cider vinegar

cheesy zucchini rice casserole

prep: 30 min. • bake: 35 min.

A college roommate gave me this heartwarming recipe a number of years ago, and it's always a hit at potluck dinners.

—Judy Hudson, Santa Rosa, California

- 1 cup uncooked long grain rice
- 3 medium zucchini, cut into 1/8-inch slices
- 1 can (4 ounces) chopped green chilies
- 4 cups (16 ounces) shredded Monterey Jack cheese, *divided*
- 2 cups (16 ounces) sour cream
- 2 tablespoons chopped green pepper
- 2 tablespoons chopped onion
- 1 tablespoon minced fresh parsley
- 1 teaspoon salt
- 1 teaspoon dried oregano
- 1 large tomato, sliced

Cook rice according to package directions. In a large saucepan, cook zucchini in 1/2 in. of water. Bring to a boil. Reduce heat; cover and simmer for 3-5 minutes or until zucchini is crisp-tender; drain and set aside.

Place rice in a greased shallow 3-qt. baking dish. Layer with chilies and 1-1/2 cups cheese. In a large bowl, combine the sour cream, green pepper, onion, parsley, salt and oregano. Spread over cheese. Layer with zucchini and tomato. Sprinkle with remaining cheese.

Cover and bake at 350° for 30 minutes. Uncover; bake 5-10 minutes longer or until casserole is heated through and cheese is melted. **yield: 12 servings.**

spinach noodle casserole

prep: 15 min. • bake: 40 min. + standing

We enjoyed a similar casserole at a friend's house many years ago. She didn't have a recipe but told me the basic ingredients. I eventually came up with my own version and have shared the recipe many times since. It goes great with ham but also is filling by itself.

—Doris Tschorn, Levittown, New York

- 4 cups uncooked egg noodles
- 1/4 cup butter, cubed
- 1/4 cup all-purpose flour
- 1 teaspoon salt
- 1/8 teaspoon pepper
- 2 cups 2% milk
- 2 packages (10 ounces *each*) frozen chopped spinach, thawed and drained
- 2 cups (8 ounces) shredded Swiss cheese
- 2 cups (8 ounces) shredded part-skim mozzarella cheese
- 1/4 cup grated Parmesan cheese

Paprika, optional

Cook noodles according to package directions; drain and rinse in cold water. Meanwhile, in a large saucepan, melt butter over medium heat. Stir in the flour, salt and pepper until smooth. Gradually add milk. Bring to a boil; cook and stir for 2 minutes or until thickened.

Arrange half of the noodles in an ungreased 11-in. x 7-in. baking dish; layer half of the spinach and half of the Swiss cheese. Spread with half of the white sauce. Repeat layers. Layer with mozzarella and Parmesan cheeses. Sprinkle with paprika if desired.

Cover and bake at 350° for 20 minutes. Uncover; bake 20 minutes longer. Let stand for 15 minutes before cutting. **yield: 12-14 servings.**

spaghetti ham bake

prep: 25 min. • bake: 30 min.

My sister passed along this easy ham bake to me. I appreciate being able to freeze one pan for a hectic day. The generous portions are bound to feed a hungry family or an extra mouth or two that show up at your table.
—Mary Killion, Hermiston, Oregon

- 2 packages (7 ounces *each*) thin spaghetti, broken into 2-inch pieces
- 4 cups cubed fully cooked ham
- 2 cans (10-3/4 ounces *each*) condensed cream of chicken soup, undiluted
- 2 cups (16 ounces) sour cream
- 1/2 pound sliced fresh mushrooms
- 1/2 cup chopped onion
- 1/2 cup sliced ripe olives, optional
- 1-1/2 teaspoons ground mustard
- 1 teaspoon seasoned salt
- 2 teaspoons Worcestershire sauce

TOPPING:
- 2 cups soft bread crumbs
- 1/4 cup butter, melted
- 2 cups (8 ounces) shredded cheddar cheese

Cook spaghetti according to package directions; drain and place in a large bowl. Stir in the ham, soup, sour cream, mushrooms, onion, olives if desired, mustard, seasoned salt and Worcestershire sauce.

Transfer to two greased 11-in. x 7-in. baking dishes. In a small bowl, toss bread crumbs and butter; add cheese. Sprinkle over casseroles.

Cover and freeze one casserole for up to 2 months. Bake the remaining casserole, uncovered, at 325° for 30 minutes or until heated through.

to use frozen casserole: Thaw in the refrigerator overnight. Bake, uncovered, at 325° for 50-55 minutes or until heated through. **yield: 2 casseroles (6 servings each).**

alphabetical index

This index lists every recipe in alphabetical order, so you can easily find your favorite recipe.

general index

This handy index lists the recipes by food category and major ingredients, so you can easily locate recipes that you need.

FOOD	EQUIVALENT
Apples	1 pound (3 medium) = 2-3/4 cups sliced
Apricots	1 pound (8 to 12 medium) = 2-1/2 cups sliced
Bananas	1 pound (3 medium) = 1-1/3 cups mashed *or* 1-1/2 to 2 cups sliced
Berries	1 pint = 1-1/2 to 2 cups
Bread	1 loaf = 16 to 20 slices
Bread Crumbs	1 slice = 1/2 cup soft crumbs *or* 1/4 cup dry crumbs
Butter *or* Margarine	1 pound = 2 cups *or* 4 sticks 1 stick = 8 tablespoons
Cheese Cottage Shredded	1 pound = 2 cups 4 ounces = 1 cup
Cherries	1 pound = 3 cups whole *or* 3-1/2 cups halved
Chocolate Chips, Semisweet	6 ounces = 1 cup
Cocoa, Baking	1 pound = 4 cups
Coconut, Flaked	14 ounces = 5-1/2 cups
Cornmeal	1 pound = 3 cups uncooked
Corn Syrup	16 ounces = 2 cups
Cranberries	12 ounces = 3 cups whole *or* 2-1/2 cups finely chopped
Cream Cheese	8 ounces = 16 tablespoons
Cream, Whipping	1 cup = 2 cups whipped
Dates, Dried	1 pound = 2-3/4 cups pitted and chopped
Dates, Dried and Chopped	10 ounces = 1-3/4 cups
Egg Whites	1 cup = 8 to 10 whites
Flour All-Purpose Cake Whole Wheat	1 pound = about 3-1/2 cups 1 pound = about 4-1/2 cups 1 pound = about 3-3/4 cup
Frozen Whipped Topping	8 ounces = 3-1/2 cups
Gelatin, Unflavored	1 envelope = 1 tablespoon
Graham Crackers	16 crackers = 1 cup crumbs
Grapefruit	1 medium = 3/4 cup juice *or* 1-1/2 cups segments

FOOD	EQUIVALENT
Grapes	1 pound = 3 cups
Honey	1 pound = 1-1/3 cups
Lemons	1 medium = 3 tablespoons juice *or* 2 teaspoons grated peel
Limes	1 medium = 2 tablespoons juice *or* 1-1/2 teaspoons grated peel
Marshmallows Large Miniature	1 cup = 7 to 9 marshmallows 1 cup = about 100 marshmallows
Nectarines	1 pound (3 medium) = 3 cups sliced
Nuts Almonds Ground Hazelnuts Pecans Walnuts	1 pound = 3 cups halves *or* 4 cups slivered 3-3/4 ounces = 1 cup 1 pound = 3-1/2 cups whole 1 pound = 4-1/2 cups chopped 1 pound = 3-3/4 cups chopped
Oats Old-Fashioned Quick-Cooking	1 pound = 5 cups 1 pound = 5-1/2 cups
Oranges	1 medium = 1/3 to 1/2 cup juice *or* 4 teaspoons grated peel
Peaches	1 pound (4 medium) = 2-3/4 cups sliced
Pears	1 pound (3 medium) = 3 cups sliced
Pineapples	1 medium = 3 cups chunks
Popcorn	1/3 to 1/2 cup unpopped = 8 cups popped
Raisins	15 ounces = 2-1/2 cups
Rhubarb	1 pound = 3 cups chopped (raw) *or* 2 cups (cooked)
Shortening	1 pound = 2 cups
Strawberries	1 pint = 2 cups hulled and sliced
Sugar Brown Sugar Confectioner's Sugar Granulated	1 pound = 2-1/4 cups 1 pound = 4 cups 1 pound = 2-1/4 to 2-1/2 cups
Yeast, Active Dry	1 envelope = 2-1/4 teaspoons

WHEN YOU NEED:	IN THIS AMOUNT:	SUBSTITUTE:
Baking Powder	1 teaspoon	1/2 teaspoon cream of tartar plus 1/4 teaspoon baking soda
Broth	1 cup	1 cup hot water plus 1 teaspoon bouillon granules *or* 1 bouillon cube
Buttermilk	1 cup	1 tablespoon lemon juice *or* white vinegar plus enough milk to measure 1 cup; let stand 5 minutes. *Or* 1 cup plain yogurt
Cajun Seasoning	1 teaspoon	1/4 teaspoon cayenne pepper, 1/2 teaspoon dried thyme, 1/4 teaspoon dried basil and 1 minced garlic clove
Chocolate, Semisweet	1 square (1 ounce)	1 square (1 ounce) unsweetened chocolate plus 1 tablespoon sugar *or* 3 tablespoons semisweet chocolate chips
Chocolate	1 square (1 ounce)	3 tablespoons baking cocoa plus 1 tablespoon shortening *or* canola oil
Cornstarch (for thickening)	1 tablespoon	2 tablespoons all-purpose flour
Corn Syrup, Dark	1 cup	3/4 cup light corn syrup plus 1/4 cup molasses
Corn Syrup, Light	1 cup	1 cup sugar plus 1/4 cup water
Cracker Crumbs	1 cup	1 cup dry bread crumbs
Cream, Half-and-Half	1 cup	1 tablespoon melted butter plus enough whole milk to measure 1 cup
Egg	1 whole	2 egg whites *or* 2 egg yolks *or* 1/4 cup egg substitute
Flour, Cake	1 cup	1 cup minus 2 tablespoons (7/8 cup) all-purpose flour
Flour, Self-Rising	1 cup	1-1/2 teaspoons baking powder, 1/2 teaspoon salt and enough all-purpose flour to measure 1 cup
Garlic, Fresh	1 clove	1/8 teaspoon garlic powder
Gingerroot, Fresh	1 teaspoon	1/4 teaspoon ground ginger
Honey	1 cup	1-1/4 cups sugar plus 1/4 cup water
Lemon Juice	1 teaspoon	1/4 teaspoon cider vinegar
Lemon Peel	1 teaspoon	1/2 teaspoon lemon extract
Milk, Whole	1 cup	1/2 cup evaporated milk plus 1/2 cup water *or* 1 cup water plus 1/3 cup nonfat dry milk powder
Molasses	1 cup	1 cup honey
Mustard, Prepared	1 tablespoon	1/2 teaspoon ground mustard plus 2 teaspoons cider *or* white vinegar
Onion	1 small (1/3 cup chopped)	1 teaspoon onion powder *or* 1 tablespoon dried minced onion
Poultry Seasoning	1 teaspoon	3/4 teaspoon rubbed sage plus 1/4 teaspoon dried thyme
Sour Cream	1 cup	1 cup plain yogurt
Sugar	1 cup	1 cup packed brown sugar *or* 2 cups sifted confectioners' sugar
Tomato Juice	1 cup	1/2 cup tomato sauce plus 1/2 cup water
Tomato Sauce	2 cups	3/4 cup tomato paste plus 1 cup water
Yeast	1 package (1/4 ounce) active dry	1 cake (5/8 ounce) compressed yeast